PMP®
Project Management
Professional
Practice Exams

ABOUT THE AUTHOR

James L. Haner, PMP, PgMP, PMI-ACP, PMI-RMP, PMI-SP, is the head of Ultimate Business Resources Consulting, specializing in "Building Better Businesses." James' management and leadership roles have included establishing a corporate web presence, creating a successful organization-wide employee development plan, and developing the IT infrastructure for a start-up company.

James brings more than three decades of dynamic experience as a distinguished college professor; award-winning author of books, articles, and blogs; and successful management and leadership consultant to each learning experience.

He is a member of the Project Management Institute (PMI) and the American Society for Training & Development (ASTD). James has won the Dale Carnegie Course "Highest Achievement Award." He earned the Vietnam Service Medal while serving in the U.S. Air Force.

About the Contributor and Technical Editor

Cate McCoy, PMP, PBA, CBAP, is the founding partner of Communi-cate, Inc., a technology management consulting and training company focused on government and corporate clients. She has been immersed in information technology projects for almost 30 years, including technical roles, project management roles, and business analysis roles. Her firsthand experience covers many industries, including government agencies, insurance, banking, and manufacturing. Ms. McCoy earned her master's degree in Information Systems and her bachelor's degree in Computer Science from Marist College, Poughkeepsie, New York, while working as a technology professional at IBM in the 1980s. The technical background serves as a solid foundation for the projects she manages and the business analysis insights she brings to projects, providing both process-oriented and logic-based insights.

Staying true to her love for writing, Cate serves as author, curriculum advisor, and seminar leader for international training companies, including Learning Tree International. Ms. McCoy is the author and technical editor of several published books on technology and management topics and is the curriculum designer and author of over 100 courses on technology, project management, and business analysis.

PMP®

Project Management Professional Practice Exams

James L. Haner

New York   Chicago   San Francisco
Athens   London   Madrid   Mexico City
Milan   New Delhi   Singapore   Sydney   Toronto

Cataloging-in-Publication Data is on file with the Library of Congress

McGraw-Hill Education books are available at special quantity discounts to use as premiums and sales promotions, or for use in corporate training programs. To contact a representative, please visit the Contact Us pages at www.mhprofessional.com.

PMP® Project Management Professional Practice Exams

1 2 3 4 5 6 7 8 9   LCR   21 20 19 18

ISBN   978-1-260-13480-3
MHID   1-260-13480-6

Sponsoring Editor Wendy Rinaldi	**Technical Editor** Cate McCoy	**Composition** Cenveo Publisher Services
Editorial Supervisor Patty Mon	**Copy Editor** Lisa McCoy	**Illustration** Cenveo Publisher Services
Project Manager Radhika Jolly, Cenveo® Publisher Services	**Proofreader** Claire Splan	**Art Director, Cover** Jeff Weeks
Acquisitions Coordinator Claire Yee	**Production Supervisor** Pamela Pelton	

This book is dedicated to Anna Mae Moss. Yo' Mom, I did it!

CONTENTS

ACKNOWLEDGMENTS

I thank Wendy Rinaldi for giving me the chance to write a different book—questions organized by the way you run a project; Claire Yee for kindly and gently keeping me on schedule; Patty Mon for understanding the need to rewrite; Radhika Jolly for finding all those foolish little inconsistencies; Joyce Fucito for the timely formatting of all 1,049 questions and answers—a herculean task; Chris Brady and Candice Ciampa for helping me help aspiring PMP candidates by using a subset of this book; Lisa McCoy, Claire Splan, Pamela Pelton, and Jeff Weeks from McGraw-Hill Education; and Cate McCoy for encouraging (forcing?) me to stick to the details.

INTRODUCTION

Why PMP?

PMI sets the bar for all project management and has made the PMP the gold standard in certification. The PMP certification is recognized worldwide as one that ensures PMP holders conform to the highest standards and ethics, and continually improve. With a PMP certification, you can be assured that you are among the best project managers in the business.

The PMP Exam

Eligibility

Before studying and sitting for the PMP examination, you will need to first check you are eligible to sit it. Full eligibility criteria can be found at the PMI website (www.pmi.org), and you should check this website to ensure the following information is up to date.

PMP Prerequisites

You must have a secondary degree (high school diploma, associate degree, or the global equivalent) and

- 7,500 hours leading and directing projects
- 35 hours of project management education

or a four-year degree (i.e., university degree or baccalaureate equivalent) and

- 4,500 hours leading and directing projects
- 35 hours of project management education

Exam-Taking Tips

- Visit the testing center before the day you have booked the exam so you know where it is and where you will park.
- Be early—allow enough time to relax.
- Take the required forms of identification as per the confirmation email PMI sent you. If you don't do this, you will not be allowed into the examination testing center.
- Take some water and some easy-to-eat food. You will not be allowed to take this in to the test center, but you should be able to store it in a locker and access it during the four hours—but remember your time doesn't stop.

- Don't panic! It's normal to feel some stress, but don't let it negatively affect your performance.
- Answer all the questions—no points are deducted for wrong answers.
- Use any remaining time to recheck answers—there are no points for leaving early.
- Check your progress throughout the exam—at the one-hour mark you should have answered about 50 questions. At two hours, you should have answered about 100 questions. At the three-hour mark, you should have answered about 150 questions.

Question-Answering Tips

- Read the question fully.
- Reread the question! Seriously, a lot of mistakes are made because people don't read the questions fully.
- Read all four answers before deciding which one is correct. Sometimes the first one looks good and you may be tempted to mark this one as correct when a better one was farther along.
- Eliminate any obviously wrong answers.
- Place the answers on a spectrum of most right to most wrong and choose the most right one.
- Organize the answers in order of which would be done first to the one which would be done last—choose the one you would do first.
- Guess! Leave no question unanswered.

About This Book

Congratulations on committing to study for the Project Management Professional (PMP) credential. This book contains enough questions with full explanations to help you pass the PMP examination on your first and only attempt.

Take your time to go through this book and complete all the questions and read the detailed answers. This way you will be prepared to pass the PMP examination.

Finally, think of me as your personal PMP coach. Not only do you have access to the content of this book, you can email me at any time with questions and I will answer.

In Every Chapter

The practice questions in each chapter are mapped to the style (situational, interpretational, general knowledge, PMBOK knowledge, formulas, specific ITTOs) and frequency of question types (from the Examination Content Outline [ECO]) on the topics you will see on the PMP exam.

In the Total Tester

Included with this book is access to the Total Tester, an online exam engine that contains even more practice questions with detailed explanations of the answers. Using this set of practice questions provided in the Total Tester exam engine is another tool to help you prepare for the PMP exam. Please see Appendix B for more information about accessing the Total Tester.

PMP Foundations

The first three chapters of PMI's *PMBOK Guide, Sixth Edition*, present the core foundation information tested on the PMI exam. From positioning project management and introducing the project documents, to discussing the environmental factors of a given enterprise, to the role of the project manager within the enterprise, the PMBOK guides project managers in core aspects that help them become oriented to a project. Although no domain tasks are associated with the first three chapters of PMI's *PMBOK Guide, Sixth Edition*, these three areas are tested on the PMP certification exam.

There are 10 to 15 questions from these three chapters on the PMP exam. The 25 practice questions in this chapter are mapped to the style and frequency of question types you will see on the PMP exam.

1. You must present your project budget to the project sponsor for approval. You are anticipating some of the questions that she may ask about how the project benefits the organization. The following table shows expected cash flow for five years, given project completion in Year 1. What is the payback period for this project?

End of Year	Cash In	Cash Out
1	-	450,000
2	250,000	200,000
3	450,000	50,000
4	350,000	50,000
5	300,000	50,000

   A. Two years
   B. Three years
   C. Four years
   D. Five years

2. When planning a project, influences that can affect the project, whether favorably or unfavorably, must be considered. Which of the following activities would you undertake as a project manager to best understand the project environment?

   A. Schedule and all resources
   B. Cultural and social issues
   C. Project budget approval process
   D. Detailed requirements analysis

3. You are the project manager for a small project team. In one of the regular meetings, a team member proposes an additional feature to the system you are developing. As project manager, you remind the team that they must concentrate on completing only the work approved. Which knowledge area is this an example of?

   A. Project Quality Management
   B. Project Change Management
   C. Project Scope Management
   D. Project Configuration Management

4. The organization you work for is very traditional, and projects must be managed within a functional organizational structure. Your functional manager assigned you to a project that is in trouble. What is your likely level of authority over the outcome of this project?

A. High

B. Moderate

C. Limited

D. Little

5. You are asked by your line manager to describe your current activities as a project manager. You list the activities as "obtain, manage and use resources to accomplish the project objectives." In what process group is this project?

A. Initiating

B. Executing

C. Planning

D. Monitoring and Controlling

6. Your organization has implemented best practices in project management processes. One function that has been set up is the project management office (PMO). What is the function of the PMO?

A. Provide hot desk facilities for all project managers

B. Coordinate the management of projects

C. Close project accounts at the end of the projects

D. Provide standard stationery for project paperwork

7. You are discussing your role as a project manager with your peers. In the conversation, another team member describes the process of defining and controlling what is, and what is not, included in the project. What is this process called?

A. Project Documentation Management

B. Project Change Control

C. Plan Scope Management

D. Formal Acceptance Documents

8. You are discussing your project roles with a colleague. She states that she is working on developing a process that ensures all scope changes go through integrated change control. What project process is she performing?

A. Define Change Control

B. Control Scope

C. Develop Risk Register

D. Validate Scope

9. You have been working on defining the procedures by which the project scope and product scope can be changed. In which process is your team engaged?

   A. Validate Scope

   B. Plan Configuration Management

   C. Initial Scope Definition

   D. Control Scope

10. As you plan a project assigned to your team, you identify the activities, dependencies, and resources needed to produce the project deliverables. What is this knowledge area you are working in called?

    A. Project Schedule Control Management

    B. Project Risk Management

    C. Project Schedule Management

    D. Project Cost Planning Management

11. Calculating the cost of the resources needed to complete the planned schedule of activities on a project is called:

    A. Project Risk Management

    B. Project Schedule Management

    C. Project Cost Management

    D. Project Resource Management

12. A new team member is monitoring and recording the results of executing quality activities to assess performance and recommend necessary changes. He asks for clarification on what his activities are related to. Which of the following is the best answer to his question?

    A. Control Quality

    B. Manage Quality

    C. Plan Quality Management

    D. Quality Improvement

13. You have delegated the task of identifying which quality standards are relevant to your current project to Sally, who is an experienced team member whom you have worked with on prior projects. You've also asked Sally to determine how to satisfy any identified quality standards. In which of the following activities is Sally engaged?

    A. Control Quality

    B. Manage Quality

    C. Plan Quality Management

    D. Improve Quality

14. You are identifying and documenting project roles, responsibilities, and reporting relationships for a project, as well as creating a staffing management plan for a project. In terms of project management, these activities are known as:

A. Plan Resource Management

B. Develop Project Management plan

C. Manage Team

D. Develop Team

15. Which of the following organizational structures can complicate the management of the project team?

A. Functional

B. Matrix

C. Project

D. Hierarchical

16. Tracking team performance, providing feedback, resolving issues, and coordinating changes to enhance project performance are all part of which process?

A. Recognition and Reward Systems

B. Team Performance Assessment

C. Manage Team

D. Build Team

17. When leading project teams, your role involves making use of knowledge, skills, and behaviors that are related to the specific domain of the project. These are examples of which key skill set?

A. Communication skills

B. Leadership

C. Strategic and business management

D. Technical aspects of project management

18. The set of project management activities that includes identification, analysis, planning responses, and monitoring and controlling risks in the project is of which knowledge area?

A. Project Risk Identification Management

B. Project Risk Analysis Management

C. Project Risk Management

D. Project Risk Mitigation Management

19. The process of project planning that involves developing options, determining actions to enhance opportunities, and reducing threats to project objectives is called:

   A. Perform Qualitative Risk Analysis

   B. Plan Risk Responses

   C. Perform Quantitative Risk Analysis

   D. Develop Probability and Impact Matrix

20. You have been asked by the project sponsor to ensure that the seller's performance meets the contractual requirements and that your organization, as the buyer, performs according to the contract. This process is called:

   A. Control Procurements

   B. Plan Procurement Management

   C. Conduct Procurements

   D. Select Sellers

21. To ensure that projects enable business value creation, you must consider tangible and intangible benefits. Which of the following are examples of intangible elements of business value?

   A. Monetary assets

   B. Utility

   C. Market share

   D. Trademarks

22. You have been assigned as project manager for a project to develop a new line of microwave cooking devices. You understand that projects drive change in organizations. The project seems to be a clever idea. What is the next thing you should do?

   A. Determine the link to the strategic objectives of the organization and the business value of the project

   B. Progressively elaborate the project management plan

   C. Start developing the project charter

   D. Set up a portfolio review board to engage with the right stakeholders

23. You have been asked by the project management team to determine the best development life cycle for the new microwave cooking devices project. Customer value and quality will be incorporated in real time during development. Your most appropriate response to this request is to:

   A. Indicate that this is not a normal project manager decision; you are willing to discuss the request with the project sponsor.

   B. Appoint a committee to investigate the idea and then interview key stakeholders about high-level business requirements.

C. Choose an adaptive life cycle: agile, iterative, or incremental. The key stakeholders will be continuously involved, and the requirements will be elaborated frequently during delivery.

D. Draw a continuum of project life cycles, and consider the risk and cost of the initial planning effort.

24. Recent research suggests three key skill sets are needed by project managers. The talent triangle focuses on all of the following competencies except:

A. Knowledge transfer and integration

B. Leadership

C. Strategic and business management

D. Technical project management

25. Andrew is a functional manager who regularly attends your retrospective meetings to check up on "his people" from the Real Estate Division who are on the project. Andrew likes to "play PM" and attracts attention to the fact that he is well liked by the project sponsor. Andrew is seen as heroic and inspiring because he orchestrated the launch of the mobile home loan application last year. What form of power is Andrew using?

A. Positional or legitimate

B. Personal or charismatic

C. Authoritarian or formal

D. Situational or substantial

1. B	**10.** C	**19.** B
2. B	**11.** C	**20.** A
3. C	**12.** A	**21.** D
4. D	**13.** C	**22.** A
5. B	**14.** A	**23.** C
6. B	**15.** B	**24.** A
7. C	**16.** C	**25.** B
8. B	**17.** D	
9. D	**18.** C	

1. You must present your project budget to the project sponsor for approval. You are anticipating some of the questions that she may ask about how the project benefits the organization. The following table shows expected cash flow for five years, given project completion in Year 1. What is the payback period for this project?

End of Year	Cash In	Cash Out
1	-	450,000
2	250,000	200,000
3	450,000	50,000
4	350,000	50,000
5	300,000	50,000

A. Two years

B. Three years

C. Four years

D. Five years

☑ **B.** One common method a project manager uses to do an economic analysis of project benefits is the payback method. This method identifies where on the project schedule income exceeds the outgoing plus the initial investment. Brigham and Houston indicate that "The payback period, defined as the expected number of years required to recover the original investment, was the first formal method used to evaluate capital budgeting projects." For this project, it will take three years for the Cash In (0 + 250,000 + 450,000) to equal the Cash Out (450,000 + 200,000 + 50,000).

☒ **A, C,** and **D** are incorrect because the answers do not match the formula.

2. When planning a project, influences that can affect the project, whether favorably or unfavorably, must be considered. Which of the following activities would you undertake as a project manager to best understand the project environment?

A. Schedule and all resources

B. Cultural and social issues

C. Project budget approval process

D. Detailed requirements analysis

☑ **B.** When planning and implementing a project, one of the considerations is the project environment, including the cultural and social issues that may affect the success of the project.

☒ **A** and **C** are incorrect because they are specific to the workings of the project rather than to the environment the project exists within. **D** is incorrect because requirements are details evaluated later in the planning processes.

3. You are the project manager for a small project team. In one of the regular meetings, a team member proposes an additional feature to the system you are developing. As project manager, you remind the team that they must concentrate on completing only the work approved. Which knowledge area is this an example of?

A. Project Quality Management

B. Project Change Management

C. Project Scope Management

D. Project Configuration Management

    ☑ **C.** Approved project scope defines the approved work that the project delivers, and only this work should be done. Any changes are managed by referring to the project scope.

    ☒ **A, B,** and **D** are incorrect because these processes are control processes used to ensure high-quality deliverables or to assist in approving changes to the project scope.

4. The organization you work for is very traditional, and projects must be managed within a functional organizational structure. Your functional manager assigned you to a project that is in trouble. What is your likely level of authority over the outcome of this project?

A. High

B. Moderate

C. Limited

D. Little

    ☑ **D.** In a functional organization, the project manager has little or no influence on project outcomes.

    ☒ **A, B,** and **C** are incorrect because the functional manager controls the budget, whereas the project manager is generally part-time and is assisted by part-time project staff.

5. You are asked by your line manager to describe your current activities as a project manager. You list the activities as "obtain, manage and use resources to accomplish the project objectives." In what process group is this project?

A. Initiating

B. Executing

C. Planning

D. Monitoring and Controlling

    ☑ **B.** The definition of the Executing process group is "obtain, manage, and use resources to accomplish the project objectives."

    ☒ **A, C,** and **D** are incorrect because Initiating, Planning, and Monitoring and Controlling do not match the description given of the activities.

6. Your organization has implemented best practices in project management processes. One function that has been set up is the project management office (PMO). What is the function of the PMO?

A. Provide hot desk facilities for all project managers

B. Coordinate the management of projects

C. Close project accounts at the end of the projects

D. Provide standard stationery for project paperwork

☑ **B.** The project management office (PMO) is a central function for coordinating and supporting management of projects in an organization.

☒ **A** is incorrect because the PMO is not responsible for hot desk implementation. **C** is incorrect because the project manager is responsible for closure of all project accounts. **D** is incorrect because items like stationery are project resources, not a function of a PMO.

7. You are discussing your role as a project manager with your peers. In the conversation, another team member describes the process of defining and controlling what is, and what is not, included in the project. What is this process called?

A. Project Documentation Management

B. Project Change Control

C. Plan Scope Management

D. Formal Acceptance Documents

☑ **C.** The Plan Scope Management process defines and controls what is and what is not included in the project.

☒ **A, B,** and **D** are incorrect. Project documentation management and project change control are procedures that allow the control of changes to scope only. Formal acceptance documents are part of the Close Project or Phase process.

8. You are discussing your project roles with a colleague. She states that she is working on developing a process that ensures all scope changes go through integrated change control. What project process is she performing?

A. Define Change Control

B. Control Scope

C. Develop Risk Register

D. Validate Scope

☑ **B.** Defining or developing a process that ensures all scope changes go through integrated change control in a project is part of the Control Scope process.

☒ **A, C,** and **D** are incorrect. The change control process supports scope control. A risk register does not ensure all changes go through change control. Scope validation occurs at the end of a project to confirm that deliverables cover the contracted scope.

9. You have been working on defining the procedures by which the project scope and product scope can be changed. In which process is your team engaged?

A. Validate Scope

B. Plan Configuration Management

C. Initial Scope Definition

D. Control Scope

☑ **D.** Defining the procedures by which the project scope and product scope can be changed is known as Control Scope.

☒ **A, B,** and **C** are incorrect. Validate Scope is done at end of a project to confirm the deliverables are as contracted. Configuration management is the process of considering changes before these are put into change control. Initial scope definition is not about controlling the scope.

10. As you plan a project assigned to your team, you identify the activities, dependencies, and resources needed to produce the project deliverables. What is this knowledge area you are working in called?

A. Project Schedule Control Management

B. Project Risk Management

C. Project Schedule Management

D. Project Cost Planning Management

☑ **C.** Identifying the activities, dependencies, and resources needed to produce the project deliverables are some of the actions required in Project Schedule Management.

☒ **A, B,** and **D** are incorrect. Project schedule control is about managing changes to the schedule. Project Risk Management is a knowledge area. Cost planning is about cost only.

11. Calculating the cost of the resources needed to complete the planned schedule of activities on a project is called:

A. Project Risk Management

B. Project Schedule Management

C. Project Cost Management

D. Project Resource Management

☑ **C.** Project activity that works out the cost of the resources needed to complete the planned schedule of activities on a project is the knowledge area called Project Cost Management.

☒ **A, B,** and **D** are incorrect. Project Risk Management is the knowledge area focused on risks, not solely on costs. Schedule management concerns the duration and dependencies of tasks. The Project Resource Management knowledge area identifies necessary resources and checks that they are available.

12. A new team member is monitoring and recording the results of executing quality activities to assess performance and recommend necessary changes. He asks for clarification on what his activities are related to. Which of the following is the best answer to his question?

   A. Control Quality

   B. Manage Quality

   C. Plan Quality Management

   D. Quality Improvement

   ☑ **A.** Monitoring and recording results of executing quality activities to assess performance and recommend necessary changes is the definition of the Control Quality.

   ☒ **B, C,** and **D** are incorrect. Manage Quality is ensuring that appropriate quality standards are used. Plan Quality Management is related to establishing the requirements and/or standards for the project. Quality improvement is an organizational development process.

13. You have delegated the task of identifying which quality standards are relevant to your current project to Sally, who is an experienced team member whom you have worked with on prior projects. You've also asked Sally to determine how to satisfy any identified quality standards. In which of the following activities is Sally engaged?

   A. Control Quality

   B. Manage Quality

   C. Plan Quality Management

   D. Improve Quality

   ☑ **C.** Quality planning is related to establishing the quality requirements and/or standards for the project as part of the Project Quality Management knowledge area.

   ☒ **A, B,** and **D** are incorrect. Monitoring and recording results of executing quality activities to assess performance and recommend necessary changes is Control Quality. Manage Quality is ensuring that appropriate quality standards are used. Quality improvement is an organizational development process.

14. You are identifying and documenting project roles, responsibilities, and reporting relationships for a project, as well as creating a staffing management plan for a project. In terms of project management, these activities are known as:

A. Plan Resource Management

B. Develop Project Management plan

C. Manage Team

D. Develop Team

☑ **A.** Identifying and documenting project roles, responsibilities, and reporting relationships, as well as creating a staffing management plan for a project, is developing the resource management plan.

☒ **B, C,** and **D** are incorrect. Develop Project Management Plan is a broader generic process. Manage Team concerns operational activities, not planning. Develop Team concerns improving competences.

15. Which of the following organizational structures can complicate the management of the project team?

A. Functional

B. Matrix

C. Project

D. Hierarchical

☑ **B.** Management of the project team is complicated when team members are accountable to both a functional and a project manager, as in a matrix organization.

☒ **A, C,** and **D** are incorrect. Functional and project organizations have clear accountability. Hierarchical organizations are the norm.

16. Tracking team performance, providing feedback, resolving issues, and coordinating changes to enhance project performance are all part of which process?

A. Recognition and Reward Systems

B. Team Performance Assessment

C. Manage Team

D. Build Team

☑ **C.** Tracking team performance, providing feedback, resolving issues, and coordinating changes to enhance project performance are all part of Manage Team.

☒ **A** and **B** are incorrect because recognition and reward systems and team performance assessment are both part of the Develop Team process. **D** is incorrect because Build Team is a made-up term.

17. When leading project teams, your role involves making use of knowledge, skills, and behaviors that are related to the specific domain of the project. These are examples of which key skill set?

   A. Communication skills

   B. Leadership

   C. Strategic and business management

   D. Technical aspects of project management

   ☑ **D.** The PMI talent triangle includes the key skill sets of technical project management, leadership, and strategic and business management. Technical project management involves the knowledge, skills, and behaviors specific to a project's domain.

   ☒ **A, B,** and **C** are incorrect. Communication skills are not a part of the talent triangle. Leadership and strategic and business management are part of the talent triangle, but do not speak to the technical aspects of performing the project manager role within a project's domain.

18. The set of project management activities that includes identification, analysis, planning responses, and monitoring and controlling risks in the project is of which knowledge area?

   A. Project Risk Identification Management

   B. Project Risk Analysis Management

   C. Project Risk Management

   D. Project Risk Mitigation Management

   ☑ **C.** Identification, analysis, planning responses, and monitoring and controlling of risks in the project are part of the Project Risk Management knowledge area.

   ☒ **A, B,** and **D** are incorrect. Risk identification, analysis, and mitigation are all parts of this overall process.

19. The process of project planning that involves developing options, determining actions to enhance opportunities, and reducing threats to project objectives is called:

   A. Perform Qualitative Risk Analysis

   B. Plan Risk Responses

   C. Perform Quantitative Risk Analysis

   D. Develop Probability and Impact Matrix

   ☑ **B.** Developing options, determining actions to enhance opportunities, and reducing threats to project objectives is known as Plan Risk Responses.

   ☒ **A, C,** and **D** are incorrect. Perform Qualitative Risk Analysis and Perform Quantitative Risk Analysis are prior steps in the overall risk management process. **D** is incorrect because Develop Probability and Impact Matrix is a made-up term.

20. You have been asked by the project sponsor to ensure that the seller's performance meets the contractual requirements and that your organization, as the buyer, performs according to the contract. This process is called:

A. Control Procurements

B. Plan Procurement Management

C. Conduct Procurements

D. Select Sellers

☑ **A.** The process of ensuring that the seller's performance meets the contractual requirements and that the buying organization performs according to the contract is called Control Procurements.

☒ **B, C,** and **D** are incorrect. Plan Procurement Management and Conduct Procurements are steps prior to administering procurements. Select sellers is an activity that inputs to contract documentation.

21. To ensure that projects enable business value creation, you must consider tangible and intangible benefits. Which of the following are examples of intangible elements of business value?

A. Monetary assets

B. Utility

C. Market share

D. Trademarks

☑ **D.** Business value in projects refers to the benefit that the results of the project provide to its stakeholders. Examples of intangible elements include goodwill, brand recognition, public benefit, trademarks, strategic alignment, and reputation.

☒ **A, B,** and **C** are incorrect because they are elements of tangible benefits.

22. You have been assigned as project manager for a project to develop a new line of microwave cooking devices. You understand that projects drive change in organizations. The project seems to be a clever idea. What is the next thing you should do?

A. Determine the link to the strategic objectives of the organization and the business value of the project

B. Progressively elaborate the project management plan

C. Start developing the project charter

D. Set up a portfolio review board to engage with the right stakeholders

☑ **A.** After the project initiation context has been mapped to one of the four fundamental categories, you need to determine the link to the strategic objectives of the organization and the business value of the project.

☒ **B** is incorrect because progressively elaborating the project management plan happens during the Planning process group. **C** is incorrect because the project charter is developed in the Initiating process group. **D** is incorrect because you do not know if you will manage this project as a project, program, or portfolio. It is not time to set up a portfolio review board to engage with the right stakeholders.

23. You have been asked by the project management team to determine the best development life cycle for the new microwave cooking devices project. Customer value and quality will be incorporated in real time during development. Your most appropriate response to this request is to:

   A. Indicate that this is not a normal project manager decision; you are willing to discuss the request with the project sponsor.

   B. Appoint a committee to investigate the idea and then interview key stakeholders about high-level business requirements.

   C. Choose an adaptive life cycle: agile, iterative, or incremental. The key stakeholders will be continuously involved, and the requirements will be elaborated frequently during delivery.

   D. Draw a continuum of project life cycles, and consider the risk and cost of the initial planning effort.

   ☑ **C.** The key stakeholders will be continuously involved and the requirements will be elaborated frequently during delivery. Customer value and quality will be incorporated in real time during development. An adaptive life cycle—agile, iterative, or incremental—maps to these elements.

   ☒ **A** is incorrect because it is normal for the project manager and the project management team to determine the best life cycle for each project. **B** is incorrect because appointing a committee to investigate the idea and then interviewing key stakeholders about high-level business requirements does not fit with the project manager's roles in the sphere of influence. **D** is incorrect because drawing a continuum of project life cycles and considering the risk and cost of the initial planning effort depend on the life cycle being employed.

24. Recent research suggests three key skill sets are needed by project managers. The talent triangle focuses on all of the following competencies except:

   A. Knowledge transfer and integration

   B. Leadership

   C. Strategic and business management

   D. Technical project management

   ☑ **A.** "Knowledge transfer and integration" is the exception.

   ☒ **B, C,** and **D** are incorrect because they are the exact three key skill sets of the talent triangle.

25. Andrew is a functional manager who regularly attends your retrospective meetings to check up on "his people" from the Real Estate Division who are on the project. Andrew likes to "play PM" and attracts attention to the fact that he is well liked by the project sponsor. Andrew is seen as heroic and inspiring because he orchestrated the launch of the mobile home loan application last year. What form of power is Andrew using?

   A. Positional or legitimate

   B. Personal or charismatic

   C. Authoritarian or formal

   D. Situational or substantial

   ☑ **B.** These two forms of power are based on charm and attraction.

   ☒ **A** is incorrect because positional or legitimate power is the formal position granted in the organization or team. **C** is incorrect because authoritarian or formal power is the formal position granted in the organization or team. **D** is incorrect because situational power is gained due to a unique situation like a specific crisis; substantial power is a distracter.

CHAPTER 2

The Initiating Domain

This chapter includes questions from the following tasks:

- **Task 1** Perform project assessment based upon available information, lessons learned from previous projects, and meetings with relevant stakeholders in order to support the evaluation of the feasibility of new products or services within the given assumptions and/or constraints.
- **Task 2** Identify key deliverables based on the business requirements in order to manage customer expectations and direct the achievement of project goals.
- **Task 3** Perform stakeholder analysis using appropriate tools and techniques in order to align expectations and gain support for the project.
- **Task 4** Identify high-level risks, assumptions, and constraints based on the current environment, organizational factors, historical data, and expert judgment in order to propose an implementation strategy.
- **Task 5** Participate in the development of the project charter by compiling and analyzing gathered information in order to ensure project stakeholders are in agreement on its elements.
- **Task 6** Obtain project charter approval from the sponsor in order to formalize the authority assigned to the project manager and gain commitment and acceptance for the project.
- **Task 7** Conduct benefit analysis with relevant stakeholders to validate project alignment with organizational strategy and expected business value.
- **Task 8** Inform stakeholders of the approved project charter to ensure common understanding of the key deliverables, milestones, and their roles and responsibilities.

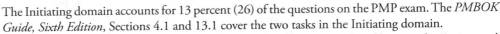

The Initiating domain accounts for 13 percent (26) of the questions on the PMP exam. The *PMBOK Guide, Sixth Edition*, Sections 4.1 and 13.1 cover the two tasks in the Initiating domain.

It is the start of the project journey and consists of defining and authorizing the project and identifying stakeholders. The 52 practice questions in this chapter are mapped to the style and frequency of question types you will see on the PMP exam.

1. You have been asked to create an end-to-end manufacturing process for your company's next-generation semiconductor fabrication line. This new fabrication line is time critical, and industry competition is fierce. Many of the older employees who have traditionally worked on the fabrication lines have helped the company be successful using ad hoc processes and heuristic knowledge. As the project manager, you want to use comprehensive project management best practices wherever possible to maximize the chances of success. Which of the following would you do first?

   A. Calculate the project timeline and initial budget

   B. Recruit the key project skills as early as possible

   C. Develop the project charter and scope of work

   D. Write a comprehensive change control process

2. You've just joined the company as a project manager for a new project. You've worked on projects at your prior company and are looking to ensure that you have the authority needed to carry out your roles and responsibilities. Which project document should you ask to see first?

   A. Work breakdown structure

   B. Project charter

   C. Requirements document

   D. Project schedule

3. You are developing the project charter for a project for an external customer. To complete the project charter, which of the following should be in place?

   A. The detailed features list to be delivered

   B. The not-to-exceed price for the project

   C. The agreed-upon contract for the project

   D. The estimated labor costs of the project

4. As a project manager, you have been given a statement of work for a project you are assigned to manage. This project is internal to your organization. Who will have provided you with this statement of work?

   A. The end-user group

   B. Your line manager

   C. The project director

   D. The project sponsor

5. You have been given a brief time to write a project charter for a project that has been fast tracked. The project will develop an IT system to help the sales team close external leads. Which of the following would be least likely to help you clarify the influences on the project when writing the project charter?

A. Existing skills and knowledge within the organization

B. Regulatory standards that are about to be approved

C. The infrastructure in place to support an IT solution

D. The likely political changes in local government

6. The project charter you have developed has not yet been approved by the project sponsor though you submitted it two weeks ago. Your direct line manager insists that you start work on the project immediately because he needs you on another project in a few months' time. What is the best course of action for you?

A. Start interviewing potential team members in anticipation of project approval

B. Start working on the project plan as a work in progress

C. State the likely impact of proceeding without approval

D. Negotiate a compromise with the line manager that considers the next project

7. The project you have been asked to develop a charter for is complex and has many inputs that are beyond your direct knowledge. Which of the following tools and techniques would best help you proceed with the project chartering process?

A. Matrix management structure

B. Available project templates

C. Lessons learned

D. Expert judgment of others

8. You have been asked to analyze a project charter that has been developed by another part of your business. Which of the following would you consider essential for the project charter to be approved?

A. Detailed work and schedule estimates

B. A list of all the resources required

C. The business need for the project

D. A list of all the risks in the project

9. You have been provided a document that contains the market demand and cost-benefit analysis that justifies the go-ahead for the project. What is this document called?

A. Contract

B. Statement of work

C. Business case

D. Organizational asset

10. You are preparing an initial stakeholder list for a project to replace the company's email system, and you believe your list is too short and is therefore likely not complete. To ensure that you take a comprehensive approach to identifying stakeholders, you decide to seek the expert judgment of this stakeholder:

   A. Data base architect

   B. Resource allocation manager

   C. Competitors

   D. Project sponsor

11. Which of the following is an output of the Identify Stakeholders process?

   A. Stakeholder register

   B. Enterprise environmental factors

   C. Change control process

   D. Communication models

12. The project statement of work that includes the business needs and high-level product requirements for the new hydroelectric plant has just been agreed to and completed. Which deliverable should be created next for this project?

   A. Scope statement

   B. Management plan

   C. Charter

   D. Requirements document

13. At which point in a project should the project manager ensure that the organizational process assets are first available?

   A. At the end of the Initiating process group

   B. Before the Initiating process group starts

   C. During the Planning process group

   D. At the end of the Planning process group

14. Project sponsors have the most influence on the scope, quality, time, and cost of the project during:

   A. Initiating

   B. Planning

   C. Executing

   D. Closing

15. Which of the following is an output of the Identify Stakeholders process?

   A. Stakeholder register

   B. RACI chart

C. Stakeholder management strategies

D. Stakeholder engagement

16. A key stakeholder is complaining to several of your project team members about the ineffectiveness of some of the risk responses. This is having a negative impact on team morale. What is the best method for handling this situation?

A. Arrange to meet with the stakeholder to clarify any concerns

B. Arrange for team-building activities to get the team back on track

C. Report the stakeholder to the project sponsor so she can handle the situation and allow you to focus on the project

D. Report the stakeholder's conduct to the stakeholder's senior management

17. You are a newly hired project manager working on your first project at a law firm with the goal of upgrading information security. The two managing partners at the law firm are used to getting their way and are pressuring you to meet only their needs and not to involve the remaining 30 lawyers in the project. How will the Identify Stakeholders process assist you with the task?

A. Planning how you will control stakeholders and their impact throughout the project

B. Establishing an approach to increase the support and minimize opposition of stakeholders

C. Creating a systematic approach to identifying stakeholders

D. Setting the tone for document creation to be used on the project

18. You are collecting and examining qualitative and quantitative information to ascertain whose interests should be considered throughout the project. In which activity are you engaging?

A. Stakeholder analysis

B. Communications planning

C. Risk analysis

D. Organizational structure analysis

19. You work for a large organization that offers risk management, quality management, and change management consulting services to other companies. Recent projects have produced disappointing results; therefore, the organization has added you to the steering committee to assist the solution search. One agreement reached is that future projects will be selected based on financial measures such as return on investment (ROI), payback period, internal rate of return (IRR), and net present value (NPV). Four such projects are currently under investigation and have the following details: Project A has an ROI of $80,000, Project B has an ROI of $85K, Project C has an ROI of $78K, and Project D has an ROI of $82K. Based on this information, which project would you select?

A. Project A

B. Project B

C. Project C

D. Project D

20. What document formally authorizes a project?

   A. Business case

   B. Project charter

   C. Project statement of work (SOW)

   D. Project management plan

21. Select the process that assigns the project manager to a project.

   A. Develop Project Charter

   B. Develop Project Management Plan

   C. Develop Business Case

   D. Develop Strategic Plan

22. You are part of an expert committee deciding which project should be implemented by your company. Your committee asks tough questions and helps decide which projects your company should select. Only the worthiest projects get through the tough scrutiny. Which project selection technique is being used?

   A. Scoring model

   B. PMO selection

   C. Murder board

   D. Defined benefit

23. Which two knowledge areas are involved in the Initiating process group?

   A. Project Integration Management and Project Scope Management

   B. Project Scope Management and Project Schedule Management

   C. Project Integration Management and Project Stakeholder Management

   D. Project Scope Management and Project Risk Management

24. Which project role is generally accountable for the development and maintenance of the business case associated with a project?

   A. Project sponsor

   B. Project manager

   C. Business stakeholder

   D. IT stakeholder

25. Expert judgment is a tool and technique of which process?

   A. Identify Resources

   B. Monitor Stakeholder Engagement

C. Manage Stakeholder Engagement

D. Manage Stakeholder Management

26. You are creating a matrix that includes all the stakeholders on the project. On your first pass at it, you decide that it's important to know each stakeholder's power (ability to impose will), urgency (need for immediate attention), and legitimacy (their involvement) within the project. What type of grid or model are you implementing?

A. Power/influence grid

B. Salience model

C. Influence/impact grid

D. Kano model

27. An ongoing endeavor to produce repetitive results with resources doing the same set of tasks is known as:

A. Project management

B. Stakeholder analysis

C. Program management

D. Operations

28. You have an active stakeholder that can directly affect your project's success. This stakeholder is a positive supporter, but is concerned about the inferior performance of previous projects. Based on your stakeholder analysis, the best way to handle this stakeholder is to:

A. Do nothing but monitor the stakeholder's actions

B. Keep the stakeholder informed of project activities

C. Manage closely to maintain the relationship

D. Try to identify the key areas of interest and work to keep the stakeholder satisfied

29. You have identified specific resource requirements in your project charter, but your company's resources are already constrained; you only need a small core team. A best practice in this situation is to include with your project charter:

A. An estimate of the resources required for the various project phases

B. A pre-assignment section on why the project is dependent upon the expertise of particular persons

C. A RACI chart showing all project resources

D. A RACI chart that includes roles and responsibilities of your project's stakeholders

30. You are preparing your project charter. You plan to have a close working relationship with the client. In the project charter, you decided to enhance your resource requirements section so you could ensure everyone understood why you need the requested resources. You decided to:

    A. Prepare a project organization chart showing cross-functional management and resources

    B. Prepare a RACI chart because you also will use resources from the client on your team

    C. Describe in an outline format the responsibilities of every member of your team

    D. Prepare both a product breakdown structure and a resource breakdown structure

31. You are attempting to identify and map your project's stakeholders. Which representation technique can you use?

    A. Sender-receiver model

    B. Stakeholder cube

    C. Probability/impact grid

    D. Code-decode model

32. While working for a secret government agency, you discover that a previous project that was very successful had a stakeholder, Winston, who was unhappy with the benefits received. Winston can have a significant impact on your project. What should you do next?

    A. Review the stakeholder register to determine exactly how much impact Winston has

    B. Communicate and work with Winston to meet his needs and expectations

    C. Ensure that the communications management plan addresses Winston's information needs

    D. Review the stakeholder management plan to determine Winston's engagement level

33. You are a project manager carrying out the first adaptive project for the company. For each iteration, you will need to ensure your team carries out all the following except:

    A. Collect Requirements

    B. Define Scope

    C. Create WBS

    D. Develop Project Charter

34. For your current project, you have determined that the probability of meeting the schedule objective is 80% and the probability of being on budget is 70%. You inherited this project from a previous manager and are disappointed that a better effort wasn't made in this forecasting when the objectives were put in place. Which of the following would you have used to assess the objectives at the beginning of the project?

    A. MoSCoW

    B. POLDAT

    C. RACI

    D. SMART

35. The training division in your company has started a new project they believe will be a best-seller, and they have brought you on board as the project manager. The project will create a series of new web-based courses to be sold external to the company targeting the health care sector. Which of the following likely influenced the need for this project?

A. Meet regulatory, legal, or social requirements

B. Satisfy stakeholder requests or needs

C. Improve or fix products, processes, or services

D. Implement or change business or technological strategies

36. You were just asked to lead a project that many people are calling a stakeholder nightmare. You will be dealing with multiple stakeholders, both inside and outside the company, and the stakeholders are all very vocal. In addition, the project is regulatory in nature. In which of the following processes would you decide how you will involve stakeholders on your current project with the goal of connecting with them based on their needs, expectations, and interests?

A. Identify Stakeholders

B. Plan Stakeholder Engagement

C. Manage Stakeholder Engagement

D. Monitor Stakeholder Engagement

37. The project charter is an input into which two Project Stakeholder Management processes?

A. Identify Stakeholders and Plan Stakeholder Engagement

B. Manage Stakeholder Engagement and Monitor Stakeholder Engagement

C. Identify Stakeholders and Manage Stakeholders

D. Plan Stakeholder Engagement and Manage Stakeholder Engagement

38. In addition to academic research, which of the following most likely highlights the importance of a structured approach to working with project stakeholders?

A. Company research

B. Analyses of high-profile project disasters

C. The increase in project successes in the past ten years

D. Program and portfolio management

39. You are taking your first pass at identifying stakeholders for your current project. Which project document should you consult as a source of information about this project's stakeholders?

A. Project charter

B. Business case

C. Stakeholder register

D. RACI chart

40. In which process group does the stakeholder identification start in a project?

   A. Initiating

   B. Planning

   C. Executing

   D. Monitoring and Controlling

41. You are working as a general contractor on behalf of a sweet old couple building a beach house with their life savings. As the general contractor, you have residential construction experience and have helped the couple decide what kind of house to build given their budget, and you found them a builder that can fulfill their requirements. You are the person managing all interactions on behalf of the homeowners, interacting with the builder, the city municipalities, and the neighbors. You have eyes on the project at every phase and are handling the problems during the build. What project role are you serving?

   A. Sponsor

   B. Project manager

   C. Business analyst

   D. None, this is not a project

42. As the general contractor for a homeowner, the project has kicked off and you need to ensure that all departments in the municipal government are on board with the plans to build a house on the beach. The house may be in a flood zone, and it is in a coastal preservation zone. To ensure that all requirements from the couple and the municipal government are met, which process is critical?

   A. Develop Project Charter

   B. Identify Stakeholders

   C. Direct and Manage Project Work

   D. Plan Communications Management

43. A couple is building a house and working with a general contractor who interacts with the builder and all other stakeholders. The house is framed and the water lines connected; however, the couple was just told that the cost to connect to the municipality's sewer system is not a task performed by the municipality, but instead is performed by a contractor hired by the homeowners to do the work. Which process should have discovered this information earlier in the project?

   A. Develop Project Charter

   B. Identify Stakeholders

   C. Direct and Manage Project Work

   D. Plan Communications Management

44. Which process has the key benefit of enabling the project team to know the right focus for engaging each stakeholder or group of stakeholders?

   A. Identify Stakeholders

   B. Plan Stakeholder Engagement

   C. Plan Communications Management

   D. Monitor Stakeholder Engagement

45. Which of the following are documents that are generally originated outside of the project but are used as input to the project?

   A. Business requirements document

   B. Business documents

   C. Stakeholder requirements document

   D. Project change control process

46. You have been hired as the project manager for a homeowners' association for an upcoming renovation. The association consists of 104 one- and two-bedroom condos. Following best practices, you have decided to involve the sponsor, customers, and all other stakeholders during the initiation phase of the project's first iteration, which is to replace the foyer door at the condo building. What is the key benefit of taking this approach?

   A. The development of a timeline for completion

   B. A division of labor for all tasks that need to be completed

   C. The creation of the business requirements

   D. A shared understanding of success criteria

47. What two things does a project charter link together?

   A. The sponsor and the project manager

   B. The objectives and the timeline

   C. The project and the strategic objectives of the company

   D. The funding and the deliverables

48. What two outputs are created in the Develop Project Charter process?

   A. Project charter and constraint list

   B. Project charter and business documents

   C. Project charter and organizational process assets

   D. Project charter and assumption log

49. You are managing the project to move the company from one database platform to another. There are business stakeholders and information technology (IT) stakeholders, and each stakeholder group seems to have different goals. Which of the following is critical to ensure that you can create a shared understanding of success criteria for this project?

   A. Listing all functional units and their detailed requirements in the project charter

   B. Involving all stakeholders during the Initiating Process group processes

   C. Listing all functional units and their detailed requirements in the project plan

   D. Creating a RACI chart to ensure all stakeholders are identified

50. You are the project manager for a local painting contractor who paints interiors and exteriors of residential houses. You've learned that there are always multiple projects going on. For each project, you use a template to create a customized communications management plan and stakeholder engagement plan. These documents are both examples of documents:

   A. Provided by the sponsor for the project

   B. Created by the business analyst during the initiating phase

   C. That are components of a project management plan

   D. Created as a part of the initiating process group

51. You are reviewing a list of high-level product characteristics for your new project. Accompanying the list is a set of approvals for the project requirements. What document are you likely reviewing?

   A. Business case

   B. Solution requirements

   C. Project charter

   D. Feasibility study

52. Which of the following is a data gathering technique used in the Identify Stakeholders process?

   A. Blamestorming

   B. Brain writing

   C. Prioritization

   D. Mind-mapping

1. C	19. B	37. A
2. B	20. B	38. B
3. C	21. A	39. B
4. D	22. C	40. A
5. D	23. C	41. B
6. C	24. A	42. B
7. D	25. C	43. B
8. C	26. B	44. A
9. C	27. D	45. B
10. D	28. C	46. D
11. A	29. B	47. C
12. C	30. B	48. D
13. B	31. B	49. B
14. A	32. A	50. C
15. A	33. D	51. C
16. A	34. D	52. B
17. B	35. B	
18. A	36. B	

1. You have been asked to create an end-to-end manufacturing process for your company's next-generation semiconductor fabrication line. This new fabrication line is time critical, and industry competition is fierce. Many of the older employees who have traditionally worked on the fabrication lines have helped the company be successful using ad hoc processes and heuristic knowledge. As the project manager, you want to use comprehensive project management best practices wherever possible to maximize the chances of success. Which of the following would you do first?

   A. Calculate the project timeline and initial budget

   B. Recruit the key project skills as early as possible

   C. Develop the project charter and scope of work

   D. Write a comprehensive change control process

   ☑ **C.** A project charter with a well-defined scope of work is necessary to calculating timelines, calculating budgets, recruiting skills, and creating a change management process. The development of the project charter is part of the project initiation process.

   ☒ **A, B,** and **D** are incorrect because they are part of scope control and detailed planning, which follow project charter creation. **A** is incorrect because a project timeline and budget cannot be created without knowing what is in scope for the project. **B** is incorrect and should be undertaken as early as possible, but skills cannot be determined until the scope of the effort is determined. **D** is incorrect because the timing for a change control process is after an understanding of the scope of the effort is complete.

2. You've just joined the company as a project manager for a new project. You've worked on projects at your prior company and are looking to ensure that you have the authority needed to carry out your roles and responsibilities. Which project document should you ask to see first?

   A. Work breakdown structure

   B. Project charter

   C. Requirements document

   D. Project schedule

   ☑ **B.** The project charter is the document that formally authorizes a project and gives the project manager the authority to apply organizational resources to project activities. A project manager is identified and assigned as early in the project as is feasible. The project manager should always be assigned prior to the start of planning, and preferably while the project charter is being developed. Without an approved charter, the project manager has no authority within the organization.

   ☒ **A** and **D** are incorrect because they are a part of the project plan, which follows from a project's charter. The work breakdown structure (WBS) itemizes the work to be done in the project. The project schedule aligns the work to be done with a calendar for completion. **C** is incorrect because a requirements document is created as a part of the executing phase and details the product planned to be created by the project charter.

3. You are developing the project charter for a project for an external customer. To complete the project charter, which of the following should be in place?

A. The detailed features list to be delivered

B. The not-to-exceed price for the project

C. The agreed-upon contract for the project

D. The estimated labor costs of the project

☑ **C.** The project charter inputs may include the contract if the project is being done for an external customer. The other options are all subsets of an agreed-upon contract or calculations that lead to an agreed-upon contract.

☒ **A** is incorrect because only a high-level list of features is created at the project charter point. **B** is incorrect because the not-to-exceed detail may be a component of the contract with the external organization; however, not all contracts have a not-to-exceed component. **D** is incorrect because although labor costs may have been estimated to arrive at pricing, those costs would be a variable used in calculating the contract price.

4. As a project manager, you have been given a statement of work for a project you are assigned to manage. This project is internal to your organization. Who will have provided you with this statement of work?

A. The end-user group

B. Your line manager

C. The project director

D. The project sponsor

☑ **D.** The project statement of work (SOW) is provided by the project initiator or sponsor for internal projects based on a business need, product, or service requirement.

☒ **A** is incorrect because the end-user group represents the stakeholders who will ultimately use the product of the project on an ongoing basis; this group may have input to the product that is needed, but would not provide the final statement of work. **B** is incorrect as it implies a matrix management organization, and in that situation the line manager is responsible for your career, not your project. **C** is incorrect because there is no project role called "project director" (in the financial industry there are often managing directors, but those still are not project managers).

5. You have been given a brief time to write a project charter for a project that has been fast tracked. The project will develop an IT system to help the sales team close external leads. Which of the following would be least likely to help you clarify the influences on the project when writing the project charter?

A. Existing skills and knowledge within the organization

B. Regulatory standards that are about to be approved

C. The infrastructure in place to support an IT solution

D. The likely political changes in local government

☑ **D.** As a project manager, you must consider many factors when developing a project charter; however, external political changes will have the least impact on an internal software solution being developed by your own company.

☒ **A** is incorrect because it is important to know the existing skills and knowledge within the organization when resourcing the project and that will be dealt with after the project charter is written and hopefully approved. **B** is incorrect because both existing and pending regulatory changes can directly influence the scope and efforts of the project. **C** is incorrect because the existing infrastructure in use by IT is extremely important, given that the solution will be developed in-house.

6. The project charter you have developed has not yet been approved by the project sponsor though you submitted it two weeks ago. Your direct line manager insists that you start work on the project immediately because he needs you on another project in a few months' time. What is the best course of action for you?

A. Start interviewing potential team members in anticipation of project approval

B. Start working on the project plan as a work in progress

C. State the likely impact of proceeding without approval

D. Negotiate a compromise with the line manager that considers the next project

☑ **C.** As a project manager you must not start a project without an approved charter. If the project starts without approval, organizational resources may be misdirected or wasted and rework may be created. Your authority to proceed should be given by the ultimate authority: the project sponsor.

☒ **A** is incorrect, as it would let people know about a project that has not yet been authorized, and in the world of dealing with the emotions of team members, it might get someone's hopes up falsely. **B** is incorrect because a project plan follows a project charter; the project plan requires the authority to manage the project, and said authority has not yet been acquired. **D** is incorrect, although an interesting answer—recall that the line manager's job and your project manager's job have two different goals and you need to be true to the goal of the project.

7. The project you have been asked to develop a charter for is complex and has many inputs that are beyond your direct knowledge. Which of the following tools and techniques would best help you proceed with the project chartering process?

A. Matrix management structure

B. Available project templates

C. Lessons learned

D. Expert judgment of others

☑ **D.** When developing a project charter, the input of expert judgment often is used to help identify the inputs that must be considered in this process.

☒ **A** is incorrect because a matrix management structure involves the line or direct managers, who would not have knowledge of the inputs needed for your project. **B** is incorrect because this may be helpful, but templates in and of themselves are skeletons of documents without specific reference to inputs you may need. **C** is incorrect because lessons learned do come from prior projects, but asking experts should be a first choice.

8. You have been asked to analyze a project charter that has been developed by another part of your business. Which of the following would you consider essential for the project charter to be approved?

   A. Detailed work and schedule estimates

   B. A list of all the resources required

   C. The business need for the project

   D. A list of all the risks in the project

   ☑ **C.** The business need for the project is an essential input to the project charter. The detailed estimates and lists of risks are produced as part of project planning, which comes after the project chartering process. Some general and top-level resources are included in the project charter, but not all the resources for the project.

   ☒ **A** is incorrect because detailed work and schedule estimates are developed during the planning phase of a project. **B** is incorrect because the detailed resources required will not be known until the full set of requirements is developed. **D** is incorrect because of the word "all." Risks are important, but the only risks identified at the initiating project charter stage are high-level risks—product risks come later.

9. You have been provided a document that contains the market demand and cost-benefit analysis that justifies the go-ahead for the project. What is this document called?

   A. Contract

   B. Statement of work

   C. Business case

   D. Organizational asset

   ☑ **C.** The business case contains the business need and cost-benefit analysis that justify the go-ahead of the project; it is created because of market demand, organizational need, customer request, technological advance, or legal requirement. All other options are inputs to the process of developing a project charter.

   ☒ **A** is incorrect because a contract implies an external entity involved with your own company, therefore, a contract would not contain cost-benefit information. **B** is incorrect because a statement of work (SOW) identifies all the deliverables for the project without regard for cost-benefit analysis. **D** is incorrect because an organizational process asset references the templates for documents used within an organization and may include policies and process references as well.

10. You are preparing an initial stakeholder list for a project to replace the company's email system, and you believe your list is too short and is therefore likely not complete. To ensure that you take a comprehensive approach to identifying stakeholders, you decide to seek the expert judgment of this stakeholder:

   A. Data base architect

   B. Resource allocation manager

   C. Competitors

   D. Project sponsor

   ☑ **D.** As part of stakeholder analysis, groups or individuals, such as senior management, project sponsor, project team, industry groups, and even technical or professional associations, should contribute to the process.

   ☒ **A** is incorrect because the data base architect may not be a member of the project team. **B** is incorrect because the resource allocation manager's job is to supply project resources as they are needed. **C** is incorrect because competitors are not a source of identifying stakeholders for an internal project, though they may be a stakeholder group that should be analyzed during the project.

11. Which of the following is an output of the Identify Stakeholders process?

   A. Stakeholder register

   B. Enterprise environmental factors

   C. Change control process

   D. Communication models

   ☑ **A.** The stakeholder register is a project document that lists identified stakeholders, including name, organizational position, location, contact details, and project role. The stakeholder register is a repository for storing assessments about each stakeholder group, including major requirements, expectations, potential for influencing project outcomes, and the phase of the project the stakeholder will likely participate in or influence. The stakeholder classification may also be useful to the project manager, and a variety of classifications can be decided for each project (e.g., internal/external).

   ☒ **B** is incorrect because enterprise environmental factors are influences on a project and serve as an input to the plan stakeholder engagement process and are not an output of identify stakeholders. **C** is incorrect because although a change control process is used by stakeholders, it does not provide information that assists in the process of identifying stakeholders. **D** is incorrect because deciding on communications models requires that stakeholders already be identified.

12. The project statement of work that includes the business needs and high-level product requirements for the new hydroelectric plant has just been agreed to and completed. Which deliverable should be created next for this project?

   A. Scope statement

   B. Management plan

C. Charter

D. Requirements document

☑ **C.** With the business need identified and high-level deliverables defined in the statement of work (SOW), the project charter is created next to give the project manager the authority to work on the project and create the product deliverables.

☒ **A, B,** and **D** are incorrect because each is an output of the planning phase, which follows the initiation phase. If the project charter does not exist, the project manager has no mandate to create the scope statement, management plan, or requirements document.

13. At which point in a project should the project manager ensure that the organizational process assets are first available?

A. At the end of the Initiating process group

B. Before the Initiating process group starts

C. During the Planning process group

D. At the end of the Planning process group

☑ **B.** Business documents, agreements, enterprise environmental factors, and organizational process assets are all inputs to the Develop Project Charter process.

☒ **A** is incorrect because organizational process assets are an input needed to help develop the project charter and are therefore needed before, not at the end, of the initiating process group. **C** and **D** are incorrect because the organizational assets must be present for the project charter to be created, which happens before the planning process group, not during or at the end.

14. Project sponsors have the most influence on the scope, quality, time, and cost of the project during:

A. Initiating

B. Planning

C. Executing

D. Closing

☑ **A.** The project sponsor is the key stakeholder in the initiating phase. The project charter is agreed to by the project sponsor and represents what they want out of the project; it also drives the direction of the project.

☒ **B** is incorrect because the project manager, not the sponsor, has the greatest influence during the planning phase. **C** is incorrect because the execution phase is carrying out what has been agreed on in the project charter during initiation and in the project plan during planning. Although there may be updates to the project plan during execution, any changes are affecting the original scope, quality, time, and cost variables and are not brand new therefore less influential in this phase. **D** is incorrect because at closing the project deliverables have been created and scope, quality, schedule, and cost are now actuals that can no longer be influenced.

15. Which of the following is an output of the Identify Stakeholders process?

    A. Stakeholder register

    B. RACI chart

    C. Stakeholder management strategies

    D. Stakeholder engagement

    ☑ **A.** This is the primary output of the Identify Stakeholders process together with updates to the project management plan and project documents. Change requests are also an output of the Identify Stakeholders process.

    ☒ **B** is incorrect because the RACI chart identifies roles and responsibilities but is not an output of Identify Stakeholders. **C** is incorrect because stakeholder management strategies are part of the stakeholder management plan. **D** is incorrect because the Manage Stakeholder Engagement process uses the stakeholder register as an input.

16. A key stakeholder is complaining to several of your project team members about the ineffectiveness of some of the risk responses. This is having a negative impact on team morale. What is the best method for handling this situation?

    A. Arrange to meet with the stakeholder to clarify any concerns

    B. Arrange for team-building activities to get the team back on track

    C. Report the stakeholder to the project sponsor so she can handle the situation and allow you to focus on the project

    D. Report the stakeholder's conduct to the stakeholder's senior management

    ☑ **A.** Arranging to meet and clarify the stakeholders confronts the situation where efforts can be made to create a win-win arrangement. This deals with the problem directly and is the recommended method. A project manager's first response should be directly with the stakeholder to understand the root cause of the concerns as a precursor to resolving the issue.

    ☒ **B** is incorrect because it does not address the root cause (stakeholder's complaint). **C** is incorrect because it is the project manager's job to solve project problems; problems that cannot be solved by the project manager should be escalated to the project sponsor, but escalating is not a first response. **D** is incorrect because the stakeholder's management chain should not be a project manager's first response.

17. You are a newly hired project manager working on your first project at a law firm with the goal of upgrading information security. The two managing partners at the law firm are used to getting their way and are pressuring you to meet only their needs and not to involve the remaining 30 lawyers in the project. How will the Identify Stakeholders process assist you with the task?

    A. Planning how you will control stakeholders and their impact throughout the project

    B. Establishing an approach to increase the support and minimize opposition of stakeholders

    C. Creating a systematic approach to identifying stakeholders

    D. Setting the tone for document creation to be used on the project

☑ **B.** Stakeholder analysis is performed during the Identify Stakeholders process to define strategies to promote stakeholder engagement. It includes key stakeholders and their impact/influence, level of participation, and stakeholder groups.

☒ **A** is incorrect because the goal is not to control stakeholders. **C** is incorrect because the stakeholders should have already been identified; however, new ones may be added. **D** is incorrect because the stakeholder management strategy information is too sensitive to share.

18. You are collecting and examining qualitative and quantitative information to ascertain whose interests should be considered throughout the project. In which activity are you engaging?

   A. Stakeholder analysis

   B. Communications planning

   C. Risk analysis

   D. Organizational structure analysis

   ☑ **A.** Stakeholder analysis focuses on stakeholder interests, influence, knowledge, etc., to determine the best approach to effectively engage them in project decisions and activities.

   ☒ **B** is incorrect because although communications planning is important when interacting with stakeholders, it is not relevant in the context of identifying stakeholders. **C** is incorrect because risk analysis uses qualitative and quantitative information to determine probability, impact, and numerical values for risks, not stakeholder identification. **D** is incorrect because there is no technique called organizational structure analysis.

19. You work for a large organization that offers risk management, quality management, and change management consulting services to other companies. Recent projects have produced disappointing results; therefore, the organization has added you to the steering committee to assist the solution search. One agreement reached is that future projects will be selected based on financial measures such as return on investment (ROI), payback period, internal rate of return (IRR), and net present value (NPV). Four such projects are currently under investigation and have the following details: Project A has an ROI of $80,000, Project B has an ROI of $85K, Project C has an ROI of $78K, and Project D has an ROI of $82K. Based on this information, which project would you select?

   A. Project A

   B. Project B

   C. Project C

   D. Project D

   ☑ **B.** Project selection is based on ROI, so the project returning the largest investment should be chosen, which is Project B at $85,000.

   ☒ **A, C,** and **D** are incorrect because the ROI values for these projects are all lower than $85,000.

20. What document formally authorizes a project?

   A. Business case

   B. Project charter

   C. Project statement of work (SOW)

   D. Project management plan

    ☑ **B.** The Develop Project Charter process assigns the project manager and produces the project charter that officially authorizes the project.

    ☒ **A** is incorrect because the business case explains the need for the project. **C** is incorrect because the SOW, part of the agreements, is a written description of the project's product, service, or result. The business case and agreements serve as inputs to the Develop Project Charter process. **D** is incorrect because the project management plan is developed after the project charter is approved and the project manager is assigned.

21. Select the process that assigns the project manager to a project.

   A. Develop Project Charter

   B. Develop Project Management Plan

   C. Develop Business Case

   D. Develop Strategic Plan

    ☑ **A.** The Develop Project Charter process assigns the project manager and produces the project charter that authorizes the project and links the need for the project to the organization's strategic plan.

    ☒ **B** is incorrect because the project management plan is created by the project manager in the planning phase. **C** is incorrect because it is a made-up process name; the business case provides the strategic and financial justification for the project and therefore precedes the project charter. **D** is incorrect because it is a made-up process name; the strategic plan precedes the project charter.

22. You are part of an expert committee deciding which project should be implemented by your company. Your committee asks tough questions and helps decide which projects your company should select. Only the worthiest projects get through the tough scrutiny. Which project selection technique is being used?

   A. Scoring model

   B. PMO selection

   C. Murder board

   D. Defined benefit

    ☑ **C.** A murder board is a process where a committee asks questions from project representatives as part of the project selection process to shoot down and eliminate projects that are not of the highest value to the company. From Wikipedia, "A murder board, also known as a 'scrub-down,' is a committee of questioners set up to critically review a proposal and/or help someone prepare for a difficult oral examination."

☒ **A** is incorrect because it is a method for ranking projects that does not involve oral questions. **B** is incorrect because the murder board may or may not be associated with a PMO. **D** is incorrect because no defined benefit threshold is mentioned in the question as a criterion for project selection.

23. Which two knowledge areas are involved in the Initiating process group?

   A. Project Integration Management and Project Scope Management

   B. Project Scope Management and Project Schedule Management

   C. Project Integration Management and Project Stakeholder Management

   D. Project Scope Management and Project Risk Management

   ☑ **C.** The knowledge area Project Integration Management contains the Develop Project Charter process, and the Project Stakeholder Management process contains Identify Stakeholders.

   ☒ **A** is incorrect because Project Scope Management has no processes in the Initiating process group. **B** is incorrect because neither Project Scope Management nor Project Schedule Management have processes in the Initiating process group. **D** is incorrect because Project Risk Management has no processes in the Initiating process group.

24. Which project role is generally accountable for the development and maintenance of the business case associated with a project?

   A. Project sponsor

   B. Project manager

   C. Business stakeholder

   D. IT stakeholder

   ☑ **A.** The project sponsor is responsible for funding the project and ensuring that it takes place. A business analyst may assist in writing the business case, but the project sponsor is accountable for the deliverable.

   ☒ **B** is incorrect because the business case precedes the project charter, which links a project manager to a project. **C** and **D** are incorrect because although either may be in the role of project sponsor, in which case they would be responsible, this would only be in the role of business or IT stakeholder—there is no power to authorize a project.

25. Expert judgment is a tool and technique of which process?

   A. Identify Resources

   B. Monitor Stakeholder Engagement

   C. Manage Stakeholder Engagement

   D. Manage Stakeholder Management

   ☑ **C.** Expert judgment is a tool and technique of the Manage Stakeholder Engagement process.

   ☒ **A** and **D** are incorrect because they are distracters—the terms are made-up. **B** is incorrect because Monitor Stakeholder Engagement does not use expert judgment.

26. You are creating a matrix that includes all the stakeholders on the project. On your first pass at it, you decide that it's important to know each stakeholder's power (ability to impose will), urgency (need for immediate attention), and legitimacy (their involvement) within the project. What type of grid or model are you implementing?

   A. Power/influence grid

   B. Salience model

   C. Influence/impact grid

   D. Kano model

   ☑ **B.** The salience model describes classes of stakeholders based on assessments of their power, urgency, and legitimacy. This model is useful in large, complex communities of stakeholders.

   ☒ **A** is incorrect because the power/influence grid does not address urgency and legitimacy. **C** is incorrect because influence/impact does not address urgency and legitimacy. **D** is incorrect because the Kano model is used in requirements prioritization.

27. An ongoing endeavor to produce repetitive results with resources doing the same set of tasks is known as:

   A. Project management

   B. Stakeholder analysis

   C. Program management

   D. Operations

   ☑ **D.** Day-to-day repetitive tasks that carry out the work of the business are known as operations. Projects are not operations.

   ☒ **A** is incorrect because projects have a definite start and end and create a unique deliverable. **B** is incorrect because although stakeholder analysis is an ongoing process during a project, it is not performed outside of a project. **C** is incorrect because programs consist of projects and therefore have the same time-based nature to them and unique deliverables.

28. You have an active stakeholder that can directly affect your project's success. This stakeholder is a positive supporter, but is concerned about the inferior performance of previous projects. Based on your stakeholder analysis, the best way to handle this stakeholder is to:

   A. Do nothing but monitor the stakeholder's actions

   B. Keep the stakeholder informed of project activities

   C. Manage closely to maintain the relationship

   D. Try to identify the key areas of interest and work to keep the stakeholder satisfied

☑ **C.** Keeping a supportive stakeholder aware of the project and potential impacts will maintain the relationship and support for the work and its outcomes.

☒ **A** is incorrect because if you do nothing, the supportive stakeholder could slip into a neutral or resistant stakeholder. **B** is incorrect because although it is important to keep the stakeholder informed of project activities, it may not help to maintain the relationship. **D** is incorrect because you will have already identified the key areas of interest in the stakeholder register.

29. You have identified specific resource requirements in your project charter, but your company's resources are already constrained; you only need a small core team. A best practice in this situation is to include with your project charter:

  A. An estimate of the resources required for the various project phases

  B. A pre-assignment section on why the project is dependent upon the expertise of particular persons

  C. A RACI chart showing all project resources

  D. A RACI chart that includes roles and responsibilities of your project's stakeholders

  ☑ **B.** When physical or team resources for a project are determined in advance, they are considered preassigned.

  ☒ **A** is incorrect because estimating resources required for the various project phases is done in the Planning process group. **C** and **D** are incorrect because the RACI chart is a useful tool to use to ensure clear assignment of roles and responsibilities when the team consists of internal and external resources.

30. You are preparing your project charter. You plan to have a close working relationship with the client. In the project charter, you decided to enhance your resource requirements section so you could ensure everyone understood why you need the requested resources. You decided to:

  A. Prepare a project organization chart showing cross-functional management and resources

  B. Prepare a RACI chart because you also will use resources from the client on your team

  C. Describe in an outline format the responsibilities of every member of your team

  D. Prepare both a product breakdown structure and a resource breakdown structure

  ☑ **B.** The RACI chart is especially useful when the team consists of internal and external resources to ensure clear division of roles and responsibilities—here your client will be actively involved.

  ☒ **A** is incorrect because a project organization chart showing cross-functional management and resources could be an input to this process. **C** is incorrect because an outline detailing the responsibilities of every member of your team is less effective than a RACI chart. **D** is incorrect because a product breakdown structure is not used for resource assignments, and a resource breakdown structure is a hierarchical list of team and physical resources related by category and resource type.

31. You are attempting to identify and map your project's stakeholders. Which representation technique can you use?

A. Sender-receiver model

B. Stakeholder cube

C. Probability/impact grid

D. Code-decode model

☑ **B.** A stakeholder cube uses the three axes of Attitude, Power, and Interest, each running from negative to positive extremes, with a node at each extreme.

☒ **A** is incorrect because the basic sender-receiver communication model is concerned with ensuring that the message is delivered, rather than understood. **C** and **D** are incorrect because they are distracters—the terms are made-up.

32. While working for a secret government agency, you discover that a previous project that was very successful had a stakeholder, Winston, who was unhappy with the benefits received. Winston can have a significant impact on your project. What should you do next?

A. Review the stakeholder register to determine exactly how much impact Winston has

B. Communicate and work with Winston to meet his needs and expectations

C. Ensure that the communications management plan addresses Winston's information needs

D. Review the stakeholder management plan to determine Winston's engagement level

☑ **A.** The stakeholder register will contain the stakeholder classification, which includes the impact/influence/power/interest grids.

☒ **B** is incorrect because meeting with Winston will enable you to identify the appropriate focus for his engagement, not his impact on the project. **C** is incorrect because the communications plan describes how project communications will be planned, structured, implemented, and monitored for effectiveness; it will be used later. **D** is incorrect because reviewing the stakeholder management plan comes after you classify stakeholders in the stakeholder register.

33. You are a project manager carrying out the first adaptive project for the company. For each iteration, you will need to ensure your team carries out all the following except:

A. Collect Requirements

B. Define Scope

C. Create WBS

D. Develop Project Charter

☑ **D.** A project charter would be created one time, at the beginning of the first iteration. In each successive iteration, small working products would be delivered through the cycle of collecting requirements, defining the scope of what will be worked on within the next iteration, and creating a work breakdown structure of tasks and deliverables in the iteration.

☒ **A** is incorrect because an iteration in an adaptive project is driven by the requirements, fine-tuning a small set of requirements and creating a working product for those requirements. **B** is incorrect because defining the scope of what will and will not be done in each iteration is crucial to the success of the iteration. **C** is incorrect because understanding the tasks of what must be done in each iteration defines who will be needed to accomplish the tasks, thus making this an essential step.

34. For your current project, you have determined that the probability of meeting the schedule objective is 80% and the probability of being on budget is 70%. You inherited this project from a previous manager and are disappointed that a better effort wasn't made in this forecasting when the objectives were put in place. Which of the following would you have used to assess the objectives at the beginning of the project?

A. MoSCoW

B. POLDAT

C. RACI

D. SMART

☑ **D.** A common test for assessing objectives is to ensure that they are SMART: specific, measurable, attainable, relevant, and time bound.

☒ **A** is incorrect because MoSCow (must, should, could, won't) is used in prioritizing requirements in an adaptive project. **B** is incorrect because POLDAT (process, organization, and location and data) is a model used to understand a company's assets. **C** is incorrect because a RACI (responsible, accountable, consulted, informed) chart is used to identify and manage stakeholders and their expectations.

35. The training division in your company has started a new project they believe will be a best-seller, and they have brought you on board as the project manager. The project will create a series of new web-based courses to be sold external to the company targeting the health care sector. Which of the following likely influenced the need for this project?

A. Meet regulatory, legal, or social requirements

B. Satisfy stakeholder requests or needs

C. Improve or fix products, processes, or services

D. Implement or change business or technological strategies

☑ **B.** High-level strategic needs are based on stakeholder needs with stakeholders at any level in the company.

☒ **A** is incorrect because regulatory, legal, and social requirements are tied to outside influences not directly related to profitability. **C** is incorrect because this is a new product, not an improvement on an existing product. **D** is incorrect because the training division preexisted, so creating courses was within the existing business strategy.

36. You were just asked to lead a project that many people are calling a stakeholder nightmare. You will be dealing with multiple stakeholders, both inside and outside the company, and the stakeholders are all very vocal. In addition, the project is regulatory in nature. In which of the following processes would you decide how you will involve stakeholders on your current project with the goal of connecting with them based on their needs, expectations, and interests?

A. Identify Stakeholders

B. Plan Stakeholder Engagement

C. Manage Stakeholder Engagement

D. Monitor Stakeholder Engagement

☑ **B.** Plan Stakeholder Engagement follows Identify Stakeholders and is where you think through how to engage the variety of stakeholders on the project based on their needs, expectations, and interests.

☒ **A** is incorrect because the goal of Identify Stakeholders is to build a comprehensive list of stakeholders. **C** is incorrect because managing engagement takes place after identifying stakeholders and planning how to engage them. **D** is incorrect because monitoring takes place throughout the project after having decided on engagement strategies.

37. The project charter is an input into which two Project Stakeholder Management processes?

A. Identify Stakeholders and Plan Stakeholder Engagement

B. Manage Stakeholder Engagement and Monitor Stakeholder Engagement

C. Identify Stakeholders and Manage Stakeholders

D. Plan Stakeholder Engagement and Manage Stakeholder Engagement

☑ **A.** The project charter is needed to define the business need, which drives the stakeholders that will be involved and the nature of their involvement.

☒ **B** is incorrect because the project charter is not an input to Manage Stakeholder Engagement or Monitor Stakeholder Engagement. **C** is incorrect because Manage Stakeholders is a made-up term. **D** is incorrect because the project charter is not an input to Manage Stakeholder Engagement.

38. In addition to academic research, which of the following most likely highlights the importance of a structured approach to working with project stakeholders?

A. Company research

B. Analyses of high-profile project disasters

C. The increase in project successes in the past ten years

D. Program and portfolio management

☑ **B.** The lessons learned from visible project disasters highlight stakeholder involvement as a critical success factor.

☒ **A** is incorrect because although company research may have taken place on this topic, it is not clear what the company research may have been about in this case. **C** is incorrect because this is a random statistic that cannot be proven by the question. **D** is incorrect because program and portfolio management are not directly involved with project stakeholders and their needs.

39. You are taking your first pass at identifying stakeholders for your current project. Which project document should you consult as a source of information about this project's stakeholders?

A. Project charter

B. Business case

C. Stakeholder register

D. RACI chart

☑ **B.** The business case is provided by the project sponsor and is a needed input to the develop project charter process.

☒ **A** is incorrect because the project charter is not a source for the initial stakeholders, but it does document the benefits once analyzed in the business case. **C** is incorrect because the stakeholder register is an output of Identify Stakeholders, not an input. **D** is incorrect because a RACI chart is developed once roles and responsibilities for identified stakeholders have been decided.

40. In which process group does the stakeholder identification start in a project?

A. Initiating

B. Planning

C. Executing

D. Monitoring and Controlling

☑ **A.** The initiating phase is where stakeholders are first identified; this identification is reviewed throughout each project phase.

☒ **B, C,** and **D** are incorrect because Identify Stakeholders is a part of the Initiating process group.

41. You are working as a general contractor on behalf of a sweet old couple building a beach house with their life savings. As the general contractor, you have residential construction experience and have helped the couple decide what kind of house to build given their budget, and you found them a builder that can fulfill their requirements. You are the person managing all interactions on behalf of the homeowners, interacting with the builder, the city municipalities, and the neighbors. You have eyes on the project at every phase and are handling the problems during the build. What project role are you serving?

   A. Sponsor

   B. Project manager

   C. Business analyst

   D. None, this is not a project

   ☑ **B.** The general contractor is managing groups of people and not actually doing the construction and is therefore acting as a project manager.

   ☒ **A** is incorrect because the homeowners are the project sponsors; they control the funding and the overall direction of the project. **C** is incorrect because the business analyst records the high-level and low-level requirements, but does not manage all the interactions. **D** is incorrect because this is a project as it has a definite start, end, and unique deliverable.

42. As the general contractor for a homeowner, the project has kicked off and you need to ensure that all departments in the municipal government are on board with the plans to build a house on the beach. The house may be in a flood zone, and it is in a coastal preservation zone. To ensure that all requirements from the couple and the municipal government are met, which process is critical?

   A. Develop Project Charter

   B. Identify Stakeholders

   C. Direct and Manage Project Work

   D. Plan Communications Management

   ☑ **B.** Identifying all stakeholders is the only way to uncover all project requirements.

   ☒ **A** is incorrect because the project has already kicked off and the charter is assumed at this point. **C** is incorrect because it will be pointless to perform the Direct and Manage Project Work process if the stakeholders have not been properly identified, as the stakeholders are the source of requirements driving the work. **D** is incorrect because planning communications can only be successful if all stakeholders have been identified.

43. A couple is building a house and working with a general contractor who interacts with the builder and all other stakeholders. The house is framed and the water lines connected; however, the couple was just told that the cost to connect to the municipality's sewer system is not a task performed by the municipality, but instead is performed by a contractor hired by the homeowners to do the work. Which process should have discovered this information earlier in the project?

A. Develop Project Charter

B. Identify Stakeholders

C. Direct and Manage Project Work

D. Plan Communications Management

☑ **B.** If the stakeholder who had knowledge of the municipalities sewer requirements and process had been identified in the beginning of the project, it would not have been a surprise communication late in the project.

☒ **A** is incorrect because the project charter does not identify all the stakeholders. **C** is incorrect because directing and managing the work can only take place if the work has been identified through stakeholder requirements first. **D** is incorrect because planning who to communicate with is ineffective if the "who" has yet to be identified.

44. Which process has the key benefit of enabling the project team to know the right focus for engaging each stakeholder or group of stakeholders?

A. Identify Stakeholders

B. Plan Stakeholder Engagement

C. Plan Communications Management

D. Monitor Stakeholder Engagement

☑ **A.** Identifying stakeholders leads to knowing who they are and what engagement focus is appropriate.

☒ **B** is incorrect because identification describes the needs of the stakeholders so that engagement can be planned. **C** is incorrect because planning communication cannot take place without knowing the stakeholders and how they wish to be engaged. **D** is incorrect because it is an ongoing task that ensures all is on track.

45. Which of the following are documents that are generally originated outside of the project but are used as input to the project?

A. Business requirements document

B. Business documents

C. Stakeholder requirements document

D. Project change control process

☑ **B.** Business documents are provided by the sponsor as an input to the develop project charter process.

☒ **A** is incorrect because the business requirements document may be developed within the project as a part of the project charter. **C** is incorrect because stakeholder requirements are documented within the Collect Requirements process. **D** is incorrect because a project's change control process is decided after the project charter is complete.

46. You have been hired as the project manager for a homeowners' association for an upcoming renovation. The association consists of 104 one- and two-bedroom condos. Following best practices, you have decided to involve the sponsor, customers, and all other stakeholders during the initiation phase of the project's first iteration, which is to replace the foyer door at the condo building. What is the key benefit of taking this approach?

   A. The development of a timeline for completion

   B. A division of labor for all tasks that need to be completed

   C. The creation of the business requirements

   D. A shared understanding of success criteria

   ☑ **D.** This approach results in a shared understanding of success criteria across all stakeholder groups and helps ensure a positive project outcome.

   ☒ **A** is incorrect because a timeline for completion is a task and deliverable, not a benefit. **B** is incorrect because the division of labor is part of delegating tasks and is not a benefit. **C** is incorrect because business requirements are not a benefit, but a must-have for a project.

47. What two things does a project charter link together?

   A. The sponsor and the project manager

   B. The objectives and the timeline

   C. The project and the strategic objectives of the company

   D. The funding and the deliverables

   ☑ **C.** Each project is undertaken for the benefit of the company, and the charter brings together the "why" of the project with how it aligns to strategic goals.

   ☒ **A** is incorrect because a project manager is given authority in the project charter; the manager may change, but the charter doesn't have to simultaneously change. **B** is incorrect because the timeline is not set in the project charter. **D** is incorrect because the funding and deliverables are both identified in the charter, but funding is not a fixed amount for most projects.

48. What two outputs are created in the Develop Project Charter process?

   A. Project charter and constraint list

   B. Project charter and business documents

   C. Project charter and organizational process assets

   D. Project charter and assumption log

   ☑ **D.** The assumptions about a project are created together with the project charter.

   ☒ **A** is incorrect because a constraint list is not created as an output of the Develop Project Charter process. **B** is incorrect because business documents are an input to the Develop Project Charter process. **C** is incorrect because organizational process assets preexist a project charter.

49. You are managing the project to move the company from one database platform to another. There are business stakeholders and information technology (IT) stakeholders, and each stakeholder group seems to have different goals. Which of the following is critical to ensure that you can create a shared understanding of success criteria for this project?

A. Listing all functional units and their detailed requirements in the project charter

B. Involving all stakeholders during the Initiating Process group processes

C. Listing all functional units and their detailed requirements in the project plan

D. Creating a RACI chart to ensure all stakeholders are identified

☑ **B.** Without stakeholder involvement, most projects will be challenged and may not succeed.

☒ **A** is incorrect because detailed requirements are not part of a project charter. **C** is incorrect because it is the project charter that creates the shared understanding of success, not the project plan. **D** is incorrect because a RACI chart assigns roles and responsibilities after stakeholders have been identified.

50. You are the project manager for a local painting contractor who paints interiors and exteriors of residential houses. You've learned that there are always multiple projects going on. For each project, you use a template to create a customized communications management plan and stakeholder engagement plan. These documents are both examples of documents:

A. Provided by the sponsor for the project

B. Created by the business analyst during the initiating phase

C. That are components of a project management plan

D. Created as a part of the initiating process group

☑ **C.** A communications plan and a stakeholder engagement plan are part of a project management plan.

☒ **A** is incorrect because the sponsor does not provide these documents; rather, they are created within the project. **B** is incorrect because these documents are created in the planning phase. **D** is incorrect because these documents are created as a part of the planning phase.

51. You are reviewing a list of high-level product characteristics for your new project. Accompanying the list is a set of approvals for the project requirements. What document are you likely reviewing?

A. Business case

B. Solution requirements

C. Project charter

D. Feasibility study

☑ **C.** A project charter contains the high-level product characteristics and is a signed-off, approved document.

☒ **A** is incorrect because a business case does not contain project requirements; rather, it presents a business problem and ways to solve it. **B** is incorrect because solution requirements are developed during the collect requirements process and contain lower-level product details. **D** is incorrect because the feasibility study would precede the project.

52. Which of the following is a data gathering technique used in the Identify Stakeholders process?

   A. Blamestorming

   B. Brain writing

   C. Prioritization

   D. Mind-mapping

   ☑ **B.** Brain writing is a refinement of brainstorming that allows individual participants time to consider the question(s) individually before the group creativity session is held.

   ☒ **A** is incorrect because blamestorming is a play on words for brainstorming. **C** is incorrect because prioritization is necessary for projects with many stakeholders. **D** is incorrect because mind-mapping consolidates ideas through individual brainstorming sessions.

The Planning Domain

This chapter includes questions from the following tasks:

- **Task 1**   Review and assess detailed project requirements, constraints, and assumptions with stakeholders based on the project charter and lessons learned and by using requirement-gathering techniques in order to establish detailed project deliverables.

- **Task 2**   Develop a scope management plan, based on the approved project scope and using scope management techniques, in order to define, maintain, and manage the scope of the project.

- **Task 3**   Develop the cost management plan based on the project scope, schedule, resources, approved project charter, and other information, using estimating techniques, in order to manage project costs.

- **Task 4**   Develop the project schedule based on the approved project deliverables and milestones, scope, and resource management plans in order to manage timely completion of the project.

- **Task 5**   Develop the human resource management plan by defining the roles and responsibilities of the project team members in order to create a project organizational structure and provide guidance regarding how resources will be assigned and managed.

- **Task 6**   Develop the communications management plan based on the project organizational structure and stakeholder requirements in order to define and manage the flow of project information.

- **Task 7**   Develop the procurement management plan based on the project scope, budget, and schedule in order to ensure that the required project resources will be available.

- **Task 8**   Develop the quality management plan and define the quality standards for the project and its products, based on the project scope, risks, and requirements, in order to prevent the occurrence of defects and control the cost of quality.

- **Task 9**   Develop the change management plan by defining how changes will be addressed and controlled in order to track and manage change.

- **Task 10**   Create a risk management plan by identifying, analyzing, and prioritizing project risk; creating the risk register; and defining risk response strategies in order to manage uncertainty and opportunity throughout the project life cycle.

- **Task 11**   Present the project management plan to the relevant stakeholders according to applicable policies and procedures in order to obtain approval to proceed with project execution.

- **Task 12**   Conduct kick-off meeting, communicating the start of the project, key milestones, and other relevant information, in order to inform and engage stakeholders and gain commitment.
- **Task 13**   Develop the stakeholder management plan by analyzing needs, interests, and potential impact in order to effectively manage stakeholders' expectations and engage them in project decisions.

The Planning process group is all about thinking through the aspects of the project at hand before moving into the execution phase. Project managers perform the planning domain with the goal of reducing project risk.

The planning domain accounts for 24% (48) of the questions on the PMP exam. The *PMBOK Guide, Sixth Edition,* namely Sections 4.2, 5.1–5.4, 6.1–6.5, 7.1–7.3, 8.1, 9.1, 9.2, 10.1, 11.1–11.5, 12.1, and 13.2, cover the 13 tasks in the planning domain.

The 96 practice questions in this chapter are mapped to the style and frequency of question types you will see on the PMP exam.

1. Calculate EMV for a risk event that has a 40% chance of occurring and that, if it occurred, would cost the project an additional $100,000.

    A. $4,000

    B. $40,000

    C. $100,000

    D. $400,000

2. Risk A has a 50% chance of happening. Unrelated Risk B has a 20% chance of happening. What is the chance they will both happen?

    A. 10%

    B. 30%

    C. 70%

    D. 100%

3. If the EMV of a risk is $200,000 and this risk exposure has been documented in the project business case, what is the maximum you could spend to remove the risk completely and be better off?

    A. $20,000

    B. $100,000

    C. $2,000,000

    D. $200,000

4. A residual risk is assessed to have a probability of 0.1 and an impact value of $50,000. What is the EMV of the residual risk?

    A. $1,000

    B. $5,000

    C. $50,000

    D. EMV does not apply to residual risk.

5. How is secondary risk assessed?

   A. E = (a + 4m + b) / 6

   B. EMV plus 10%

   C. Determine probability and multiply by impact

   D. The same way as original or residual risks

6. Your project charter has been approved. You are seeking approval of your project management plan. You have a meeting coming up with your project management team next week. They will be most interested in:

   A. Needed project team members

   B. The overall approach you will use to manage the project

   C. How progress will be measured and reported

   D. The project contracts you plan to put in place

7. You will be using earned value management (EVM) on your current project because it is mandated by the project management office (PMO). This means you will need to use:

   A. A PMO member on your team

   B. A project management information system

   C. A dedicated EVM specialist within your team

   D. Project-specific contract officers

8. As you plan your project's resources, you should emphasize the:

   A. Quality metrics to be collected to evaluate the product, service, or result

   B. Costs for each resource

   C. Desirability of having a dedicated team for each phase of the project

   D. Need to allocate and account for all resources

9. As you prepare your project management plan, you decide to attach your subsidiary plans, one of which is the:

   A. Benefits management plan

   B. Contract management plan

   C. Schedule management plan

   D. Stakeholder involvement plan

10. An effective project management practice is to enable contractors assigned to your project to have access to information in your Project Management Information System (PMIS) such as:

   A. Project budget information

   B. Buy or lease decision rules

   C. Change control/revision tools

   D. Requirements management information

11. Having been a project manager before, you were pleased to be selected to manage a software upgrade project on a nuclear power plant and have set up specific team ground rules for your project, including that:

   A. The steering committee members are part of the staffing management plan

   B. The resource management plan includes all project resources

   C. The Project Management Office (PMO) forms the dedicated project team

   D. Your project team is part of the PMO

12. You are the lead project manager on a government contract, and you are preparing the cost management plan for the project. Given that your project is for a government agency, which of the following should you be sure to consider?

   A. Policy compliance and audit procedures

   B. Annual nature of government funding

   C. Multiple civilian and military resources that will be available to you

   D. How the Federal Reserve decisions may affect interest rate hikes

13. You are a construction project manager working on a new office building in the outskirts of your city. You are developing your project management plan that assumes a dedicated project team. The plan for the project forecasts a two-year schedule. As part of the plan, you need to consider:

   A. Potential increases in resource costs

   B. The payback period for every year of the project

   C. Design changes based on external dependencies

   D. The need for annual cost/benefit analyses

14. You are working as a project manager on a project that involves protecting grizzly bears in Alaska. Not everyone is onboard with this effort, including several external stakeholders. In developing your communications management plan, you should consider:

   A. Updating the communications issues log

   B. Local laws about grizzly bears

   C. Building a RACI chart to ensure that all stakeholders are engaged

   D. The use of a communications assessment for unsupportive stakeholders

15. Given the planning data for your project, SEMAJ, you have identified the need to use several contractors for three parts of the multiyear project. As you determine specific procurement strategies after analyzing the involved WBS elements, your next step is to:

   A. Analyze the project scope statement

   B. Analyze the product description

   C. Prepare a procurement management plan

   D. Consider make-or-buy analysis

16. Your project will include the hiring of multiple third-party vendors, and you are considering the elements to include in the procurement management plan for the project. Before completing the procurement management plan, you should first:

    A. Review project assets on procurement

    B. Develop activity cost estimates

    C. Prepare a prequalified seller list

    D. Review the WBS

17. The PMO is recommending that you use fixed price (FP, or lump sum, or firm fixed price) contracts on all vendor contracts because you will have the least cost risk. The contract information should be:

    A. Included in the contract management plan

    B. Part of the procurement management plan

    C. Part of the procurement statement of work

    D. Developed by the contracts department

18. As you prepare your quality plan, it is important to understand:

    A. Quality is a variable cost in projects

    B. Quality is cost based

    C. Quality activities tend to be about equal from a QA and QC perspective

    D. Quality should be determined after test cases are complete

19. You are the project manager setting up a new production line for innovative gadget gifts for techies. You and your team are preparing the risk management plan. You first need to define:

    A. Your organization's risk appetite

    B. The functional requirements document you plan to use to identify risks

    C. Who the resistor stakeholders are

    D. Budget assumptions and constraints

20. You understand that positive and negative risks may affect your project, and you have set up risk categories to help as you work on your risk management plan. One obvious category of opportunities and threats is associated with resource availability. Which type of risk is this?

    A. Portfolio-related

    B. Product-level

    C. Program-level

    D. Project-related

21. As you prepare your project's risk management plan, and since the project involves setting up a new production line for innovative gadget gifts for techies, you should review the:

   A. Occupational safety and health issues

   B. Business case

   C. Potential suppliers on the prequalified sellers list

   D. Cultural differences in the production workers

22. You have a team of 12 people who are working on various parts of a project whose purpose is to facilitate the buying and selling of big-box stores that have closed. You have a WBS, and now you are developing your scope baseline. Which of the following should you include in your project schedule?

   A. Schedule decomposition

   B. Stakeholder issue tracking

   C. Activities related to stakeholder engagement

   D. A requirements traceability matrix

23. On a buying and selling closed big-box stores project, you acknowledge the desire to control risk through planning and therefore conclude that your scope management approach should be:

   A. Predictive

   B. Adaptive

   C. Iterative

   D. Lean

24. As you develop the project scope statement as the foundation for work your company is performing for a very demanding client, you should:

   A. Ask the project team to list the major deliverables to tie to major milestones

   B. Identify any new job seekers for open positions

   C. Use the resource traceability matrix in your data analysis

   D. Include acceptance criteria to use as closure guidelines

25. When you prepare your project schedule, you focus on identifying those activities that are on your critical path and that you intend to manage aggressively. As a part of the project schedule, it is also important for you to:

   A. Perform level-of-effort estimating for summary activities

   B. Use the critical chain method to include buffers

   C. Monitor the Iron Triangle for value and quality of the deliverables

   D. Ensure each key stakeholder's project deliverable expectations are met

26. Having been a PM for three years, you realize that a collective understanding of the success of the project among the project stakeholders can assist you in managing stakeholder expectations. Such a mutual understanding is best documented as part of the:

   A. Stakeholder management plan

   B. Project scope statement

   C. Scope management plan

   D. Project charter

27. On your project, you prepared a detailed stakeholder analysis. Realizing there was not a mutual understanding of the project's direction, you should prepare a:

   A. Feasibility study

   B. Stakeholder engagement plan

   C. Governance plan

   D. Project scope statement

28. Because the WBS is used to capture all project and nonproject work, this means that project management office support deliverables should be considered a(n):

   A. Top-level milestone

   B. External deliverable

   C. Work package

   D. Project management artifact

29. In developing project scope, one approach is to:

   A. Describe scope in user stories

   B. Determine scope through a high-level infrastructure

   C. Use the project's budget to set a financial baseline

   D. Include nonfunctional requirements for products, services, or results

30. You are creating your WBS. You realize that a generally accepted business practice is to:

   A. Structure it so product scope and project scope are easily managed

   B. Set it up so that it shows the complete scope of the work to be carried out on the project

   C. Use it to define the management control points for each of the major deliverables

   D. Define the solution to the problem in terms of a product, service, or result

31. Your organization's long-term goal is to build and sell electric bicycles. For now, your company will continue to produce motorcycles until the electric bicycles are online. You have a design team of 6 members and a production team of 18 people; these numbers are about half of what you believe you need. These limits are:

   A. Constraints to document in your project scope statement

   B. Limitations to document in your project charter

C. Known risks to set aside management reserves

D. Key issues to document in the risk log

32. You are the PM on a high-priority project. Your company has limited human resources. You have been told that the completion date cannot change. You are developing the resource management plan. You have decided to:

A. Prepare a resource plan

B. Use a resource breakdown structure linked to your WBS

C. Use resource smoothing

D. Conduct a Monte Carlo analysis to identify resource supply and demand on the project

33. You are in the military stationed near the North Pole. Your project is to rebuild all the runways at your air base, and you have one year to complete the project. Since it usually snows for nine months of the year, the construction team will be able to work on the runways in June, July, and August ... and maybe May and September. You understand your organizational culture, have the latest version of the scheduling software, and ESTICOR is used for standardized estimating data. What should you do now?

A. You should prepare a scope management plan.

B. The agile release approach should be followed.

C. The critical path may change as you use resource leveling.

D. You should adjust the start and end times with leads and lags.

34. Your new project, the SecureAI Project, will view threats and security breaches of corporate data involving artificial intelligence (AI). You have a dedicated project team of 16 people. Maciej is the domain expert and is frequently used in expert systems software development. Maciej's expertise has been a major advantage so far on your project. To be prudent, you need to:

A. Make sure there is a succession plan in place if Maciej leaves the project

B. Set up a process to debrief team members if they make plans to leave the project

C. Have everyone on your team go to advanced AI training

D. Have daily meetings with Maciej to make sure the project team knows what he is doing

35. You know that projects are unique endeavors, and you also know that they can be similar in some ways to other projects regarding work performance data and information. Which of the following will help ensure that project knowledge is a focus of your project team?

A. A project management information system

B. A chief information officer on your dedicated team

C. A chief data management officer in the PMO

D. A detailed human resource information system

36. As you manage the SecureAI Project, you know you will encounter some risks and issues. Issues can be risks that have occurred, but also are areas of concern to the project. A generally accepted business practice to follow regarding risks and issues is to:

    A. Use the risk register to capture operational-level issues

    B. Set up a risk control board for risks and issues that may occur

    C. Set up an escalation process for you to help resolve risks and issues

    D. Ensure a risk or issue is isolated to a singular project phase

37. In your project to set up a new production line for innovative gadget gifts for techies, you have decided to use two contractor companies for the work: one for the software and one for the hardware. You have developed the procurement management plan, and you have created a WBS. You recently met with the software contract officer and she had an issue to discuss with you, and in thinking about it, you realized it also affected the hardware contractor team. You should immediately:

    A. Meet with the entire project team.

    B. Inform your executive sponsor of this issue.

    C. Escalate it to the steering committee for resolution.

    D. Analyze your response so it is consistent with project objectives.

38. You just graduated from a prestigious university and you have been appointed to your first job as a project manager. Your project charter has been approved, and you now have a dedicated team who is working with you in planning the project. So far, you have prepared your scope and quality management plans and now are beginning to work on other plans that will be included in your project management plan. In the project management plan, you need to describe how performance reports will be prepared and distributed. Your program manager pointed out that she wanted regular updates, but she did not want to see many metrics collected that did not add value. You and your team have decided that the best approach is to choose metrics that:

    A. Show how your project contributes to the organization's bottom line

    B. Show the progress according to the triple constraints

    C. Use earned value management to assess project performance and progress

    D. Show project management and team delivery rates

39. You must develop a scope statement for a cross-department project. Many people will be involved in this project with multiple stakeholders represented from each of the departments. In this case, who would approve the scope statement that you develop?

    A. The project team members

    B. The project sponsor

C. The project manager

D. The financial manager

40. A project manager is stepping in as a take-over role and has been given a completed project scope statement prepared by the previous project manager. What is the first action she should take at this point?

A. Create a complete network diagram for the tasks and milestones in the project.

B. Confirm that the project management team agrees with the scope statement.

C. Develop a detailed project plan based on the existing work breakdown structure.

D. Call a meeting of the project management team to agree on a procurement plan.

41. You have just acquired a new team member on the project you are managing. This is the first project for the team member, and she asks you the purpose of the WBS. What do you describe as its primary purpose?

A. Clarify the responsibility for project tasks.

B. Communicate with all stakeholders.

C. Define the business need for the project.

D. Detail the dates for the work packages.

42. The project has produced a requirements traceability matrix that links requirements to their origin and traces them throughout the project life cycle. Which statement describes the purpose of the requirements traceability matrix?

A. It describes in detail the project's deliverables and the work required to create those deliverables and includes product and project scope description.

B. It ensures that requirements approved in the requirements documentation are delivered at the end of the project and helps manage changes to the product scope.

C. It is a narrative description of products or services to be delivered by the project and is received from the customer for external projects.

D. It provides the necessary information from a business standpoint to determine whether the project is worth the required investment.

43. You have been developing a scope statement for a project you have been given authority to manage. During this process, you came across areas of technical details that you were not familiar with. Which of the following would you use to help clarify the related issues and their impact on the project scope?

A. Experienced managers

B. Special interest groups

C. Expert judgment

D. Similar project plans

44. You have been given the responsibility for a project that you have not been involved with to date. The project is at the beginning of the execution stage. What is the main document to which you would refer to guide you on what you should be doing on this project?

   A. Project management plan

   B. Procurement management plan

   C. Communication management plan

   D. Project scope management plan

45. You are involved in a project and regularly receive work packages to complete from the project manager. The project manager describes some of the results of your work as project deliverables. The processes that describe project deliverables from your work are defined in which of the following?

   A. The completed task contract form

   B. The initial work breakdown structure

   C. The project management plan

   D. The initial project scope document

46. The project has produced a requirements management plan. What is the purpose of this document?

   A. The requirements management plan links requirements to their origin and traces them throughout the project.

   B. The requirements management plan documents how requirements will be analyzed, documented, and managed throughout the project.

   C. The requirements management plan describes how individual requirements meet the business need for the project.

   D. The requirements management plan provides guidance on how project scope will be defined, documented, verified, managed, and controlled.

47. You are discussing your role as a project manager with your peers. In the conversation, another team member describes the process of defining and controlling what is, and what is not, included in the project. What are these activities called?

   A. Project documentation management

   B. Project change control

   C. Plan scope management

   D. Formal acceptance documents

48. You have been involved in a workshop at which the project management team created an initial work breakdown structure (WBS). Which of the following best describes the process in which you were involved?

   A. Calculating the total duration of the project from the start

   B. Counting the total number of work packages in the project

C. Allocating responsibilities for the project work to individuals in the team

D. Subdividing the project work into smaller, more manageable components

49. The scope management plan is produced by the project management team as part of the Plan Scope Management process. Which statement best describes the scope management plan?

   A. The scope management plan provides guidance on how project scope will be defined, documented, verified, managed, and controlled.

   B. The scope management plan documents how requirements will be analyzed, documented, and managed throughout the project.

   C. The scope management plan describes in detail the project's deliverables and the work required to create those deliverables.

   D. The scope management plan is a deliverable-oriented hierarchical decomposition of the work to be executed by the project team.

50. A team member who has just joined your project asks what is involved in this project. You refer her to the project scope statement, which contains all the following except:

   A. Deferred change requests

   B. Product scope description

   C. Project assumptions

   D. Product acceptance criteria

51. The project you are working on is running behind schedule, is over budget, and is failing to deliver the features originally promised. The project manager says that the work must now be focused on a list of activities. What defines this list of activities?

   A. Shortest-duration tasks

   B. Requirements documentation

   C. Critical-path tasks

   D. Lowest-cost tasks

52. You are assigned to manage a new project. Your line manager suggests that you should use a tool to help you plan the new project. She suggests that you use a work breakdown structure (WBS) template. Which of the following is the best description of this tool?

   A. A document that lists WBS elements

   B. An all-purpose WBS from the Internet

   C. A WBS from a previous project

   D. A definition of WBS colors and shapes

53. The project meeting you are attending is becoming heated, and arguments are starting about the work completed and the work to be done. The project manager stops the discussion and refers to one document that is used as a reference. What is this document called?

- **A.** Approved changes
- **B.** Newly identified risks
- **C.** The WBS template
- **D.** The scope baseline

54. After some changes to your project scope, you have revised the schedule, costs, and work package assignments, and these changes have been approved. What action do you now complete?

- **A.** Wait for resources to complete current assignments.
- **B.** Reissue the project management plan.
- **C.** Immediately look for other changes to submit.
- **D.** Let the project schedule continue as previously.

55. You have asked a team member to perform many actions on a project plan. These actions are decomposing the work packages into smaller components and activities that are to be the basis for estimating, scheduling, and running the project. What is this team member's activity called?

- **A.** Schedule work
- **B.** Estimate tasks
- **C.** Schedule activities
- **D.** Define activities

56. You note that your weekly time sheet report shows that you have identified activities, scoped the work needed on each, and provided sufficient detail to allow a team member to understand what is required to complete that work. What description summarizes the time you have spent this week?

- **A.** Producing an activity list
- **B.** Defining the project scope
- **C.** Developing the project schedule
- **D.** Identifying the WBS elements

57. The precedence diagramming method can be used to clarify the dependencies between activities. One type of dependency used is to ensure that the successor activity does not start until the completion of the predecessor activity. What is the name given to this type of dependency?

   A. Start-to-start

   B. Finish-to-finish

   C. Finish-to-start

   D. Start-to-finish

58. One tool of project management is a table that identifies and describes the types and quantities of each resource required to complete all project work packages. What is this table known as?

   A. Resource calendar updates

   B. Activity attribute updates

   C. Resource breakdown structure

   D. Activity resource requirements

59. You are completing the planning for a project schedule. Because you do not have much information about one activity, you decide to estimate its duration by referring to the actual duration of a similar activity on another project. This calculation method is called:

   A. Analogous estimating

   B. Expert judgment

   C. Parametric estimating

   D. Reserve analysis

60. Your project manager asks you to calculate the theoretical early start and finish dates on your project schedule, along with late start and finish dates, for all the project activities. He suggests you use a forward and backward pass analysis. This technique is known as (the):

   A. Critical chain method

   B. Critical path method

   C. Schedule compression

   D. What-if analysis

61. You are asked to review a project that another department has planned for your organization. Your line manager asks you to show her a project overview that shows only the start and end dates of major deliverables, along with key external dependencies. This graphic is known as a:

   A. Network diagram

   B. Summary bar chart

   C. Milestone chart

   D. Schedule baseline

62. While reviewing a work package that you have assigned to a member of your team, you look at a graphic that shows the activity start, duration, and finish on a time base. This chart is commonly known as a(n):

 A. Activity float list

 B. Network diagram

 C. Work breakdown structure

 D. Project bar chart

63. The project you have been planning has been approved by the project management team, and you can now start the execution stage. You have authority for a reference that contains an activity schedule and project start and finish dates. This reference is called:

 A. The project schedule baseline

 B. A network diagram

 C. A milestone chart

 D. The project calendar

64. You are asked to develop a table that includes the schedule milestones, schedule activities, activity attributes, and documented assumptions and constraints. You also include resource requirements by time period, alternative schedules, and scheduling of contingency reserves. The table that you prepare is known as the:

 A. Project schedule

 B. Schedule data

 C. Resource schedule

 D. Project bar chart

65. You have been working on a project in the planning stage, developing the likely costs. The project sponsor expects a narrower estimate of the costs because more information is now known. Which of the following is considered a suitable range for this request?

 A. −100% to +100%

 B. −5% to +10%

 C. −25% to +25%

 D. −50% to +50%

66. A project team member is building the costs for a current project, using costs from a previous similar project that has been completed in your organization. This estimating technique is known as:

 A. Analogous

 B. Bottom-up

 C. Parametric

 D. Three-point

67. Building the costs for a current project using characteristics from a mathematical model to help predict the project costs is known as what type of estimating technique?

   A. Analogous

   B. Bottom-up

   C. Parametric

   D. Three-point

68. A team member has been given the task of identifying which quality standards are relevant to this project and determining how to satisfy these standards. In which of the following processes is she engaged?

   A. Control Quality

   B. Manage Quality

   C. Plan Quality Management

   D. Quality Improvement

69. You have been asked to detail the steps for analyzing processes to identify activities that enhance the value of those processes. This is called:

   A. Establishing the quality baseline

   B. Developing quality checklists

   C. Establishing quality metrics

   D. Process improvement planning

70. You have been asked to perform the quality planning for a project. One of the first actions you take is to clarify what some of the measurements on the project are and how the Control Quality process measures these. This action is known as:

   A. Define quality metrics

   B. Develop quality checklists

   C. Set the quality baseline

   D. Plan process improvements

71. A team member is following the steps outlined in the process improvement plan. This is needed to improve organizational and project performance. What reference document would the team member use to help with this activity?

   A. Quality metrics

   B. Quality audits

   C. Process analysis

   D. Quality checklists

72. You are identifying and documenting project roles, responsibilities, and reporting relationships for a project, as well as creating a staffing management plan for a project. In terms of project management, these activities are known as:

    A. Planning resource management

    B. Developing project management plan

    C. Managing team

    D. Developing team

73. As part of the project plan documentation, you find a diagram that illustrates the link between work packages and project team members. This diagram is called a(n):

    A. Hierarchy-type chart

    B. Responsibility assignment matrix

    C. Organizational chart

    D. Dependency diagram

74. You are planning the resourcing for a project and create a visual representation that illustrates the number of hours that each person will be needed each week over the course of the project schedule. This visual representation is commonly known as a:

    A. Work breakdown structure

    B. Task network diagram

    C. Resource histogram

    D. Detailed Gantt chart

75. You are managing a project and ask for additional time to enable you to meet new roles. You list the additional activities, such as setting clear expectations, developing processes for managing conflict, including the team in decision making, and sharing credit for success. The name given to this process is:

    A. Management by objectives

    B. Matrix management

    C. Negotiate for resources

    D. Plan Communications Management

76. You are in the final stages of planning a project and are considering ways to best influence the team over the course of the project, including bonus structures, perks, and a project website. What best describes what you are defining?

    A. Staff roles and responsibilities

    B. Organizational process assets

    C. Staffing management plan

    D. Team performance assessment

77. A project manager must perform many activities when planning and managing a project. These include developing an approach for stakeholder information needs; creating, collecting, distributing, storing, and disposing of project information; and monitoring and controlling communications. These activities are examples of:

   A. Recommended preventive actions

   B. Project performance appraisals

   C. Recommended corrective actions

   D. Project communications management

78. A section of your project plan lists methods and technologies to be used to convey memoranda, email, press releases, and how frequently these should be used. The document that defines these is called a(n):

   A. Communications management plan

   B. Organizational assets

   C. Communications technology

   D. Project management plan

79. During the planning stage of a project, you decide to assign a member of your project team to be responsible for the distribution of information about the project. Where should you document this decision?

   A. Project management plan

   B. Communications management plan

   C. Project roles and responsibilities

   D. Project team assessment

80. To be successful, how often should an organization address risk management?

   A. At every management meeting

   B. Only in the planning phase

   C. On high-risk projects only

   D. Consistently throughout

81. The project director advises you that a project should have a balance between risk taking and risk avoidance. This policy is implemented in a project using:

   A. Risk responses

   B. Risk analysis

   C. Risk identification

   D. Risk classification

82. Who is responsible for identifying risks in a new project?

  A. The project manager

  B. The project sponsor

  C. Any project personnel

  D. The main stakeholders

83. The document that contains a list of identified risks and, against each a list of potential responses, the root cause of the risk, and the risk category is called the:

  A. Risk management plan

  B. Project issues log

  C. Risk category checklist

  D. Risk register

84. As part of your responsibility for managing risks in your project, you rate risks as low, medium, or high. What tool would you typically use to define these categories?

  A. Probability impact matrix

  B. Risk register updates

  C. Assumption analysis

  D. Checklist analysis

85. A new member of your project team suggests that you should quantify risks using the lowest, highest, and most likely costs of the WBS elements in the project plan. What is the name for the technique being suggested?

  A. Three-point estimating

  B. Probability impact analysis

  C. Probability distributions

  D. Sensitivity analysis

86. The process of project planning that involves developing options, determining actions to enhance opportunities, and reducing threats to project objectives is called:

  A. Perform Qualitative Risk Analysis

  B. Plan Risk Responses

  C. Perform Quantitative Risk Analysis

  D. Probability and Impact Matrix

87. Your team is developing a part of the risk management plan. For some of the risks, the team decides that a response plan will be executed only when certain predefined conditions exist. What is the term given to this type of risk strategy?

  A. Contingent

  B. Sharing

C. Exploit

D. Enhance

88. Information such as outcomes of risk reassessments, risk audits, and periodic risk reviews are examples from which of the following?

   A. Risk management plan

   B. Approved change requests

   C. Project documents updates

   D. Work performance information

89. During the Plan Procurement Management process for a project, you decide whether a product or service can be produced by the project team or instead should be purchased. This decision-making process is called:

   A. Procurement management

   B. Expert judgment

   C. Risk management

   D. Make-or-buy analysis

90. The contract you are negotiating with a subcontractor involves a set price for a well-defined requirement and incentives for meeting selected objectives. This type of contract is:

   A. Time and material

   B. Cost-reimbursable

   C. Fixed-price

   D. Cost plus incentive

91. The procurement and contracting process involves asking such questions as how well the seller meets the contract statement of work, whether the seller has the capacity to meet future requirements, and whether the seller can provide references from previous customers. What is the name given to this list and/or its use?

   A. Contract management

   B. Source selection criteria

   C. Supplier risk analysis

   D. Contract negotiation

92. Your contract and procurement consultant recommends that you establish source selection criteria for each of your sellers' proposals. What part of the procurement process will this assist?

   A. Bidder conference

   B. Plan Procurement Management

   C. Conduct Procurements

   D. Buyer requests

93. Using the following part of a WBS, what do you know about Activity 3.1.1?

3.1 Requirements
3.1.1 Interview Stakeholders

- **A.** It is a control account.
- **B.** It is used for cost reporting.
- **C.** It is the work package.
- **D.** It is the milestone above the work package.

94. You and your team are estimating the duration of the coding/unit testing phase. Your optimistic estimate is 1,200 hours, your most likely estimate is 1,700 hours, and your pessimistic estimate is 2,000 hours. The resource rate is $150 per hour. What is your cost estimate of the coding/unit test phase using the PERT estimating technique?

- **A.** $255,000
- **B.** $250,050
- **C.** $280,325
- **D.** $270,175

95. The business case stated a project cost of $2,500,000. You and your team just received the signed project charter and are ready to present a high-level estimate to the project management team. What is the acceptable accuracy range for this estimate?

- **A.** $1,187,500 to $4,375,000
- **B.** $1,200,000 to $3,300,000
- **C.** $1,225,000 to $4,312,500
- **D.** $1,237,500 to $3,275,000

96. A project estimate generated during the initiation phase may have an accuracy of:

- **A.** –25% to +75%
- **B.** –10% to +25%
- **C.** –5% to +10%
- **D.** –50% to +150%

1. B	**25.** D	**49.** A	**73.** B
2. A	**26.** B	**50.** A	**74.** C
3. D	**27.** D	**51.** B	**75.** D
4. B	**28.** C	**52.** C	**76.** B
5. D	**29.** A	**53.** D	**77.** D
6. B	**30.** B	**54.** B	**78.** A
7. B	**31.** A	**55.** D	**79.** B
8. D	**32.** B	**56.** A	**80.** D
9. C	**33.** A	**57.** C	**81.** A
10. D	**34.** B	**58.** D	**82.** C
11. B	**35.** A	**59.** A	**83.** D
12. B	**36.** C	**60.** B	**84.** A
13. A	**37.** D	**61.** C	**85.** A
14. D	**38.** A	**62.** D	**86.** B
15. D	**39.** B	**63.** A	**87.** A
16. D	**40.** B	**64.** B	**88.** C
17. B	**41.** B	**65.** B	**89.** D
18. A	**42.** B	**66.** A	**90.** C
19. A	**43.** C	**67.** C	**91.** B
20. D	**44.** A	**68.** C	**92.** B
21. B	**45.** C	**69.** D	**93.** C
22. C	**46.** B	**70.** A	**94.** B
23. A	**47.** C	**71.** C	**95.** A
24. D	**48.** D	**72.** A	**96.** A

1. Calculate EMV for a risk event that has a 40% chance of occurring and that, if it occurred, would cost the project an additional $100,000.

   A. $4,000

   B. $40,000

   C. $100,000

   D. $400,000

   ☑ **B.** 40% × $100,000 = $40,000. The three steps to calculate EMV are as follows: 1) Assign a probability of occurrence for the risk. 2) Assign the monetary value of the impact of the risk when it occurs. 3) Multiply Step 1 and Step 2. The value you get after performing Step 3 is the expected monetary value (EMV). This value is positive for opportunities (positive risks) and negative for threats (negative risks). Managing project risk requires you to address both types of project risks.

   ☒ **A, C,** and **D** are incorrect because the answers do not come from following the three steps of calculating EMV.

2. Risk A has a 50% chance of happening. Unrelated Risk B has a 20% chance of happening. What is the chance they will both happen?

   A. 10%

   B. 30%

   C. 70%

   D. 100%

   ☑ **A.** 10% because 0.50 × 0.20 = 0.10 = 10%. When two events are independent, the EMV (probability) of both occurring is the product of the probabilities of the individual events. More formally, if events A and B are independent, then the probability of both A and B occurring is: P(A and B) = P(A) × P(B).

   ☒ **B, C,** and **D** are incorrect because they were not arrived at by calculating the probability of two independent events through multiplication of the probabilities of the two events.

3. If the EMV of a risk is $200,000 and this risk exposure has been documented in the project business case, what is the maximum you could spend to remove the risk completely and be better off?

   A. $20,000

   B. $100,000

   C. $2,000,000

   D. $200,000

☑ **D.** $200,000 is the maximum amount you would spend to eliminate the risk completely, which is equal to the amount of risk exposure.

☒ **A, B,** and **C** are incorrect because spending any more or less than the amount of risk exposure is not a sound project management practice.

4. A residual risk is assessed to have a probability of 0.1 and an impact value of $50,000. What is the EMV of the residual risk?

   A. $1,000

   B. $5,000

   C. $50,000

   D. EMV does not apply to residual risk.

   ☑ **B.** $5000. The three steps to calculate EMV are as follows: 1) Assign a probability of occurrence for the risk. 2) Assign a monetary value for the impact of the risk when it occurs. 3) Multiply Step 1 and Step 2. The value you get after performing Step 3 is the expected monetary value (EMV). This value is positive for opportunities (positive risks) and negative for threats (negative risks). Managing project risk requires requires you to address both types of project risks.

   ☒ **A, C,** and **D** are incorrect because the answers do not come from following the three steps for calculating EMV.

5. How is secondary risk assessed?

   A. E = (a + 4m + b) / 6

   B. EMV plus 10%

   C. Determine probability and multiply by impact

   D. The same way as original or residual risks

   ☑ **D.** Secondary risk is a risk that happens because you implemented a risk response. A residual risk is the risk that remains after a risk response has been taken. Secondary risks should be assessed for proper action in the same way as original risks and residual risks.

   ☒ **A** is incorrect because it is the formula for three-point estimating. **B** is incorrect because it is an improper calculation. **C** is incorrect because it is the definition of risk exposure.

6. Your project charter has been approved. You are seeking approval of your project management plan. You have a meeting coming up with your project management team next week. They will be most interested in:

   A. Needed project team members

   B. The overall approach you will use to manage the project

C. How progress will be measured and reported

D. The project contracts you plan to put in place

☑ **B.** The project management plan development process integrates the project's subsidiary plans and establishes the overall approach for managing the project.

☒ **A** is incorrect because you are responsible for acquiring, managing, and developing the project team members. **C** is incorrect because at this point it is too early to select the project performance measurements. **D** is incorrect because procurements and contracts are decided after you create a WBS.

7. You will be using earned value management (EVM) on your current project because it is mandated by the project management office (PMO). This means you will need to use:

A. A PMO member on your team

B. A project management information system

C. A dedicated EVM specialist within your team

D. Project-specific contract officers

☑ **B.** A project management information system (PMIS) is the coherent arrangement of the information required for an organization to execute projects successfully. A PMIS is typically one or more software applications, together with a methodical process for collecting and using project information.

☒ **A** is incorrect because PMP members are support staff and not dedicated team members. **C** is incorrect because you do not need a specialist added to the team to use EVM. PMs can use spreadsheets to calculate EVM. **D** is incorrect because it is too early in the project to know about contracts.

8. As you plan your project's resources, you should emphasize the:

A. Quality metrics to be collected to evaluate the product, service, or result

B. Costs for each resource

C. Desirability of having a dedicated team for each phase of the project

D. Need to allocate and account for all resources

☑ **D.** Resource planning is done at an early stage. Work performance reports can show the details of resource allocation and usage throughout the project.

☒ **A** is incorrect because quality metrics are a description of the product or project attributes and how to measure them. **B** is incorrect because the costs for each resource are collected and used in the Determine Budget process. **C** is incorrect because the skills and competencies needed for each team member—within each phase of the project—is the Plan Resource Management process.

9. As you prepare your project management plan, you decide to attach your subsidiary plans, one of which is the:

A. Benefits management plan

B. Contract management plan

C. Schedule management plan

D. Stakeholder involvement plan

☑ **C.** The schedule management plan is a subsidiary plan of the project management plan and is the only output of the Plan Schedule Management process.

☒ **A** is incorrect because the benefits management plan complements the project management plan. It is not a subsidiary plan. **B** is incorrect because although a contract management plan can be used by the contracting officer, it is not a subsidiary plan. **D** is incorrect because the stakeholder involvement plan does not exist; instead it is the stakeholder engagement plan that includes strategies or approaches for engaging with stakeholders.

10. An effective project management practice is to enable contractors assigned to your project to have access to information in your Project Management Information System (PMIS) such as:

A. Project budget information

B. Buy or lease decision rules

C. Change control/revision tools

D. Requirements management information

☑ **D.** Requirements management information is stored in a PMIS. Contractors can be more productive when allowed to use tools to capture and manage requirements for your projects/products in a structured, collaborative fashion.

☒ **A** and **B** are incorrect because budget information and buy-or-lease decisions are sensitive, company-specific information and better controlled within the company. **C** is incorrect because the PM is responsible for maintaining the integrity of modifications to project deliverables and documentation.

11. Having been a project manager before, you were pleased to be selected to manage a software upgrade project on a nuclear power plant and have set up specific team ground rules for your project, including that:

A. The steering committee members are part of the staffing management plan

B. The resource management plan includes all project resources

C. The Project Management Office (PMO) forms the dedicated project team

D. Your project team is part of the PMO

☑ **B.** The resource management plan is a subsidiary plan of the project management plan that describes how all project resources are acquired, allocated, measured, and corrected.

☒ **A** is incorrect because a steering committee should be selected at the beginning of a project, usually in the preinitiation stage. In general, the steering committee is a senior management team that guides and is accountable for the project and gains management commitment. **C** is incorrect because the PMO is a support group. **D** is incorrect because your dedicated project team members are assigned to your project and are not assigned to the PMO.

12. You are the lead project manager on a government contract, and you are preparing the cost management plan for the project. Given that your project is for a government agency, which of the following should you be sure to consider?

A. Policy compliance and audit procedures

B. Annual nature of government funding

C. Multiple civilian and military resources that will be available to you

D. How the Federal Reserve decisions may affect interest rate hikes

☑ B. DoD's annual funding policy states that the budget request for a fiscal year should be restricted to the budget authority necessary to cover all 1) expenditures expected to be made during that fiscal year and 2) costs of goods and services expected to be required during that fiscal year.

☒ A is incorrect because policy compliance is a goal set by an organization in its attempt to encourage and achieve compliance by its members/employees about the organization's policies. Audits are performed to ensure compliance. C is incorrect because resource allocation and usage are handled through the project life cycle. D is incorrect because interest rate hikes affect borrowing capacity, not funding.

13. You are a construction project manager working on a new office building in the outskirts of your city. You are developing your project management plan that assumes a dedicated project team. The plan for the project forecasts a two-year schedule. As part of the plan, you need to consider:

A. Potential increases in resource costs

B. The payback period for every year of the project

C. Design changes based on external dependencies

D. The need for annual cost/benefit analyses

☑ A. Direct costs include the salaries for dedicated team members on your project and contractors that provide support exclusively to your project. In multiyear projects it is likely that resource costs will increase each year, and a prudent project manager will budget for these increases.

☒ B. The payback period formula is used to determine the length of time it will take to recoup the initial amount invested on a project or investment. It is calculated at the beginning of the project. C is incorrect because "design changes based on external dependencies" may affect the project, but the PM controls these changes. D is incorrect because cost/benefit analysis is part of the business case and completed in the initiation stage of the project.

14. You are working as a project manager on a project that involves protecting grizzly bears in Alaska. Not everyone is onboard with this effort, including several external stakeholders. In developing your communications management plan, you should consider:

A. Updating the communications issues log

B. Local laws about grizzly bears

C. Building a RACI chart to ensure that all stakeholders are engaged

D. The use of a communications assessment for unsupportive stakeholders

☑ **D.** PMs face the challenges of communicating with stakeholders who have a different style of communication than their own. One of the best ways to quickly improve the effectiveness of your communication is to adapt your communication style to match theirs. This is especially true with unwilling/unsupportive/challenging stakeholders.

☒ **A** is incorrect because although there is disagreement about your project, after you complete the communications assessments, you could update the communications issues log. **B** is incorrect because obeying all local laws about grizzly bears is an external factor. **C** is incorrect because a RACI chart assigns roles and responsibilities to stakeholders during a project; however, it would be preferable to do a communications assessment prior to a RACI chart.

15. Given the planning data for your project, SEMAJ, you have identified the need to use several contractors for three parts of the multiyear project. As you determine specific procurement strategies after analyzing the involved WBS elements, your next step is to:

A. Analyze the project scope statement

B. Analyze the product description

C. Prepare a procurement management plan

D. Consider make-or-buy analysis

☑ **D.** Make-or-buy analysis (which can lead to a make-or-buy decision) is a process that PMs follow to know whether it's better for them to do the work in-house or pay for a third-party company to help the project team.

☒ **A** is incorrect because you have already analyzed the project scope statement to determine specific procurement strategies. **B** is incorrect because the product scope description is completed as part of scope definition. **C** is incorrect because the procurement management plan will include your procurement decisions after you complete the make-or-buy analysis.

16. Your project will include the hiring of multiple third-party vendors, and you are considering the elements to include in the procurement management plan for the project. Before completing the procurement management plan, you should first:

A. Review project assets on procurement

B. Develop activity cost estimates

C. Prepare a prequalified seller list

D. Review the WBS

☑ **D.** The procurement management plan is a part of the overall project management plan, and the WBS is the best predictor of the success of a new project, including vendor assets. By reviewing the work breakdown structure before you prepare the procurement plan, it is relatively easy to determine what procurements are needed throughout the life of the project. The WBS identifies items to be procured, and the procurement plan defines the items to be procured, the types of contracts to be used in support of the project, the contract approval process, and decision criteria.

☒ **A** is incorrect because you are not at the point that assets for procurement would be available. **B** is incorrect because you prepare activity cost estimates after you create the WBS. **C** is incorrect because a prequalified seller list is prepared in conducting procurements, which follows the creation of the procurement management plan.

17. The PMO is recommending that you use fixed price (FP, or lump sum, or firm fixed price) contracts on all vendor contracts because you will have the least cost risk. The contract information should be:

   A. Included in the contract management plan

   B. Part of the procurement management plan

   C. Part of the procurement statement of work

   D. Developed by the contracts department

   ☑ **B.** Contract terms for a project are included in the procurement management plan.

   ☒ **A** is incorrect because the contract management plan is not a plan used by the PM. It may be a plan used by the contracts office. **C** is incorrect because the work to be done on each procurement is called a procurement statement of work (PSOW), which describes the work and activities that the seller is required to complete. The activities also include meetings, reports, and communications. Contract types are part of the PSOW. **D** is incorrect because the project management team is responsible for receiving bids or proposals and the application of evaluation criteria to select a seller.

18. As you prepare your quality plan, it is important to understand:

   A. Quality is a variable cost in projects

   B. Quality is cost based

   C. Quality activities tend to be about equal from a QA and QC perspective

   D. Quality should be determined after test cases are complete

   ☑ **A.** Quality is a variable cost in all projects and should be considered as such in project quality planning.

   ☒ **B** is incorrect because the cost of quality includes the cost impact of conformance versus nonconformance. It can also include quick cost reductions versus long-term costs to prevent product problems later in the life cycle. **C** is incorrect because QA activities are preferred over QC activities. QA means keeping the defect out of the process. QC means keeping the defect out of the hands of the customer. Prevention over inspection. **D** is incorrect because test cases should be created before quality is measured.

19. You are the project manager setting up a new production line for innovative gadget gifts for techies. You and your team are preparing the risk management plan. You first need to define:

A. Your organization's risk appetite

B. The functional requirements document you plan to use to identify risks

C. Who the resistor stakeholders are

D. Budget assumptions and constraints

☑ **A.** In risk management, risk appetite is the level of risk an organization is prepared to accept. Risk appetite constraints are not easy to define; every organization can tolerate different levels of risk.

☒ **B** is incorrect because the functional requirements document may indicate project objectives that are particularly at risk and is an input to the risk management plan. **C** is incorrect because a resistant stakeholder will be identified in the stakeholder engagement assessment matrix in the stakeholder management plan. **D** is incorrect because budget assumptions and constraints will be used to keep the known risks within the identified risk thresholds.

20. You understand that positive and negative risks may affect your project, and you have set up risk categories to help as you work on your risk management plan. One obvious category of opportunities and threats is associated with resource availability. Which type of risk is this?

A. Portfolio-related

B. Product-level

C. Program-level

D. Project-related

☑ **D.** Resource availability risk is a category of potential causes of positive and negative risk and can affect the day-to-day work on the project.

☒ **A** and **C** are incorrect because each are higher-level risks and do not happen at the same time as the project work. **B** is incorrect because product-level risks are not usually related to resourcing.

21. As you prepare your project's risk management plan, and since the project involves setting up a new production line for innovative gadget gifts for techies, you should review the:

A. Occupational safety and health issues

B. Business case

C. Potential suppliers on the prequalified sellers list

D. Cultural differences in the production workers

☑ **B.** When managing risk, market factors that apply to the project should be included as an enterprise environmental factor. Market demand, a high risk, is included in the business case.

☒ **A** is incorrect because although you will comply with OSHA regulations in your new building, it is a low risk compared to no market for your gadgets. **C** is incorrect because the question does not imply the use of potential sellers. **D** is incorrect because resource risks are known risks and are mitigated later in the risk management processes.

22. You have a team of 12 people who are working on various parts of a project whose purpose is to facilitate the buying and selling of big-box stores that have closed. You have a WBS, and now you are developing your scope baseline. Which of the following should you include in your project schedule?

   A. Schedule decomposition

   B. Stakeholder issue tracking

   C. Activities related to stakeholder engagement

   D. A requirements traceability matrix

   ☑ **C.** The project schedule should include activities related to stakeholder engagement, risk mitigation, and project reviews.

   ☒ **A** is incorrect because the activities/tasks are already decomposed in a project schedule to work packages and then aggregated to build a project schedule. **B** is incorrect because stakeholder issues are listed in the stakeholder issue log. **D** is incorrect because a requirements traceability matrix is not included in a project schedule.

23. On a buying and selling closed big-box stores project, you acknowledge the desire to control risk through planning and therefore conclude that your scope management approach should be:

   A. Predictive

   B. Adaptive

   C. Iterative

   D. Lean

   ☑ **A.** In a predictive (plan-driven) life cycle, the three major constraints (scope, schedule, and cost) are determined ahead of time, not just at a high level, but in detail. This is where the high-level planning is done for the entire project, but the detailed planning is done only for the work that needs to be done soon. In a plan-driven life cycle, the detailed scope of the project is determined right from the start.

   ☒ **B** and **C** are incorrect because the adaptive life cycle is based upon the iterative and incremental process models and focuses upon adaptability to changing product requirements and enhancing customer satisfaction through rapid delivery of working product features and client participation. **D** is incorrect because lean is also an adaptive life cycle approach and controls risk through rapid delivery of small amounts of working product.

24. As you develop the project scope statement as the foundation for work your company is performing for a very demanding client, you should:

A. Ask the project team to list the major deliverables to tie to major milestones

B. Identify any new job seekers for open positions

C. Use the resource traceability matrix in your data analysis

D. Include acceptance criteria to use as closure guidelines

  ☑ **D.** Acceptance criteria are documented in the project scope statement. Acceptance criteria are also considered an important part of contractual agreements on external projects and are used as project closure guidelines.

  ☒ **A** is incorrect because major deliverables are sometimes tied to major milestones and are displayed in a milestone chart, which is an output of developing the schedule. **B** is incorrect because new team members are added as part of acquiring the project team. **C** is incorrect because resource traceability matrix is a made-up term. A responsibility assignment matrix shows the project resources assigned to each work package.

25. When you prepare your project schedule, you focus on identifying those activities that are on your critical path and that you intend to manage aggressively. As a part of the project schedule, it is also important for you to:

A. Perform level-of-effort estimating for summary activities

B. Use the critical chain method to include buffers

C. Monitor the Iron Triangle for value and quality of the deliverables

D. Ensure each key stakeholder's project deliverable expectations are met

  ☑ **D.** Each stakeholder group has needs and expectations. Getting the right deliverables to the right stakeholders at the right time is paramount.

  ☒ **A** is incorrect because although prudent project managers use duration estimates for work package estimates and aggregate those estimates for summary activities, level of effort estimates are the number of labor hours required to complete an activity and therefore are not summaries. **B** is incorrect because the critical chain method of planning and managing projects emphasizes the resources (people, equipment, physical space) required to execute project tasks and therefore excludes buffers. **C** is incorrect because the Iron Triangle measures scope, time, and cost, not value and quality; however, the Agile Triangle measures value and quality in addition to Iron Triangle constraints.

26. Having been a PM for three years, you realize that a collective understanding of the success of the project among the project stakeholders can assist you in managing stakeholder expectations. Such a mutual understanding is best documented as part of the:

A. Stakeholder management plan

B. Project scope statement

C. Scope management plan

D. Project charter

    ☑ **B.** The PM ensures that the context and framework of the project are properly defined, assessed, and documented in the form of a project scope statement. Project stakeholders should verify and approve the project scope statement.

    ☒ **A** is incorrect because the stakeholder management plan has been replaced with the stakeholder engagement plan. **C** is incorrect because the scope management plan is an input to defining the scope, which produces the project scope statement. **D** is incorrect because the project charter ensures a mutual understanding of deliverables and milestones.

27. On your project, you prepared a detailed stakeholder analysis. Realizing there was not a mutual understanding of the project's direction, you should prepare a:

A. Feasibility study

B. Stakeholder engagement plan

C. Governance plan

D. Project scope statement

    ☑ **D.** The PM ensures that the context and framework of the project are properly defined, assessed, and documented in the form of a project scope statement. Project stakeholders should verify and approve the project scope statement.

    ☒ **A** is incorrect because a feasibility study is conducted as part of preproject work and is used to justify the project. **B** is incorrect because the stakeholder engagement plan identifies the project partnership—shared accountability and responsibility—a two-way engagement in project decision making and actions. **C** is incorrect because governance relates to managing change, which is not a natural follow-on to preparing a detailed stakeholder analysis.

28. Because the WBS is used to capture all project and nonproject work, this means that project management office support deliverables should be considered a(n):

A. Top-level milestone

B. External deliverable

C. Work package

D. Project management artifact

    ☑ **C.** The work to create project management office support deliverables is indeed work and therefore should be represented in the WBS as a work package. A work package is a group of related tasks within a project. Work packages are the smallest unit of work (typically 8 to 80 hours) that a project can be broken down to when creating your work breakdown structure (WBS).

☒ **A** is incorrect because a high-level milestone is a deliverable or major event to be achieved on a specified date. **B** is incorrect because an external deliverable is a product, service, or result delivered to a customer outside the company. **D** is incorrect because project management artifacts are created because of carrying out the work packages in a WBS (e.g., user stories, class diagrams, UML models).

29. In developing project scope, one approach is to:

    A. Describe scope in user stories

    B. Determine scope through a high-level infrastructure

    C. Use the project's budget to set a financial baseline

    D. Include nonfunctional requirements for products, services, or results

    ☑ **A.** User stories are an effective approach on all time-constrained projects and are a wonderful way to begin introducing a bit of agility to your projects and requirement management approach. In the adaptive approach, you are more likely to create a scope statement as project requirements in terms of user stories, as compared with a functional requirements document created as part of a predictive life cycle project.

    ☒ **B** is incorrect because the high-level infrastructure is determined as part of high-level design (HLD). Scope drives the design. **C** is incorrect because the project's budget is used to set a cost performance baseline. **D** is incorrect because nonfunctional requirements (speed, maintainability, robustness, etc.) are classified as solution requirements and are documented when collecting requirements.

30. You are creating your WBS. You realize that a generally accepted business practice is to:

    A. Structure it so product scope and project scope are easily managed

    B. Set it up so that it shows the complete scope of the work to be carried out on the project

    C. Use it to define the management control points for each of the major deliverables

    D. Define the solution to the problem in terms of a product, service, or result

    ☑ **B.** The WBS is the total scope of work to be done on the project—what's *in* scope.

    ☒ **A** is incorrect because product scope is the features and functions of the product. Project scope is the work performed to deliver the product. The WBS provides the framework of what must be delivered. **C** is incorrect because management control points are normally key review points, such as end of design, or a major management review, such as after the release of the risk management plan. **D** is incorrect because the "how" of the problem is left to the technical team after the business team has described the "what" of the product, service, or result.

31. Your organization's long-term goal is to build and sell electric bicycles. For now, your company will continue to produce motorcycles until the electric bicycles are online. You have a design team of 6 members and a production team of 18 people; these numbers are about half of what you believe you need. These limits are:

    A. Constraints to document in your project scope statement

    B. Limitations to document in your project charter

C. Known risks to set aside management reserves

D. Key issues to document in the risk log

☑ **A.** These are examples of constraints. Constraints and assumptions should be included in the scope statement.

☒ **B** is incorrect because resource limitations are not documented in the project charter. High-level boundaries are listed in the project charter. **C** is incorrect because contingency reserves are set aside for known risks. Unknown risks are covered by management reserves. Risks are documented in the risk register. **D** is incorrect because key issues are documented in the issues log.

32. You are the PM on a high-priority project. Your company has limited human resources. You have been told that the completion date cannot change. You are developing the resource management plan. You have decided to:

A. Prepare a resource plan

B. Use a resource breakdown structure linked to your WBS

C. Use resource smoothing

D. Conduct a Monte Carlo analysis to identify resource supply and demand on the project

☑ **B.** A resource breakdown structure shows you the resources related by function/category and resource type. It can be decomposed to a level usable with the WBS to show the work to be performed, measured, and corrected.

☒ **A** is incorrect because the scope management plan is complete and you are still in the Planning process group. **C** is incorrect because resource smoothing is used when the schedule is top priority—when the goal is to complete the work by the required date while avoiding the peaks and valleys of resource demand. It is a resource optimization technique used in schedule development (Executing process group). **D** is incorrect because Monte Carlo simulation uses randomness to solve problems. Limited human resources is a specific problem.

33. You are in the military stationed near the North Pole. Your project is to rebuild all the runways at your air base, and you have one year to complete the project. Since it usually snows for nine months of the year, the construction team will be able to work on the runways in June, July, and August ... and maybe May and September. You understand your organizational culture, have the latest version of the scheduling software, and ESTICOR is used for standardized estimating data. What should you do now?

A. You should prepare a scope management plan.

B. The agile release approach should be followed.

C. The critical path may change as you use resource leveling.

D. You should adjust the start and end times with leads and lags.

☑ **A.** The "rebuild the runways" project is clearly defined, and the schedule management plan will show the scheduling methodology to be used.

☒ **B** is incorrect because the scope of the project is fully defined and it has a high degree of certainty. **C** is incorrect because you are in the execution phase and the scope management plan is complete. As you use resource leveling, it can cause the original critical path to change, especially if certain resources can only work at certain times. It is a resource optimization technique used in schedule development (Executing process group). **D** is incorrect because leads and lags are used to accelerate or delay activities. The weather is controlling the project, and the activities are finish-to-start.

34. Your new project, the SecureAI Project, will view threats and security breaches of corporate data involving artificial intelligence (AI). You have a dedicated project team of 16 people. Maciej is the domain expert and is frequently used in expert systems software development. Maciej's expertise has been a major advantage so far on your project. To be prudent, you need to:

    A. Make sure there is a succession plan in place if Maciej leaves the project

    B. Set up a process to debrief team members if they make plans to leave the project

    C. Have everyone on your team go to advanced AI training

    D. Have daily meetings with Maciej to make sure the project team knows what he is doing

    ☑ **B.** Most everyone on the project team will have some intellectual knowledge because of working on the project. A process is needed to capture Maciej's knowledge when he leaves the project.

    ☒ **A** is incorrect because a succession plan will identify who can replace Maciej. It will not solve the immediate problem of capturing and transferring his knowledge. **C** is incorrect because going to AI training is a good start and will help in the short term. **D** is incorrect because a daily meeting with Maciej will take away time from his work and is not practical for all team members to attend.

35. You know that projects are unique endeavors, and you also know that they can be similar in some ways to other projects regarding work performance data and information. Which of the following will help ensure that project knowledge is a focus of your project team?

    A. A project management information system

    B. A chief information officer on your dedicated team

    C. A chief data management officer in the PMO

    D. A detailed human resource information system

    ☑ **A.** A PMIS, among other things, is helpful in sharing knowledge with the project team. It can include documents, data, and knowledge repositories.

    ☒ **B** is incorrect because a CIO is an executive-level position concerned with IT strategies and tactics, not day-to-day project management. **C** is incorrect because chief data management officer is a made-up job title. **D** is incorrect because a human resources system is not focused on project data.

36. As you manage the SecureAI Project, you know you will encounter some risks and issues. Issues can be risks that have occurred, but also are areas of concern to the project. A generally accepted business practice to follow regarding risks and issues is to:

A. Use the risk register to capture operational-level issues

B. Set up a risk control board for risks and issues that may occur

C. Set up an escalation process for you to help resolve risks and issues

D. Ensure a risk or issue is isolated to a singular project phase

☑ **C.** Risks or issues related to project objectives, resource and intergroup conflicts, ambiguous roles and responsibilities, scope disagreements, and third-party dependencies are some known situations calling for escalations. Such issues require higher-level intervention because many times the authority, decision making, resources, or effort required to resolve them are beyond a project manager's scope.

☒ **A** is incorrect because issues are recorded in the issues log, not the risk register. **B** is incorrect because although there is a change control board, there is not a separate risk control board, as risks are evaluated by the change control board during an impact assessment. **D** is incorrect because the risk management processes identify risks by category and select risk strategies to address overall risk exposure throughout the project, including when risks and issues span project phases.

37. In your project to set up a new production line for innovative gadget gifts for techies, you have decided to use two contractor companies for the work: one for the software and one for the hardware. You have developed the procurement management plan, and you have created a WBS. You recently met with the software contract officer and she had an issue to discuss with you, and in thinking about it, you realized it also affected the hardware contractor team. You should immediately:

A. Meet with the entire project team.

B. Inform your executive sponsor of this issue.

C. Escalate it to the steering committee for resolution.

D. Analyze your response so it is consistent with project objectives.

☑ **D.** When you resolve an issue, you need to determine a course of action that is consistent with the project's objectives to achieve project benefits and deliver business value.

☒ **A** is incorrect because the issue is with the software contractor and may affect the hardware contractor. This is an issue resolution meeting and should include the appropriate stakeholders involved. The whole team may not be affected by the topics addressed and does not need to attend the meeting. Perhaps any team member who has a defined role in the meeting could attend. **B** is incorrect because the PM is responsible for conflict resolution. If the disruptive conflict continues, formal procedures (escalation) and disciplinary actions can be used. **C** is incorrect because the project manager is responsible for conflict resolution. If the disruptive conflict continues, formal procedures (escalation) and disciplinary actions can be used.

38. You just graduated from a prestigious university and you have been appointed to your first job as a project manager. Your project charter has been approved, and you now have a dedicated team who is working with you in planning the project. So far, you have prepared your scope and quality management plans and now are beginning to work on other plans that will be included in your project management plan. In the project management plan, you need to describe how performance reports will be prepared and distributed. Your program manager pointed out that she wanted regular updates, but she did not want to see many metrics collected that did not add value. You and your team have decided that the best approach is to choose metrics that:

A. Show how your project contributes to the organization's bottom line

B. Show the progress according to the triple constraints

C. Use earned value management to assess project performance and progress

D. Show project management and team delivery rates

☑ **A.** Key performance indicators (KPIs) should measure how the project contributes to tangible and intangible, as well as internal and external, benefits, such as profitability, goodwill, loyalty, etc.

☒ **B** is incorrect because reaching a reasonable trade-off among the three project constraints does not necessarily mean that the project is delivering business value. **C** is incorrect because EVM is used at the project level and does not show the direct and indirect measurements used to show the benefits (business value) realized. **D** is incorrect because there is no indication in the answer of what is being measured for project management or team delivery.

39. You must develop a scope statement for a cross-department project. Many people will be involved in this project with multiple stakeholders represented from each of the departments. In this case, who would approve the scope statement that you develop?

A. The project team members

B. The project sponsor

C. The project manager

D. The financial manager

☑ **B.** The project sponsors or initiators drive the business need for the project, and they approve the project scope statement.

☒ **A** is incorrect because although project team members may provide input to the project scope statement, they are not approvers. **C** is incorrect because the project manager has created the project scope statement and must seek approval from the project sponsor. **D** is incorrect because although the financial manager has input to creating the scope statement, approving their own input would be inappropriate.

40. A project manager is stepping in as a take-over role and has been given a completed project scope statement prepared by the previous project manager. What is the first action she should take at this point?

A. Create a complete network diagram for the tasks and milestones in the project.

B. Confirm that the project management team agrees with the scope statement.

C. Develop a detailed project plan based on the existing work breakdown structure.

D. Call a meeting of the project management team to agree on a procurement plan.

☑ **B.** The project management team is responsible for taking the project charter and creating a scope statement. They are included in the set of all project stakeholders. It is important that all stakeholders have had input to the project scope statement and there is consensus before doing anything else.

☒ **A** is incorrect because she has not verified the project scope statement and therefore cannot continue forward to planning the work. **C** is incorrect because the WBS may not align to the project scope statement. **D** is incorrect because developing a procurement plan would be premature without a valid scope statement and WBS.

41. You have just acquired a new team member on the project you are managing. This is the first project for the team member, and she asks you the purpose of the WBS. What do you describe as its primary purpose?

A. Clarify the responsibility for project tasks.

B. Communicate with all stakeholders.

C. Define the business need for the project.

D. Detail the dates for the work packages.

☑ **B.** The WBS serves as a communication mechanism to and from project stakeholders.

☒ **A** is incorrect because the WBS does not show responsibilities for tasks. **C** is incorrect because the business need is defined in the project charter. **D** is incorrect because dates are decided based on more detailed schedule planning.

42. The project has produced a requirements traceability matrix that links requirements to their origin and traces them throughout the project life cycle. Which statement describes the purpose of the requirements traceability matrix?

A. It describes in detail the project's deliverables and the work required to create those deliverables and includes product and project scope description.

B. It ensures that requirements approved in the requirements documentation are delivered at the end of the project and helps manage changes to the product scope.

C. It is a narrative description of products or services to be delivered by the project and is received from the customer for external projects.

D. It provides the necessary information from a business standpoint to determine whether the project is worth the required investment.

☑ **B.** The requirements traceability matrix ensures that requirements approved in the requirements documentation are delivered at the end of the project. The requirements traceability matrix also provides a structure for managing changes to product scope.

☒ **A** is incorrect because it describes the project scope statement. **C** is incorrect because this is the project statement of work used in developing the project charter. **D** is incorrect because it describes the project business case. Identifying all stakeholders is the only way to uncover all project requirements.

43. You have been developing a scope statement for a project you have been given authority to manage. During this process, you came across areas of technical details that you were not familiar with. Which of the following would you use to help clarify the related issues and their impact on the project scope?

   A. Experienced managers

   B. Special interest groups

   C. Expert judgment

   D. Similar project plans

   ☑ **C.** The use of expert judgment is recommended when a project manager comes across an area that is unfamiliar.

   ☒ **A** is incorrect because "experienced managers" is not a clear answer. **B** and **D** are incorrect because special interest groups (SIGs) are a possibility, as are similar project plans, but expert judgment is considered the best answer because of the technical detail that can be provided by a subject matter expert.

44. You have been given the responsibility for a project that you have not been involved with to date. The project is at the beginning of the execution stage. What is the main document to which you would refer to guide you on what you should be doing on this project?

   A. Project management plan

   B. Procurement management plan

   C. Communication management plan

   D. Project scope management plan

   ☑ **A.** The project management plan is the main reference for the project manager during the execution stage of a project.

   ☒ **B, C,** and **D** are incorrect because the procurement management plan, communications management plan, and project scope management plan are all subsets of the project management plan.

45. You are involved in a project and regularly receive work packages to complete from the project manager. The project manager describes some of the results of your work as project deliverables. The processes that describe project deliverables from your work are defined in which of the following?

A. The completed task contract form

B. The initial work breakdown structure

C. The project management plan

D. The initial project scope document

☑ **C.** Deliverables are produced as outputs from the processes described in the project management plan.

☒ **A** is incorrect because not all tasks produce project deliverables and are not tracked with a task contract. **B** is incorrect because not all WBS elements produce project deliverables. **D** is incorrect because the initial project scope document does not list project deliverables.

46. The project has produced a requirements management plan. What is the purpose of this document?

A. The requirements management plan links requirements to their origin and traces them throughout the project.

B. The requirements management plan documents how requirements will be analyzed, documented, and managed throughout the project.

C. The requirements management plan describes how individual requirements meet the business need for the project.

D. The requirements management plan provides guidance on how project scope will be defined, documented, verified, managed, and controlled.

☑ **B.** The requirements management plan documents how requirements will be analyzed, documented, and managed throughout the project.

☒ **A** is incorrect because it is the definition of the requirements traceability matrix. **C** is incorrect because it describes the requirements document. **D** is incorrect because it describes the scope management plan.

47. You are discussing your role as a project manager with your peers. In the conversation, another team member describes the process of defining and controlling what is, and what is not, included in the project. What are these activities called?

A. Project documentation management

B. Project change control

C. Plan scope management

D. Formal acceptance documents

☑ **C.** The Plan Scope Management process defines and controls what is, and what is not, included in the project.

☒ **A** and **B** are incorrect because project documentation management and project change control are procedures to allow the control of changes to scope only. **D** is incorrect because formal acceptance documents are part of the Close Project or Phase process.

48. You have been involved in a workshop at which the project management team created an initial work breakdown structure (WBS). Which of the following best describes the process in which you were involved?

   A. Calculating the total duration of the project from the start

   B. Counting the total number of work packages in the project

   C. Allocating responsibilities for the project work to individuals in the team

   D. Subdividing the project work into smaller, more manageable components

   ☑ **D.** The Create WBS process subdivides the major project deliverables and project work into smaller, more manageable components.

   ☒ **A** is incorrect because the WBS does not concern project duration. **B** is incorrect because determining the total work package count is not a function of the Create WBS process. **C** is incorrect because the allocation of responsibilities is not a function of the initial WBS.

49. The scope management plan is produced by the project management team as part of the Plan Scope Management process. Which statement best describes the scope management plan?

   A. The scope management plan provides guidance on how project scope will be defined, documented, verified, managed, and controlled.

   B. The scope management plan documents how requirements will be analyzed, documented, and managed throughout the project.

   C. The scope management plan describes in detail the project's deliverables and the work required to create those deliverables.

   D. The scope management plan is a deliverable-oriented hierarchical decomposition of the work to be executed by the project team.

   ☑ **A.** The scope management plan provides guidance on how project scope will be defined, documented, verified, managed, and controlled. It may be formal or informal, highly detailed, or broadly framed, based on the project needs.

   ☒ **B** is incorrect because detailed requirements are not part of a project charter. **C** is incorrect because it describes the project scope statement. **D** is incorrect because it describes the WBS.

50. A team member who has just joined your project asks what is involved in this project. You refer her to the project scope statement, which contains all the following except:

    A. Deferred change requests

    B. Product scope description

    C. Project assumptions

    D. Product acceptance criteria

      ☑ **A.** Deferred change requests could be approved at some time in the future, but have not yet been approved and do not authorize the work that implies a change in scope.

      ☒ **B, C,** and **D** are incorrect because the detailed project scope statement *does* include product scope description, product acceptance criteria, project deliverables, exclusions, constraints, and assumptions.

51. The project you are working on is running behind schedule, is over budget, and is failing to deliver the features originally promised. The project manager says that the work must now be focused on a list of activities. What defines this list of activities?

    A. Shortest-duration tasks

    B. Requirements documentation

    C. Critical-path tasks

    D. Lowest-cost tasks

      ☑ **B.** The requirements documentation helps define the priorities of the requirements as part of the Collect Requirements process. This is where the project team determines how resources can be best used to obtain contract acceptance.

      ☒ **A** is incorrect because shortest-duration tasks will give an impression of progress, but that focus may be on the wrong tasks. **C** is incorrect because focusing on critical-path tasks will preserve or shorten the duration but may not ensure meeting the overall contract. **D** is incorrect because focusing on lowest-cost tasks will help short-term cash flow but may not meet the contract or stakeholders' expectations.

52. You are assigned to manage a new project. Your line manager suggests that you should use a tool to help you plan the new project. She suggests that you use a work breakdown structure (WBS) template. Which of the following is the best description of this tool?

    A. A document that lists WBS elements

    B. An all-purpose WBS from the Internet

    C. A WBS from a previous project

    D. A definition of WBS colors and shapes

      ☑ **C.** A work breakdown template is often a WBS from a previous project within your organization, because projects within an organization often share many common elements and processes.

☒ **A** and **B** are incorrect because generic or general-purpose lists of elements or structures are not necessarily the best fit for your organization. **D** is incorrect because WBS colors and shapes are cosmetic definitions of standards to be referenced.

53. The project meeting you are attending is becoming heated, and arguments are starting about the work completed and the work to be done. The project manager stops the discussion and refers to one document that is used as a reference. What is this document called?

    A. Approved changes

    B. Newly identified risks

    C. The WBS template

    D. The scope baseline

    ☑ **D.** The work to be done in a project is defined in the WBS and is part of the approved project scope statement and associated WBS. This is known as the scope baseline.

    ☒ **A** is incorrect because approved changes are only one part of the scope. **B** is incorrect because newly identified risks are not necessarily translated to impact on the work or scope. **C** is incorrect because the WBS template is a generic starting point for defining the scope or final WBS.

54. After some changes to your project scope, you have revised the schedule, costs, and work package assignments, and these changes have been approved. What action do you now complete?

    A. Wait for resources to complete current assignments.

    B. Reissue the project management plan.

    C. Immediately look for other changes to submit.

    D. Let the project schedule continue as previously.

    ☑ **B.** Reissuing the project management plan is a major output of controlling scope once the changes have been approved.

    ☒ **A** is incorrect because some assignments may have to be changed. **C** is incorrect because looking for other changes without issuing the new plan may cause rework. **D** is incorrect because letting the project schedule continue and ignoring the recent changes may compromise the project.

55. You have asked a team member to perform many actions on a project plan. These actions are decomposing the work packages into smaller components and activities that are to be the basis for estimating, scheduling, and running the project. What is this team member's activity called?

    A. Schedule work

    B. Estimate tasks

C. Schedule activities

D. Define activities

☑ **D.** As part of the Project Schedule Management knowledge area, the project manager must define activities, which allows for decomposing the work packages into smaller components and activities that are to be the basis for estimating, scheduling, and running the project.

☒ **A, B,** and **C** are incorrect because work scheduling is part of the follow-on process, as are estimating tasks and scheduling activities.

56. You note that your weekly time sheet report shows that you have identified activities, scoped the work needed on each, and provided sufficient detail to allow a team member to understand what is required to complete that work. What description summarizes the time you have spent this week?

A. Producing an activity list

B. Defining the project scope

C. Developing the project schedule

D. Identifying the WBS elements

☑ **A.** The activity list is a comprehensive list of all scheduled activities, including scope and activity identifier, that is in sufficient detail for a team member to complete the work.

☒ **B** is incorrect because defining the project scope is an earlier stage and does not break the project into detailed work packages. **C** is incorrect because defining and developing the project schedule is a later stage of planning. **D** is incorrect because the WBS elements already will have been identified prior to this activity.

57. The precedence diagramming method can be used to clarify the dependencies between activities. One type of dependency used is to ensure that the successor activity does not start until the completion of the predecessor activity. What is the name given to this type of dependency?

A. Start-to-start

B. Finish-to-finish

C. Finish-to-start

D. Start-to-finish

☑ **C.** The type of dependency in which the successor activity does not start until the completion of a predecessor activity is known as finish-to-start.

☒ **A** is incorrect because in the start-to-start dependency a successor activity cannot start until a predecessor activity has started. **B** is incorrect because in the finish-to-finish dependency a successor activity cannot finish until a predecessor activity has finished. **D** is incorrect because in the start-to-finish dependency a successor activity cannot finish until a predecessor activity has started.

58. One tool of project management is a table that identifies and describes the types and quantities of each resource required to complete all project work packages. What is this table known as?

A. Resource calendar updates

B. Activity attribute updates

C. Resource breakdown structure

D. Activity resource requirements

☑ **D.** A list that identifies and describes the types and quantities of each resource required to complete all project work packages is known as the activity resource requirements.

☒ **A, B,** and **C** are incorrect because the resource calendar, activity attribute updates, and resource breakdown structure are outputs of activity resource estimating but are not the correct answers.

59. You are completing the planning for a project schedule. Because you do not have much information about one activity, you decide to estimate its duration by referring to the actual duration of a similar activity on another project. This calculation method is called:

A. Analogous estimating

B. Expert judgment

C. Parametric estimating

D. Reserve analysis

☑ **A.** Estimating the duration of a project activity by referring to the actual duration of a similar activity on another project is known as analogous estimating.

☒ **B** is incorrect because expert judgment uses other specialists to modify historical data. **C** is incorrect because parametric estimating uses pro-rata data. **D** is incorrect because reserve analysis refers to contingency or time buffers.

60. Your project manager asks you to calculate the theoretical early start and finish dates on your project schedule, along with late start and finish dates, for all the project activities. He suggests you use a forward and backward pass analysis. This technique is known as (the):

A. Critical chain method

B. Critical path method

C. Schedule compression

D. What-if analysis

☑ **B.** Calculating the theoretical early start and finish dates, along with late start and finish dates, for all the project activities using a forward and backward pass analysis is known as the critical path method.

☒ **A** is incorrect because the critical chain method is specifically related to resource constraints. **C** is incorrect because schedule compression is about reducing project duration. **D** is incorrect because what-if analysis relates to calculating the durations of multiple combinations of tasks.

61. You are asked to review a project that another department has planned for your organization. Your line manager asks you to show her a project overview that shows only the start and end dates of major deliverables, along with key external dependencies. This graphic is known as a:

   A. Network diagram

   B. Summary bar chart

   C. Milestone chart

   D. Schedule baseline

   ☑ **C.** A project overview that shows only the start and end of major deliverables, along with key external dependencies, is known as a milestone chart.

   ☒ **A** and **B** are incorrect because network diagrams and summary bar charts are used for more detailed presentation; they also show dependencies and durations of tasks. **D** is incorrect because the schedule baseline is a detailed chart.

62. While reviewing a work package that you have assigned to a member of your team, you look at a graphic that shows the activity start, duration, and finish on a time base. This chart is commonly known as a(n):

   A. Activity float list

   B. Network diagram

   C. Work breakdown structure

   D. Project bar chart

   ☑ **D.** A graphic that shows the activity start, duration, and finish on a time base is known as a project bar chart.

   ☒ **A** is incorrect because an activity float list does not represent the duration of an activity. **B** is incorrect because the network diagram shows dependencies. **C** is incorrect because the WBS identifies the activities only.

63. The project you have been planning has been approved by the project management team, and you can now start the execution stage. You have authority for a reference that contains an activity schedule and project start and finish dates. This reference is called:

   A. The project schedule baseline

   B. A network diagram

   C. A milestone chart

   D. The project calendar

☑ **A.** The activity schedule, with project start and finish dates, is known as the project schedule baseline.

☒ **B** is incorrect because a network diagram shows dependencies only. **C** is incorrect because a milestone chart is a summary that does not show the activity schedule. **D** is incorrect because the project calendar is a detailed view of working and nonworking days for the project and resources.

64. You are asked to develop a table that includes the schedule milestones, schedule activities, activity attributes, and documented assumptions and constraints. You also include resource requirements by time period, alternative schedules, and scheduling of contingency reserves. The table that you prepare is known as the:

   A. Project schedule

   B. Schedule data

   C. Resource schedule

   D. Project bar chart

   ☑ **B.** The schedule data includes the schedule milestones, schedule activities, activity attributes, and documented assumptions and constraints, as well as resource requirements by time period, alternative schedules, and scheduling of contingency reserves.

   ☒ **A** is incorrect because the project schedule is a detail of activity start and end dates. **C** is incorrect because the resource schedule does not show weekends and vacations. **D** is incorrect because the project bar chart does not show the working days and shifts.

65. You have been working on a project in the planning stage, developing the likely costs. The project sponsor expects a narrower estimate of the costs because more information is now known. Which of the following is considered a suitable range for this request?

   A. −100% to +100%

   B. −5% to +10%

   C. −25% to +25%

   D. −50% to +50%

   ☑ **B.** As more information becomes known later in the project, estimates could narrow to a range of −5% to +10% (a definitive estimate).

   ☒ **A, C,** and **D** are incorrect because earlier in a project, for example, in the initiation stage, estimates could use a rough order of magnitude (ROM) estimate in the range of −25 to +75%.

66. A project team member is building the costs for a current project, using costs from a previous similar project that has been completed in your organization. This estimating technique is known as:

   A. Analogous

   B. Bottom-up

   C. Parametric

   D. Three-point

   ☑ **A.** Using costs from a previous similar project that has been completed in your organization is known as analogous estimating.

   ☒ **B** is incorrect because bottom-up estimating is based on WBS activities. **C** is incorrect because parametric estimating is based on pro-rata calculations from standard rates. **D** is incorrect because three-point estimating requires three data points.

67. Building the costs for a current project using characteristics from a mathematical model to help predict the project costs is known as what type of estimating technique?

   A. Analogous

   B. Bottom-up

   C. Parametric

   D. Three-point

   ☑ **C.** Parametric estimating is based on pro-rata calculations from standard rates based on a mathematical model.

   ☒ **A** is incorrect because using costs from a previous similar project that has been completed in the organization is known as analogous estimating. **B** is incorrect because bottom-up estimating is based on WBS activities. **D** is incorrect because three-point estimating requires three data points.

68. A team member has been given the task of identifying which quality standards are relevant to this project and determining how to satisfy these standards. In which of the following processes is she engaged?

   A. Control Quality

   B. Manage Quality

   C. Plan Quality Management

   D. Quality Improvement

   ☑ **C.** Quality planning is related to establishing the quality requirements and/or standards for the project.

   ☒ **A** is incorrect because monitoring and recording results of executing quality activities to assess performance and recommend necessary changes is Control Quality. **B** is incorrect because Manage Quality is ensuring that appropriate quality standards are used. **D** is incorrect because quality improvement is an organizational development process.

69. You have been asked to detail the steps for analyzing processes to identify activities that enhance the value of those processes. This is called:

A. Establishing the quality baseline

B. Developing quality checklists

C. Establishing quality metrics

D. Process improvement planning

☑ **D.** A plan that details the steps for analyzing processes to identify activities that enhance the value of those processes in a project is known as the process improvement plan.

☒ **A** is incorrect because the quality baseline records the quality objectives for the project. **B** is incorrect because quality checklists are component specific. **C** is incorrect because quality metrics define the quality control measurements.

70. You have been asked to perform the quality planning for a project. One of the first actions you take is to clarify what some of the measurements on the project are and how the Control Quality process measures these. This action is known as:

A. Define quality metrics

B. Develop quality checklists

C. Set the quality baseline

D. Plan process improvements

☑ **A.** Clarifying what some of the measurements on the project are and how the Control Quality process measures these is defining the project quality metrics.

☒ **B** is incorrect because quality checklists are component specific. **C** is incorrect because the quality baseline records the quality objectives for the project. **D** is incorrect because a plan that details the steps for analyzing processes to identify activities that enhance the value in a project is known as the process improvement plan.

71. A team member is following the steps outlined in the process improvement plan. This is needed to improve organizational and project performance. What reference document would the team member use to help with this activity?

A. Quality metrics

B. Quality audits

C. Process analysis

D. Quality checklists

☑ **C.** Following the steps outlined in the process improvement plan to improve organizational and project performance is known as process analysis.

☒ **A** is incorrect because quality metrics are an input to Manage Quality and define the quality control measurements. **B** is incorrect because performing a quality audit is identifying inefficient and ineffective policies, processes, and procedures. **D** is incorrect because quality checklists are component specific.

72. You are identifying and documenting project roles, responsibilities, and reporting relationships for a project, as well as creating a staffing management plan for a project. In terms of project management, these activities are known as:

A. Planning resource management

B. Developing project management plan

C. Managing team

D. Developing team

☑ **A.** Identifying and documenting project roles, responsibilities, and reporting relationships, as well as creating a staffing management plan for a project, is developing the resource management plan.

☒ **B** is incorrect because develop project management plan is a broader generic process. **C** is incorrect because the Manage Team process concerns operational activities, not planning. **D** is incorrect because the Develop Team process concerns improving competences.

73. As part of the project plan documentation, you find a diagram that illustrates the link between work packages and project team members. This diagram is called a(n):

A. Hierarchy-type chart

B. Responsibility assignment matrix

C. Organizational chart

D. Dependency diagram

☑ **B.** A diagram that illustrates the link between work packages and project team members is a responsibility assignment matrix (RAM).

☒ **A** is incorrect because hierarchy-type charts show the reporting structure or work, such as a WBS. **C** is incorrect because organizational charts show roles and responsibilities. **D** is incorrect because dependency diagrams show the logical work flow in a project.

74. You are planning the resourcing for a project and create a visual representation that illustrates the number of hours that each person will be needed each week over the course of the project schedule. This visual representation is commonly known as a:

A. Work breakdown structure

B. Task network diagram

C. Resource histogram

D. Detailed Gantt chart

☑ **C.** A chart that illustrates the number of hours that each person will be needed each week over the course of the project schedule is known as a resource histogram.

☒ **A** is incorrect because a WBS does not show weekly allocation. **B** is incorrect because a task network diagram is not used to show schedule information for resources. **D** is incorrect because a Gantt chart shows task schedule information.

75. You are managing a project and ask for additional time to enable you to meet new roles. You list the additional activities, such as setting clear expectations, developing processes for managing conflict, including the team in decision making, and sharing credit for success. The name given to this process is:

A. Management by objectives

B. Matrix management

C. Negotiate for resources

D. Plan Communications Management

☑ **D.** Asking for additional time to enable you to meet your new roles, such as setting clear expectations, developing processes for managing conflict, including the team in decision making, and sharing credit for success, is known as Plan Communications Management.

☒ **A** is incorrect because management by objectives (MBO) is a directive style of management, not a role or activity as described. **B** is incorrect because matrix management is related to organizational structure. **C** is incorrect because negotiating is not as described.

76. You are in the final stages of planning a project and are considering ways to best influence the team over the course of the project, including bonus structures, perks, and a project website. What best describes what you are defining?

A. Staff roles and responsibilities

B. Organizational process assets

C. Staffing management plan

D. Team performance assessment

☑ **B.** The organizational process assets that can influence the Manage Team process can include certificates of appreciation, newsletters, websites, bonus structures, corporate apparel, and other organizational perquisites.

☒ **A** is incorrect because staff roles and responsibilities are related to individuals, not the performance. **C** is incorrect because the staffing management plan is a list or schedule of work for staff. **D** is incorrect because team performance assessment is related to the team members explicitly.

77. A project manager must perform many activities when planning and managing a project. These include developing an approach for stakeholder information needs; creating, collecting, distributing, storing, and disposing of project information; and monitoring and controlling communications. These activities are examples of:

A. Recommended preventive actions

B. Project performance appraisals

C. Recommended corrective actions

D. Project communications management

☑ **D.** Developing an approach for stakeholder information needs; creating, collecting, distributing, storing, and disposing of project information; and monitoring and controlling communications are examples of project communications planning.

☒ **A, B,** and **C** are incorrect because recommended preventive actions, project performance appraisals, and recommended corrective actions are all inputs to the team management process in operation during a project.

78. A section of your project plan lists methods and technologies to be used to convey memoranda, email, press releases, and how frequently these should be used. The document that defines these is called a(n):

   A. Communications management plan

   B. Organizational assets

   C. Communications technology

   D. Project management plan

   ☑ **A.** Methods and technologies to be used to convey memoranda, emails, press releases, and how frequently these should be used are examples of the contents of a communications management plan.

   ☒ **B** is incorrect because organizational assets are related to processes and procedures that the organization has in place. **C** is incorrect because communications technology is about the technology only. **D** is incorrect because the project management plan is a higher-level document that does not contain the detail of the communications management plan.

79. During the planning stage of a project, you decide to assign a member of your project team to be responsible for the distribution of information about the project. Where should you document this decision?

   A. Project management plan

   B. Communications management plan

   C. Project roles and responsibilities

   D. Project team assessment

   ☑ **B.** The staff member responsible for the distribution of information about the project is defined in the communications management plan.

   ☒ **A** is incorrect because the project management plan is the higher-level document that contains the communications management plan within it. **C** is incorrect because project roles and responsibilities are related to task responsibilities. **D** is incorrect because project team assessment is a process of measurement performed during a project.

80. To be successful, how often should an organization address risk management?

   A. At every management meeting

   B. Only in the planning phase

C. On high-risk projects only

D. Consistently throughout

☑ **D.** An organization should be committed to addressing risk management proactively and consistently throughout the project.

☒ **A, B,** and **C** are incorrect because risk needs to be identified early with mitigation strategies in place and then constantly monitored as the details of the project are progressively elaborated to ensure that new risks have not been introduced.

81. The project director advises you that a project should have a balance between risk taking and risk avoidance. This policy is implemented in a project using:

A. Risk responses

B. Risk analysis

C. Risk identification

D. Risk classification

☑ **A.** A balance between risk taking and risk avoidance is the application of risk responses.

☒ **B, C,** and **D** are incorrect because risk analysis, risk identification, and risk classification are parts of prior steps to the responses in the risk management process.

82. Who is responsible for identifying risks in a new project?

A. The project manager

B. The project sponsor

C. Any project personnel

D. The main stakeholders

☑ **C.** Any project personnel can identify risks in a project.

☒ **A, B,** and **D** are incorrect because the project manager manages the risk management process with input from the sponsor and main stakeholders.

83. The document that contains a list of identified risks and, against each a list of potential responses, the root cause of the risk, and the risk category is called the:

A. Risk management plan

B. Project issues log

C. Risk category checklist

D. Risk register

☑ **D.** A list of identified risks, and against each a list of potential responses, the root cause of the risk, and the risk category, are the basic fields in a risk register.

☒ **A** is incorrect because the risk management plan is the overall management document and processes definitions for managing risk in the project. **B** is incorrect because the project issues log contains the list of all issues, not solely risks. **C** is incorrect because the risk category checklist contains weighting information on probability and impact.

84. As part of your responsibility for managing risks in your project, you rate risks as low, medium, or high. What tool would you typically use to define these categories?

A. Probability impact matrix

B. Risk register updates

C. Assumption analysis

D. Checklist analysis

☑ **A.** Rating risks into a low, medium, or high category is done and presented on a probability impact matrix.

☒ **B** is incorrect because risk register updates are an output from the risk management process. **C** and **D** are incorrect because assumption analysis and checklist analysis are tools used for risk identification.

85. A new member of your project team suggests that you should quantify risks using the lowest, highest, and most likely costs of the WBS elements in the project plan. What is the name for the technique being suggested?

A. Three-point estimating

B. Probability impact analysis

C. Probability distributions

D. Sensitivity analysis

☑ **A.** A technique that is often used for risk analysis that calculates or obtains information on the lowest, highest, and most likely costs of the WBS elements in the project plan is called three-point estimating.

☒ **B** is incorrect because probability impact analysis is a ranking of risks. **C** is incorrect because probability distributions are the application of three-point estimates in differing ways. **D** is incorrect because sensitivity analysis is used to test the major project variables independently for risks.

86. The process of project planning that involves developing options, determining actions to enhance opportunities, and reducing threats to project objectives is called:

A. Perform Qualitative Risk Analysis

B. Plan Risk Responses

C. Perform Quantitative Risk Analysis

D. Probability and Impact Matrix

☑ **B.** Developing options, determining actions to enhance opportunities, and reducing threats to project objectives is known as Plan Risk Responses.

☒ **A** and **C** are incorrect because Perform Qualitative Risk Analysis and Perform Quantitative Risk Analysis are prior steps in the risk management process. **D** is incorrect because the probability and impact matrix is a means of classifying the ranking of risks.

87. Your team is developing a part of the risk management plan. For some of the risks, the team decides that a response plan will be executed only when certain predefined conditions exist. What is the term given to this type of risk strategy?

   A. Contingent

   B. Sharing

   C. Exploit

   D. Enhance

   ☑ **A.** For some of the risks in a project, particularly those that pose a threat as well as an opportunity, a response plan that will be executed only when certain predefined conditions exist is called a contingent response strategy.

   ☒ **B, C,** and **D** are incorrect because sharing, exploiting, and enhancing are responses to opportunities related to risk events.

88. Information such as outcomes of risk reassessments, risk audits, and periodic risk reviews are examples from which of the following?

   A. Risk management plan

   B. Approved change requests

   C. Project documents updates

   D. Work performance information

   ☑ **C.** Information such as outcomes of risk reassessments, risk audits, and periodic risk reviews are examples of project document updates from the Monitor Risk process.

   ☒ **A** is incorrect because the risk management plan defines the process and resources involved in managing the risks. **B** and **D** are incorrect because approved change requests and work performance information do not match the question items.

89. During the Plan Procurement Management process for a project, you decide whether a product or service can be produced by the project team or instead should be purchased. This decision-making process is called:

   A. Procurement management

   B. Expert judgment

   C. Risk management

   D. Make-or-buy analysis

   ☑ **D.** The process of deciding whether a particular product or service can be produced by the project team or instead should be purchased is known as make-or-buy analysis.

   ☒ **A** is incorrect because procurement management is the process used to manage contracts. **B** is incorrect because expert judgment is a technique used in many decision-making processes. **C** is incorrect because risk management is a process related to risks in the project and does not document into the make-or-buy analysis.

90. The contract you are negotiating with a subcontractor involves a set price for a well-defined requirement and incentives for meeting selected objectives. This type of contract is:

A. Time and material

B. Cost-reimbursable

C. Fixed-price

D. Cost plus incentive

☑ **C.** A contract that involves a fixed price for a well-defined requirement, possibly with incentives for meeting selected objectives, is a fixed-price contract.

☒ **A** is incorrect because time and material contracts contain both cost-reimbursable and fixed-price arrangements. **B** is incorrect because a cost-reimbursable contract defines allowable costs plus profit. **D** is incorrect because a cost plus incentive contract contains fixed agreed-upon costs plus incentives based on performance.

91. The procurement and contracting process involves asking such questions as how well the seller meets the contract statement of work, whether the seller has the capacity to meet future requirements, and whether the seller can provide references from previous customers. What is the name given to this list and/or its use?

A. Contract management

B. Source selection criteria

C. Supplier risk analysis

D. Contract negotiation

☑ **B.** How well the seller meets the contract statement of work, whether the seller has the capacity to meet future requirements, and whether the seller can provide references from previous customers are examples of contract source selection criteria.

☒ **A** is incorrect because contract management is the overall process of managing contracts. **C** is incorrect because supplier risk analysis is part of risk management. **D** is incorrect because contract negotiation occurs after source selection criteria have been decided and analyzed.

92. Your contract and procurement consultant recommends that you establish source selection criteria for each of your sellers' proposals. What part of the procurement process will this assist?

A. Bidder conference

B. Plan Procurement Management

C. Conduct Procurements

D. Buyer requests

☑ **B.** Establishing source selection criteria for each of your sellers' proposals helps to rate or score seller proposals. These source selection criteria are an output of the Plan Procurement Management.

A is incorrect because the bidder conference is an open meeting prior to the proposals being delivered. **C** is incorrect because the source selection criteria are used as an input in the Conduct Procurements process, but are created in the earlier process. **D** is incorrect because buyer requests refer to the customer's needs.

93. Using the following part of a WBS, what do you know about Activity 3.1.1?

3.1 Requirements

3.1.1 Interview Stakeholders

   A. It is a control account.

   B. It is used for cost reporting.

   C. It is the work package.

   D. It is the milestone above the work package.

   ☑ **C.** The WBS entry 3.1.1 Interview Stakeholders is a work package and identifies activity tasks to be carried out to complete the project.

   ☒ **A, B,** and **D** are incorrect because 3.1.1 is a work package, not a control account, and although each work package is part of a control account, which enables the project manager to compare work completed to earned value objectives, the work package itself is not a control account.

94. You and your team are estimating the duration of the coding/unit testing phase. Your optimistic estimate is 1,200 hours, your most likely estimate is 1,700 hours, and your pessimistic estimate is 2,000 hours. The resource rate is $150 per hour. What is your cost estimate of the coding/unit test phase using the PERT estimating technique?

   A. $255,000

   B. $250,050

   C. $280,325

   D. $270,175

   ☑ **B.** PERT = (o + 4m + p) / 6 with o = 1200, m = 1700, and p = 2000. Substituting these numbers, PERT = (1200 + 4(1700) + 2000) / 6, or (1200 + 6800 + 2000) / 6 or 10,000 / 6, or 1,667 hours. Because the labor rate is $150/hour, 1667 × 150 = $250,050.

   ☒ **A, C,** and **D** are incorrect because the answers do not come from using the PERT formula.

95. The business case stated a project cost of $2,500,000. You and your team just received the signed project charter and are ready to present a high-level estimate to the project management team. What is the acceptable accuracy range for this estimate?

   A. $1,187,500 to $4,375,000

   B. $1,200,000 to $3,300,000

C. $1,225,000 to $4,312,500

D. $1,237,500 to $3,275,000

☑ **A.** $1,187,500 – $4,375,000 is the correct answer using an order of magnitude range of –25% to +75%. The math is $2,500,000 × –25% = $1,187,500 and $2,500,000 × 75% = $4,375,000. Order of magnitude (OOM) estimates are rough guesses made at the very beginning of the project. In the initiation stage of a project, not much is known about the project, and things change as planning progresses.

☒ **B, C,** and **D** are incorrect because they did not use estimates at initiation that may have a range of –25 to +75%.

96. A project estimate generated during the initiation phase may have an accuracy of:

A. –25% to +75%

B. –10% to +25%

C. –5% to +10%

D. –50% to +150%

☑ **A.** –25% to +75% are the percentages for a rough order of magnitude (ROM) estimate that is a rough guess made at the initiation stage of the project. At this time not much is known about the project, and things change as planning progresses.

☒ **B** is incorrect because these percentages apply to a budgetary estimate. **C** is incorrect because these percentages apply to a definitive estimate. **D** is incorrect because it is a made-up percentage for estimating.

The Executing Domain

This chapter includes questions from the following tasks:

- **Task 1** Acquire and manage project resources by following the human resource and procurement management plans in order to meet project requirements.
- **Task 2** Manage task execution based on the project management plan by leading and developing the project team in order to achieve project deliverables.
- **Task 3** Implement the quality management plan using the appropriate tools and techniques in order to ensure that work is performed in accordance with required quality standards.
- **Task 4** Implement approved changes and corrective actions by following the change management plan in order to meet project requirements.
- **Task 5** Implement approved actions by following the risk management plan in order to minimize the impact of the risks and take advantage of opportunities on the project.
- **Task 6** Manage the flow of information by following the communications plan in order to keep stakeholders engaged and informed.
- **Task 7** Maintain stakeholder relationships by following the stakeholder management plan in order to receive continued support and manage expectations.

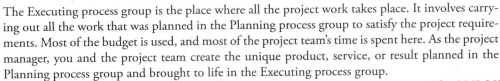

The Executing process group is the place where all the project work takes place. It involves carrying out all the work that was planned in the Planning process group to satisfy the project requirements. Most of the budget is used, and most of the project team's time is spent here. As the project manager, you and the project team create the unique product, service, or result planned in the Planning process group and brought to life in the Executing process group.

The Executing domain accounts for 31% (62) of the questions on the PMP exam. The *PMBOK Guide, Sixth Edition,* namely, Sections 4.3, 4.4, 8.2, 9.3–9.5, 10.2, 11.6, 12.2, and 13.3, cover the 10 tasks in the Executing domain.

The 124 practice questions in this chapter are mapped to the style and frequency of question types you will see on the PMP exam.

1. You are managing a construction project. At 75% through the project, you determine that you are behind schedule. You review the project schedule to determine how to complete the project on time. The project sponsor will not give you any more resources. When analyzing the project schedule, you see a lot of soft logic—the remaining activities are sequenced based on the project team's knowledge of best practices. What can you do to adjust the project schedule and finish the project on the expected due date?

    A. Crash the schedule.

    B. Keep the soft logic decisions and fast-track the activities on the critical path.

    C. Fast-track the schedule.

    D. Remove the soft logic and do more of the remaining tasks/activities concurrently.

2. A generally accepted practice in project management is to use lessons learned to capitalize on effective and ineffective events that have happened in past projects and to take corrective actions for future work. In addition, the project manager uses lessons learned and communication techniques to keep stakeholders informed. Lessons learned will be compiled and archived at project closure time, and a final report will be written and distributed. When is the best time to inform stakeholders about lessons learned?

    A. During all phases of the project life cycle

    B. During the execution phase of the project life cycle

    C. At the beginning of the project during the project kick-off meeting

    D. When a major deliverable is completed during any phase of the project

3. You decide to conduct regular QA audits on the SCAN project. The major purpose is to:

    A. Document best practices and noncompliance issues and forward these to the PMO

    B. Confirm the implementation of approved change requests

    C. Verify that the quality management plan is being followed

    D. Determine if policies, processes, and procedures are complying with benefits realization

4. You are managing a project focused on optimizing company processes to increase efficiencies by taking advantage of economies of scale. A major challenge in the company is the knowledge silos that have appeared in project teams. You are determined to change the culture of your projects to one of information sharing, not hoarding. You have one person skilled in product development and another person who is the marketing guru on your project team. The product development person seems overallocated, and she is complaining about all the work. As the project manager you should:

   A. Rely on the functional manager to assign the proper amount of work

   B. Use the resource allocation team (RAT) to work with your project team to outsource some of the work

   C. Use the resource calendar to document the time periods she is working

   D. Meet with the product development person and prioritize her work

5. The product development specialist on your current project has the PMP certification. The marketing expert on your team has a master's degree in project management. To ensure all your project team members, including these two, receive feedback on their performance, you decide to:

   A. Meet with each of them weekly to generate decisions, actions, or awareness

   B. Set up work performance reports for each one to determine recognition and rewards

   C. Ask each of them to prepare an individual development plan for your review

   D. Conduct a formal review with each of them at the end of each phase

6. As part of implementing risk responses, you are updating your risk report. You should include:

   A. Any changes to overall risk exposure

   B. Impact of identified risks on achieving project benefits

   C. A change request process for risks that occur that affect project team assignments

   D. A revised list of prioritized issues that affect the project's objectives

7. As part of your Implement Risk Responses process, for a risk you should:

   A. Specify the risk thresholds based on the risk appetite of the sponsor

   B. Encourage risk owners to take necessary action, if required

   C. Document the risk description and impact if it happens

   D. Inform project stakeholders of all ranked risks

8. You are establishing a Project Management Office (PMO) in your global company. You know you need to set up knowledge management tools. You also have a chief knowledge officer in your company. She is on the project management team and is recommending the project use library services. Why?

   A. To connect every team member so they can share knowledge management

   B. To make reverse shadowing mandatory to build trust

   C. To share explicit knowledge for your team

   D. To focus the team on organizational learning

9. Your team is a weak matrix one, and given travel restrictions, you will not have any face-to-face meetings during this two-year project. During this two-year period, you do not want to lose any project members to either other projects or their functional work. To be successful in this environment, you need to:

   A. Get commitments in writing that the functional manager will allocate the team member to your project for two years

   B. Encourage the project team to collaborate/problem-solve to build consensus and commitment

   C. Give certificates of appreciation to the functional team members at key milestone points to influence them to stay on the project

   D. Have each team member sign a letter of intent stating that he or she will stay on the project until completion

10. Your last assignment before retirement is to design and develop the next-generation handheld device. You have used functional decomposition to create three subprojects in your project: video, audio, and AI. You must consider maintenance and customer support for your new product. Your three teams—one for each subproject—are geographically located in the United States, Ireland, and Russia. You expect team members to be committed to the success not only of their subproject but also to the overall project. You want to increase team cohesiveness and minimize staff turnover rate. To measure team effectiveness, you should:

    A. Use structured interviews and focus group tools

    B. Conduct individual team member assessments

    C. Evaluate the openness of information sharing and experiences among the team

    D. Formally establish a job shadowing program and encourage teams from each country to participate

11. Although people may say they can identify, assess, and manage their personal feelings, many teams experience tension and uncooperative behaviors among teammates. You have recognized this on projects where you have been a team member, especially virtual teams. Now that you are a project manager, you want to establish an environment in which teammates can reduce tension and increase cooperation. A best practice to follow is to:

    A. Use emotional intelligence to control the sentiments of team members

    B. Focus on goals to be served and ask that emotions be left outside the project

C. Emphasize areas of agreement rather than areas of difference

D. Maintain a good relationship with the project sponsor

12. You have been working on the SecureAI project for six months. You are scheduled to meet with your steering committee to review project performance next week. You have met individually with each member of the steering committee to better understand their concerns and issues. You found that one person does not believe the project has delivered any benefits to date based on the reports he has received. Another member of the team is concerned because even though you are only in the first six months of this two-year project, already you have had seven change requests. The third steering committee team member was out of the office last week, but her administrative assistant seems to think she is happy—so far. In this meeting you will explain how you are evaluating overall project progress. One approach to use is to:

A. Switch to a critical success factor approach

B. Tell them you are relying on the Project Management Information System (PMIS) as one way to evaluate progress

C. Enable them to have full access to the lessons learned repository

D. Set up a red-amber-green dashboard that emphasizes value and quality rather than the Triple Constraint Triangle

13. You are outlining and guiding the selection of resources and assigning them to their respective activities. Which of the following tools and techniques would be least helpful to you?

A. Decision making

B. Resource calendars

C. Negotiation

D. Pre-assignment

14. You are leading and performing the work defined in the project management plan. Which of the following actions would be least helpful to you?

A. Allocate available resources

B. Manage organizational interfaces

C. Analyze work performance data

D. Leverage prior organizational knowledge

15. Leadership and management are about getting things done. In the execution phase, leadership differs from management in that:

A. Leadership is about demonstrating the value of project management

B. Management is about delivering better strategic outcomes

C. Leadership includes making sure the project is delivered on target, on schedule, and on budget

D. Leadership involves guiding, motivating, and directing the project team

16. Decision making is the ability to negotiate and influence the project team. A guideline for effective decision making is:

A. Follow a decision-making process

B. Seek a compromise/reconcile solution

C. Improve the efficiency of conflict resolution

D. Apply both leadership and management techniques

17. One of your key stakeholders is upset about the quality of the demo from the last iteration. During the retrospective, one of the developers openly blames the other team members through the entire meeting to the point of hurting people's feelings. You step in and remind the team that the retrospective is a time for them to learn from previous work and make small improvements. Two weeks later, at the next retrospective, the same team member repeats the same "blamestorming" behavior. The team development behavior that you can improve is:

A. Establishing high team performance

B. Encouraging collaborative problem solving

C. Providing "stretch" objectives

D. Setting up a project room

18. Translating the quality management plan into executable quality activities during the execution phase is:

A. Execute Quality Management

B. Manage Quality

C. Control Quality

D. Project Quality Management

19. A structured, independent process to determine whether project activities comply with project policies, processes, and procedures is called a:

A. Quality inspection

B. Quality audit

C. Retrospective

D. Quality demo

20. A key benefit of the Manage Team process is that it:

A. Requires subject matter experts to create sustainable solutions

B. Selects team members who can deal with high rates of change

C. Implements a zero-sum reward and recognition system for the team

D. Influences team behavior to optimize project performance

21. Which of the following is a tool and technique of the Manage Communications process?

    A. Reporting performance

    B. Project reporting

    C. Work performance reports

    D. Project communications

22. Which of the following trends and emerging practices in procurement management could have a negative effect on the success of your project?

    A. Advances in tools

    B. Permanent engagements

    C. More advanced risk management

    D. Changing contracting processes

23. An effective way to ensure that no prospective bidders receive preferential treatment is to hold a vendor conference. A vendor conference should be held:

    A. Before you prepare the request for quotation (RFQ) so prices can be submitted by prospective sellers

    B. Before prospective sellers submit their proposals and after procurement documents have been distributed

    C. Before you issue the statement of work to the prospective sellers

    D. After the contract is awarded so that unsuccessful vendors can improve their bid packages

24. Seller proposals is an input to:

    A. Plan Procurement Management

    B. Request Procurements

    C. Procurement Strategy

    D. Conduct Procurements

25. You are translating the quality management plan into executable quality activities. Which of the following inputs will be least helpful to you?

    A. Quality control measurements

    B. Process improvement plan

    C. Lessons learned register

    D. Risk report

26. Finally, after three months of negotiating with the resource allocation manager, a new business analyst, Sharon, has been added to your current project team. Given the introduction of a new team member, which team development stage might your team fall into?

   A. Forming

   B. Storming

   C. Norming

   D. Performing

27. Negotiation is a key interpersonal and team skill used in the Conduct Procurements process. The negotiation should be led by:

   A. The project manager working on behalf of the project sponsor

   B. The senior member of the steering committee

   C. A member of the procurement team who is authorized to sign contracts

   D. The contracting officer representative assigned to the project

28. You are a junior project manager assigned to your first takeover project. The team does not feel confident in their own abilities. In fact, they show feelings of inferiority for assignments. What level of Maslow's hierarchy of needs is not being met?

   A. Safety

   B. Self-esteem

   C. Physiological

   D. Love/belonging

29. You have an optimistic, positive opinion of your project team, and you use a decentralized, participative management style. Douglas McGregor called this:

   A. Theory Y

   B. Theory X

   C. Theory W

   D. Theory Z

30. Effective project managers know that resources needed for the project can be acquired internally or externally. Which of the following outputs of the Acquire Resources process documents the material, equipment, and supplies that will be used in the project?

   A. Project team assignments

   B. Resource management plan

   C. Resource breakdown structure

   D. Physical resource assignments

31. The Manage Project Knowledge process consists of:

   A. Managing tacit and explicit knowledge

   B. Knowledge sharing and codifying implicit knowledge

   C. Making sure tools and techniques are shared by the stakeholders

   D. Ensuring that all stakeholder knowledge needs are met

32. Corporate communications requirements are an example of:

   A. Organizational process assets

   B. A best practice in information management

   C. A knowledge requirement for knowledge management

   D. Enterprise environmental factors

33. Design for X (DfX) is a(n):

   A. Set of technical guidelines for the optimization of a specific aspect of the product design

   B. Situational guideline for using agile approaches

   C. Specific design tool that addresses specific aspects of a mature product

   D. Agile tool used by everybody throughout the project

34. Which of the following inputs for the Develop Team process documents the team values and operating guidelines?

   A. Team charter

   B. Project team assignments

   C. Agile team manifesto

   D. Single-team process framework

35. Two of the common quality improvement tools are:

   A. Define, Measure, Analyze, Improve and Control (DMAIC) and three-point estimating

   B. Design of experiments (DOE) and Mean time between failure (MTBF)

   C. Logical data models and Suppliers, inputs, process, outputs, and customers (SIPOC)

   D. Plan-do-check-act (PDCA) and Six Sigma

36. The least effective way to motivate team members is to ensure there is adequate:

   A. Opportunity to grow

   B. Application of professional skills

   C. Financial reward

   D. Appreciation

37. Conflict is a reality that project managers face every day. Successful conflict resolution can produce positive results for everyone. When the project manager actively works to increase stakeholder support and minimize resistance, it is an example of which process?

   A. Plan Conflict Management

   B. Manage Stakeholder Engagement

   C. Manage Stakeholder Conflict

   D. Manage Communications

38. In David McClelland's needs-based motivational model, this determined results-driven approach is almost invariably present in the character makeup of all successful project managers:

   A. People with strong achievement motivation

   B. A strong power/authority motivation

   C. Strong affiliation motivation

   D. Motivational or needs "mix"

39. Frederick Herzberg's two-factor theory, also known as motivation-hygiene theory or intrinsic vs. extrinsic motivation, concludes that certain factors in the workplace can cause job satisfaction and a separate set of factors can cause dissatisfaction. Which of the following factors would be least effective in increasing motivation?

   A. Sense of achievement

   B. Job recognition and potential for promotion

   C. The work itself and responsibility

   D. Lifetime employment

40. You are working in an adaptive environment. You want to streamline team member access to information and have transparent decision making. The most effective project reporting technique in this situation would be to:

   A. Set up an intranet site

   B. Email and fax project status reports

   C. Form an online community

   D. Use information radiators

41. Which of the following project communications artifacts would be most useful in managing communications?

   A. Issue log

   B. Schedule progress

   C. Risk register

   D. Communications management plan

42. You are in the process of implementing agreed-upon risk response plans. Which of the following actions is least likely to occur?

    A. A change request to the cost baseline

    B. A change request to the schedule baseline

    C. A change request to the scope baseline

    D. An update to the project team assignments

43. You have been hired by a large organization to apply agile techniques and approaches. Your job is to move the organization from being internally focused to being focused outwardly on the customer experience. The PMO is a stumbling block; their lack of support in establishing an organizational change management (OCM) group is a major concern. You are pushing the PMO to adopt an agile mind-set. Your agile implementation strategy depends on the PMO and the OCM. Addressing this concern is an example of:

    A. Manage Communications

    B. Manage Team Members

    C. Manage Stakeholder Engagement

    D. Direct and Manage Project Work

44. Your project team is collecting requirements. Sally has proposed interviewing as an elicitation technique to gather information from three system operators working three different shifts to cover their job tasks in a 24-hour period. She anticipates she will need two hours per shift from each person for a three-week period. In the meeting with the system operators' manager, she confirms listening by nodding, eye contact, and asking questions for clarification. Sally summarizes the conversation along the way. What communication skill is being practiced here?

    A. Language management

    B. Verbal feedback

    C. Effective listening

    D. Active listening

45. You are obtaining seller responses, selecting a seller, and awarding a contract. Which of the following is an enterprise environmental factor that can influence the Conduct Procurements process?

    A. List of preferred sellers that have been prequalified

    B. Resource management systems

    C. Prior agreements already in place

    D. Resource pre-assignment in the project charter

46. Who is primarily responsible for execution of the project management plan?

   A. Project manager and project team

   B. Project sponsor and project manager

   C. Program sponsor and project manager

   D. Program manager and project manager

47. You will be producing many outputs during the execution phase, such as deliverables, work performance data, and the issue log. You will also be implementing which of the following during the execution phase?

   A. Project scope, business case, project charter

   B. Project management plan, communications plan, work breakdown structure (WBS)

   C. Procurement management plan, contract statement of work, contract management plan

   D. Defect repairs, corrective actions, preventive actions

48. Key skills are needed to manage project data and the flow of information in and out of project processes. Which of the following is least useful in consolidating project data?

   A. Organizing various data metrics

   B. Using reporting tools to create and assemble the reports

   C. Clarifying requirements

   D. Communicating and presenting complex information

49. A major automotive manufacturer is working hard to adjust to recent legislative changes to the fuel mileage ratings on new vehicles. The government has changed the calculation methods to make the determination for gas mileage more realistic. This has caused the distance ratings to decline and resulted in a decline in sales due to consumer expectations to get better fuel economy. When the project was established, which of the following were most likely involved in developing governance for project tracking and updating?

   A. Project board

   B. Project managers

   C. Project office

   D. Project management office (PMO)

50. Which of the following tool sets will be most useful in facilitating project management activities to deliver the benefits of the project?

   A. Creation of the milestone plan

   B. Measuring project performance

   C. Estimation of task schedule

   D. Estimating resource usage

51. A new project needs to be chartered to ensure adjustments are made to keep the project work aligned with new strategic goals related to the reductions in fuel economy. Which of the following techniques/notations is least useful in chartering new projects?

A. The "rich picture" approach

B. The "context diagram" from structured analysis

C. Lean manufacturing's "A3"

D. eXtreme programming (XP) best practice

52. Many key resources from other projects in the organization will be needed on the new project you are starting. Which of the following should you apply as constraints when you level the related resources?

A. Schedule, budget, quality

B. Schedule, availability, level of expertise

C. Time, schedule, availability

D. Availability, level of expertise, commitment

53. Even though your matrix management organization uses projects extensively to bring change to the company, nearly all decisions are made by and are the responsibility of functional managers. Project managers are primarily facilitators for their respective projects. Which of the following will be most useful in managing this circumstance?

A. Identifying market trends for benefits planning

B. Negotiating trade-offs with functional managers

C. Identifying personal aspirations

D. Identifying tools for resource determination

54. Which of the following processes is focused on creating the project's intended benefits?

A. Plan Risk Management

B. Manage Quality

C. Direct and Manage Project Work

D. Manage Project Knowledge

55. Most of your staff has been assigned to you temporarily from various functional departments. Even so, you want to motivate them as much as possible and make sure their level of commitment is high. Which of the following will help you manage their career development the most?

A. Identify career path within available and potential roles

B. Identify competence assessment techniques

C. Identify intellectual property

D. Create team ground rules and techniques

56. To motivate the team, it is essential to use appropriate tools and techniques to increase commitment to the project objectives. Which of the following skills will be most useful in generating the highest level of commitment?

A. Conflict resolution between team members

B. Analyzing data and reports

C. Scenario analysis

D. Maintaining work/life balance

57. More and more organizations today are becoming globally diversified. Outsourcing resources from around the world and having staff work remotely are two optimization methods that will increase your need to manage diversity in your project. Awareness of the diverse population in your project will benefit least from which of the following?

A. Describing the organization's culture

B. Describing the team structure and individual cultures

C. Maintaining cohesiveness among all teams

D. Establishing workgroups that consist of individual cultural groups

58. The project you are managing is complex and challenging. This has resulted in concerns by several of the staff on this project that their performance may be viewed poorly in relation to others on less complex and demanding projects. Which of the reward and recognition policies will assist you in managing this dilemma best?

A. Facilitate coaching and mentoring across the teams

B. Measure resource retention and personal achievement

C. Map results to rewards

D. Complete a skill set inventory

59. What Project Resource Management processes do you manage as a part of the Executing process group?

A. Acquire Resources, Develop Team, Manage Team

B. Initiate Team, Develop Team, Close Team

C. Human Resource Planning, Acquire Project Team, Develop Project Team

D. Initiate Team, Acquire Team, Develop Team

60. A major educational institution is late in developing a project that allows students to attend classes and complete educational requirements online. This has resulted in a 20% reduction in enrollment and led the executive board to establish a project that will increase enrollment in the next year by 10%. Part of your project is delayed pending availability of resources. The programming can start in the next two weeks. The delayed projects will maintain the staff, regardless of changes, because no other resources are available and the budget does not support hiring contractors who have the necessary expertise. Which of the following will be least useful in developing the teams for these projects under these conditions?

A. Training plan

B. Staffing management plan

C. Project preferred-vendor list

D. Training records

61. Your current project is construction oriented with a variety of subcontractors bidding on various parts of the work. Which of the following will be least useful in assessing potential contractors you will use?

A. Request for proposal (RFP)

B. Request for information (RFI)

C. Return on investment (ROI)

D. Request for quotation (RFQ)

62. Your construction project has identified four possible vendors who can connect the water and sewer lines to the municipality's main water and sewer trunk. To select a subcontractor for this work, which of the following will be most useful in managing the selection process fairly and equitably?

A. Request for proposal (RFP)

B. Source selection criteria

C. Project budget

D. Lease agreements

63. You establish a formal documented procedure to define how work will be authorized to ensure work is done by the right people at the right time and in the right sequence. Which of the following is this a description of?

A. Work authorization system

B. Project management information system

C. Manage quality

D. Performance monitoring system

64. To make sure there is an evaluation of overall project performance, you manage the quality on a regular basis to provide confidence that the project will comply with the quality policy and standards. Which of the following is least useful as an input for managing quality?

A. Quality control measurements

B. Quality metrics

C. Risk report

D. Resource capabilities and availability

65. Several options are available to you in formulating the team on a project. Which of the following is a common method for staffing projects?

    A. Requesting resources from the directors of functional managers through the project management office

    B. Procuring resources from family members

    C. Negotiating with functional managers

    D. Preassigning external resources before internal resources

66. A major metropolitan city has lost over 40% of its manufacturing jobs due to outsourcing overseas. Left with a large volume of skilled workers from the manufacturing sector, the city and businesses have combined their efforts to generate a new class of manufacturing jobs building ecofriendly products. The consortium has launched a project that will provide training to existing workers in the area, focusing on currently unemployed members. A consulting firm did a study and found there are currently 1,700 electrical tradesmen in the community that are not employed. One project, already funded, will build a facility to manufacture solar panels. The unemployed tradesmen are skeptical of potentially working at the solar panel plant because their skills are related to other types of electrical products. Which of the following will be most useful in convincing the workers to accept these immediately available jobs?

    A. Change the project scope.

    B. Build trust and establish good working relationships.

    C. Define a process for budget allocation.

    D. Complete a skills inventory.

67. You've been assigned as the replacement project manager for a project that is already in the executing phase. After a brief period of ramping up on the project, you have determined you will need to make changes to the project as you go forward. Which of the following will you need least to manage changes effectively?

    A. Change control board

    B. Stage gates

    C. Change request reviews

    D. Resource leveling

68. While executing the Solar Panel Retraining project, you need to capture status and store data in the project management information system. To maintain accurate and current information for the diverse set of stakeholders on this project, you will need to consolidate the approach to information and decide on a set of data points that matter to a large cross-section of the stakeholders. Which of the following steps will benefit you least as you consolidate the information?

    A. Demonstrating the benefits of the project

    B. Applying resource-leveling techniques

C. Developing a project data retrieval process

D. Applying the data retrieval process

69. You are managing project communications and are wondering what tools to use as part of the PMIS. The least effective tool to use so that stakeholders can easily retrieve the information they need in a timely manner is:

A. Work performance reports

B. Social media

C. Web conferencing

D. Blogs

70. As you execute a project, you use appropriate project plans to ensure all facets of the project are managed and carried out consistent with the project governance criteria you established. Which plan do you review and adjust to reflect needed changes to personnel that are moved from project to project based on skill sets needed to support technical activities?

A. Risk management plan

B. Human resource management plan

C. Communications management plan

D. Staffing management plan

71. You plan to staff your project using internal company staff and to avoid the use of consultants and contractors. Which of the following will be least useful to you in trying to staff internally?

A. Identifying existing personnel qualified for open positions

B. Negotiating for existing personnel with their functional management

C. Balancing the needs of the individual with the individual's career path

D. Transitioning them to their project positions

72. You are focused on creating new knowledge that helps achieve the project's objectives while simultaneously contributing to organizational learning for the company and the project team. Which of the following is the most important part of knowledge management?

A. Reporting project data

B. Creating an atmosphere of trust

C. Coaching and mentoring members of the project team

D. Analyzing appropriate project data

73. One technique you can use to develop a project team is to place the team members in the same physical location. This technique enhances the team's ability to perform and is commonly referred to as:

A. Co-location

B. Geographic leveling

C. Remote staffing

D. Peer transfer

74. There are many methods for communicating key information within the project team. Which of the following methods is most useful for collecting, sharing, and distributing timely information to stakeholders?

A. Written reports distributed through a channeling system

B. Meetings and conferences with all the key players

C. Electronic communications and conferencing tools

D. Monthly or quarterly reviews

75. What are the key outputs of the Conduct Procurements process?

A. Evaluation criteria, proposals, and qualified sellers lists

B. Evaluation criteria and project preferred-vendor lists

C. RFIs, RFPs, and RFQs

D. Procurement statement of work, selected sellers, and change requests

76. As a project manager, you are assuring that benefits management and stakeholder engagement are carried out according to established policies and plans. Where in the project life cycle do these activities occur?

A. Pre-project setup

B. Initiation

C. Project planning

D. Execution

77. You are a project manager and are periodically verifying that team leaders are adhering to established project management methodologies and delivering products that meet business and technical requirements. What major project management theme do these activities most support?

A. Manage quality

B. Stakeholder engagement

C. Project governance

D. Benefits delivery

78. Samantha is the newly assigned project manager for a proposed project to provide basic cable service to retirement facilities nationwide. She establishes a formal documented procedure to define how work will be authorized to ensure work is done by the right organization, at the right time, and in the right sequence. This is a description of:

A. Work authorization system

B. Project management information system

C. Quality assurance system

D. Performance monitoring system

79. Samantha is performing an evaluation of her project using the Manage Quality process to provide confidence that the project will comply with the quality policy and standards. Which of the following is least useful as an input for performing the Manage Quality process?

A. Quality management plan

B. Quality metrics

C. Resource availability

D. Lessons learned register

80. Gary is using appropriate project plans to ensure all phases of his project are managed and carried out according to criteria that have been established. Which plan will he review and adjust to reflect needed changes to personnel based on skill sets and the need to be moved from one project to another?

A. Human resource management plan

B. Quality management plan

C. Personnel assignment plan

D. Resource management plan

81. You have just been appointed as the project manager for a new project at Smart Planes, Inc., and are responsible for the development of a new innovative unmanned aerial vehicle. This is your first large-scale project, and you know that the project management plan execution is your primary responsibility once the initial planning activities are completed and execution of the project has begun. Who else is primarily responsible for the project management plan execution?

A. Business analyst

B. Project team

C. Project managers

D. PMO

82. In addition to producing deliverables, the Direct and Manage Project Work process implements which of the following the least?

    A. Approved change requests

    B. Corrective actions

    C. Key performance indicators

    D. Preventive actions

83. Which project management processes in the Executing process group provide change requests as an input to the Perform Integrated Change Control process?

    A. Direct and Manage Project Execution, Schedule Control

    B. Manage Quality, Project Contract Administration

    C. Direct and Manage Project Work, Perform Quality Control

    D. Implement Risk Responses, Manage Quality, Direct and Manage Project Work

84. A household appliance company has established a major project to upgrade numerous products using projects for each product. The director of research and development will oversee all the projects, and the CFO will ensure that the benefits are realized from these upgrades by conducting independent reviews. The director of research and development is managing a:

    A. Large project

    B. Program

    C. Operation

    D. Functional area

85. A major filmmaker has established a large project to enhance the technologies for special effects development for several upcoming productions. Several teams are working on the project, and resources are shared between the project and ongoing operations. To develop some of your project team, you decide to have your team work in pairs, with experienced members working side by side with less experienced members. Which tool or technique of developing a team have you implemented?

    A. Centralized staffing

    B. Remote staffing

    C. Co-location

    D. Peer transfer

86. A large defense contractor has an established safety project to support manufacturing operations. Recent regulatory changes from government regulators and increased risks related to new work have increased operational cost substantially. You have instituted a process to provide timely and accurate information to project stakeholders and to use formats and media that are useful to the clients, sponsors, and the project team. Which of the following tools is most consistent with these actions?

A. Meetings

B. RACI (responsible, accountable, inform, consult) chart

C. Project management information system

D. Resource breakdown structure

87. Outsourcing resources from around the world and having staff resources work remotely are two resource optimization methods that will increase your need to manage diversity in your project. Given the global nature of team resourcing present in your company, awareness of the diverse population in your project will benefit least from which of the following?

A. Establishing work groups that consist of individual cultural groups

B. Identifying and understanding the organization's culture

C. Describing the team structure and individual cultures

D. Maintaining cohesiveness among all cross-divisional teams

88. You sent out RFPs to three vendors and received their offers. Currently you are reviewing the offers to choose potential vendors and negotiate contract conditions and are involved in the Conduct Procurements process. Which of the following are you expected to have to complete this process?

A. Seller responses

B. Executed seller risk plans

C. Selected sellers

D. Planned project contracting

89. A large defense contractor has an established safety project to support manufacturing operations. Recent regulatory changes from government regulators and increased risks related to new work have increased operational cost substantially. You need to select contractors. Which of the following will be most useful in managing the selection process fairly and equitably?

A. Evaluation criteria

B. Request for proposal (RFP)

C. Project budget

D. Lease agreements

90. The specific technique for evaluating sellers' proposals that involves evaluation of the proposals by a multidiscipline team containing members with specialist knowledge in each of the areas covered by the proposed contract is called a(n):

A. Seller rating system

B. Expert judgment

C. Screening system

D. Bidder conference

91. Within the Conduct Procurements process, the procurement management plan, seller proposals, and source selection criteria are examples of:

    A. Contract types

    B. Tools and techniques

    C. Inputs

    D. Outputs

92. The project sponsor asks you to be certain that you ensure that all prospective sellers have a clear and collective understanding of the procurement you require. He suggests you have a structured meeting to do this. What type of meeting is being suggested?

    A. Request seller responses

    B. Contract status meeting

    C. Project progress meeting

    D. Bidder conference

93. The part of the procurement process involving obtaining seller responses, selecting a seller, and awarding a contract is called:

    A. Qualified sellers list

    B. Bidder conference

    C. Conduct procurements

    D. Selected sellers

94. You are part of a team running a complex project spanning several years and involving several subcontractors. The contracts signed for this project might or will end during:

    A. Any phase of the project

    B. The completion phase

    C. The execution phase

    D. The acceptance phase

95. Documenting the effectiveness of risk responses in dealing with identified risks and the root causes and of the effectiveness of managing risk is called (a):

    A. Implement risk responses

    B. Risk identification

    C. Risk analysis

    D. Risk audit

96. When engaging project stakeholders, you may use many different techniques, including written and oral and both giving and receiving. These techniques are examples of what type of skills?

    A. Influence

    B. Negotiating

C. Delegation

D. Communications

97. You have completed an end-of-phase review meeting. Several actions and suggestions have been given to you as the project manager. You must document these and ensure that they become part of the project and organizational process assets (OPAs) from this point on. These actions and suggestions are called (the):

A. Project issues list

B. Lessons learned

C. Risk register items

D. Project documentation

98. Which of the following is the recommended way of reporting on project progress to stakeholders?

A. Regularly at preset times

B. Comprehensively at the end of the project

C. Regularly and on exception

D. On exception and at the end of the project

99. You have been asked to collect and provide performance information to the project stakeholders. This action is called:

A. Baselining the schedule

B. Stakeholder management

C. Performance analysis

D. Performance reporting

100. Work performance reports on the status of deliverables and what has been accomplished in the project is part of which process group?

A. Initiating

B. Executing

C. Closing

D. Planning

101. You have many reports, including analysis of project forecasts, status of issues and risks, and work completed during the Manage Communications process. The collective name for this information is:

A. Performance measurements

B. Forecast completion

C. Performance reports

D. Deliverables status reports

102. You have been asked to give details of how you propose to develop the project team. What description best describes what you should be doing?

    A. Improve the competencies of team members

    B. Document the resource calendars of team members

    C. Assign the appropriate people to activities on the project

    D. Finalize roles and responsibilities in the project plan

103. You are discussing the work that you have been doing with a colleague. The activities include assisting others when the workload is unbalanced, sharing information, and communicating in diverse ways to suit individual team members. This group of activities is related to:

    A. Communications planning

    B. Effective team working

    C. Improving team competencies

    D. Management by objectives (MBO)

104. At your personal performance review, your line manager suggests many areas in which you can improve. These include understanding better the sentiments of the project team members and acknowledging their concerns. These skills are most related to:

    A. Effective team working

    B. Communication planning

    C. Interpersonal skills

    D. Negotiating techniques

105. You are required to develop a recognition and reward system for your project office. Which of the following is an appropriate basis for this system?

    A. Reward only desirable behavior

    B. Reward the team member of the month

    C. Reward all team members who work overtime

    D. Reward individualism, regardless of culture

106. Which type of organization complicates the management of the project team?

    A. Functional

    B. Matrix

    C. Projectized

    D. Hierarchical

107. Tracking team performance, providing feedback, resolving issues, and coordinating changes to enhance project performance are all part of which process?

    A. Develop Team

    B. Perform Team

C. Manage Team

D. Build Team

108. Checking skills improvements, recording current competencies, and monitoring reduction in team turnover rates are related to:

A. Project staff assignments

B. Project team building activities

C. Recognition and reward systems

D. Team performance assessment

109. To help you manage the project team, you are using a system that documents who is responsible for resolving a specific problem by a target date. This system is called using (a):

A. Project risk register

B. Change control

C. Project issue log

D. Performance reports

110. You meet with the project sponsor, and the conversation covers the following topics: availability, competencies, experience, interests, and costs of the potential project team. A list or chart of these items is known as a(n):

A. Enterprise environmental factor (EEF)

B. Project resource histogram

C. Responsibility assignment matrix (RAM)

D. Organizational hierarchy chart

111. Which of the following is an input to the Manage Quality process?

A. Quality metrics

B. Project requirements

C. Change requests

D. Validated deliverables

112. A project manager is reviewing a project that is in progress. She is trying to identify the best project practices being used and gaps between best practices and current practices, as well as sharing the best practices introduced or implemented in similar projects in the organization. This is known as:

A. Developing the quality metrics

B. Performing a quality audit

C. Setting the quality baseline

D. Building quality checklists

113. You are coaching a new team member in your project. One of her functions is to recommend corrective actions to increase the effectiveness and efficiency of the organization. This falls under the Manage Quality process ITTOs (inputs, tools and techniques, and outputs). This list of actions is documented as:

    A. Change requests

    B. Organizational process assets (OPAs) updates

    C. Project management plan updates

    D. Recommended preventive actions

114. As a project manager you must audit the quality requirements and the results from quality control measurements to ensure that appropriate quality standards and operational definitions are used. This is part of which of the following processes?

    A. Improve Quality Standards

    B. Manage Quality

    C. Plan Quality

    D. Plan Quality Improvement

115. You are managing the execution stage of a project. Your responsibilities include gathering data on actual start and finish dates of activities, along with remaining durations for work in progress. The work you are doing is involved with:

    A. Cost variance analysis

    B. Performance measurement

    C. Performance reviews

    D. Critical path analysis

116. You are managing a project that is running late. You have proposed corrective actions that will affect the schedule baseline. These actions are called:

    A. Change requests

    B. Action change control

    C. Schedule baseline updates

    D. Project scope updates

117. You are managing the execution of a project in your organization. You work with many people and groups regularly during this stage of a project. With whom do you work closely to direct, manage, and execute the project?

    A. The project initiator and sponsor

    B. The business unit as the customer

    C. No one; as project manager, you assume full responsibility

    D. The project management team

118. You are asked by your line manager to describe your current activities as a project manager. You list the activities as "obtain, manage, and use resources to accomplish the project objectives." In what process group is this project?

A. Initiating

B. Executing

C. Planning

D. Monitoring and Controlling

119. During the execution of a project, many influences drive a project manager's activities. Which of the following is an input to this process?

A. Outstanding defects and faults

B. Administrative procedure edits

C. Approved change requests

D. Postponed change requests

120. You are managing a project that is time critical and essential for the survival of the business. You have many changes on this project. Which of the following do you spend your time scheduling into the work for the project team?

A. Likely changes to the schedule

B. Change requests to the scope

C. Requested changes to the budget

D. Approved change requests

121. A new team member has joined your project team and asks you what is a project deliverable from a generic perspective rather than for your project. Which of the following is the best answer to this question?

A. All items consumed in the project during the execution

B. The goods that are delivered to the shipping dock and are signed for

C. A product purchased according to the procurement plan

D. Something that is produced to complete the project

122. A quantitative standard of measurement typically used in projects to measure performance and progress is a:

A. Metric

B. Process

C. Tool

D. Technique

123. Which of the following tool sets will be most useful in facilitating project management activities to deliver the benefits of the project?

A. Creating the milestone plan

B. Estimating the task schedule

C. Estimating resource usage

D. Measuring project performance

124. What Project Integration Management processes do you manage as a part of the Executing process group?

A. Integrate Team, Develop Team, Close Team

B. Project Integration Planning, Acquire Project Team, Integrate Team

C. Direct and Manage Project Work, Manage Project Knowledge

D. Acquire Project Team, Develop Project Team, Manage Project Team

1. D	**32.** A	**63.** A	**94.** A
2. A	**33.** A	**64.** D	**95.** D
3. B	**34.** A	**65.** C	**96.** D
4. D	**35.** D	**66.** B	**97.** B
5. B	**36.** C	**67.** D	**98.** C
6. A	**37.** B	**68.** B	**99.** D
7. B	**38.** A	**69.** A	**100.** B
8. C	**39.** D	**70.** D	**101.** C
9. B	**40.** D	**71.** C	**102.** A
10. C	**41.** B	**72.** B	**103.** B
11. A	**42.** C	**73.** A	**104.** C
12. B	**43.** C	**74.** C	**105.** A
13. B	**44.** D	**75.** D	**106.** B
14. D	**45.** C	**76.** D	**107.** C
15. D	**46.** A	**77.** C	**108.** D
16. A	**47.** D	**78.** A	**109.** D
17. B	**48.** C	**79.** C	**110.** B
18. B	**49.** B	**80.** D	**111.** A
19. B	**50.** B	**81.** B	**112.** B
20. D	**51.** D	**82.** C	**113.** C
21. B	**52.** A	**83.** D	**114.** B
22. B	**53.** B	**84.** A	**115.** C
23. B	**54.** C	**85.** C	**116.** A
24. D	**55.** A	**86.** C	**117.** D
25. B	**56.** D	**87.** A	**118.** B
26. B	**57.** D	**88.** C	**119.** C
27. C	**58.** C	**89.** A	**120.** D
28. B	**59.** A	**90.** B	**121.** D
29. A	**60.** C	**91.** C	**122.** A
30. D	**61.** C	**92.** D	**123.** D
31. A	**62.** B	**93.** C	**124.** C

Chapter 4: The Executing Domain

1. You are managing a construction project. At 75% through the project, you determine that you are behind schedule. You review the project schedule to determine how to complete the project on time. The project sponsor will not give you any more resources. When analyzing the project schedule, you see a lot of soft logic—the remaining activities are sequenced based on the project team's knowledge of best practices. What can you do to adjust the project schedule and finish the project on the expected due date?

   A. Crash the schedule.

   B. Keep the soft logic decisions and fast-track the activities on the critical path.

   C. Fast-track the schedule.

   D. Remove the soft logic and do more of the remaining tasks/activities concurrently.

   ☑ **D.** When you remove the discretionary dependencies, you are now ready to fast-track and do more task activities in parallel, leaving the rest of the work on the critical path.

   ☒ **A** is incorrect because crashing is a way to shorten the schedule by adding more resources. **B** is incorrect because when fast tracking is used, soft logic should be reviewed and considered for modification or removal. **C** is incorrect because just fast tracking alone will not overcome the discretionary dependencies.

2. A generally accepted practice in project management is to use lessons learned to capitalize on effective and ineffective events that have happened in past projects and to take corrective actions for future work. In addition, the project manager uses lessons learned and communication techniques to keep stakeholders informed. Lessons learned will be compiled and archived at project closure time, and a final report will be written and distributed. When is the best time to inform stakeholders about lessons learned?

   A. During all phases of the project life cycle

   B. During the execution phase of the project life cycle

   C. At the beginning of the project during the project kick-off meeting

   D. When a major deliverable is completed during any phase of the project

   ☑ **A.** Lessons learned can occur at key times in a project: the team delivers something, the end of a phase, and the end of the project.

   ☒ **B, C,** and **D** are incorrect because they are all too limiting. Stakeholders need to know about what could be improved, what to incorporate in the rest of the project, and what to add to organizational process assets.

3. You decide to conduct regular QA audits on the SCAN project. The major purpose is to:

   A. Document best practices and noncompliance issues and forward these to the PMO

   B. Confirm the implementation of approved change requests

C. Verify that the quality management plan is being followed

D. Determine if policies, processes, and procedures are complying with benefits realization

☑ **B.** Approved change requests, including updates, corrective actions, defect repairs, and preventive actions, are confirmed in a quality audit.

☒ **A** is incorrect because documenting best practices is part of lessons learned, and the results of the quality audit are forwarded to the requester of the audit, not necessarily the PMO. **C** is incorrect because the quality management plan should be reviewed to ensure that decisions are based on accurate information. **D** is incorrect because the benefits management plan is evaluated later to determine if benefits are realized.

4. You are managing a project focused on optimizing company processes to increase efficiencies by taking advantage of economies of scale. A major challenge in the company is the knowledge silos that have appeared in project teams. You are determined to change the culture of your projects to one of information sharing, not hoarding. You have one person skilled in product development and another person who is the marketing guru on your project team. The product development person seems overallocated, and she is complaining about all the work. As the project manager you should:

A. Rely on the functional manager to assign the proper amount of work

B. Use the resource allocation team (RAT) to work with your project team to outsource some of the work

C. Use the resource calendar to document the time periods she is working

D. Meet with the product development person and prioritize her work

☑ **D.** Assigning and prioritizing work is a primary responsibility of the project manager.

☒ **A** is incorrect because the project manager assigns the work, not the functional area manager. **B** is incorrect because a risk assessment team (RAT) may be the name of a company team that assesses risks, but this is not a PMI term, nor are risks directly related to who assigns work in a project. **C** is incorrect because a resource calendar identifies the working days for each resource.

5. The product development specialist on your current project has the PMP certification. The marketing expert on your team has a master's degree in project management. To ensure all your project team members, including these two, receive feedback on their performance, you decide to:

A. Meet with each of them weekly to generate decisions, actions, or awareness

B. Set up work performance reports for each one to determine recognition and rewards

C. Ask each of them to prepare an individual development plan for your review

D. Conduct a formal review with each of them at the end of each phase

☑ **B.** Work performance reports will help you manage the team and make decisions about recognition and rewards.

☒ **A** is incorrect because meeting weekly is too frequent to discuss the performance of each team member. Monthly or quarterly meetings are recommended. **C** is incorrect because an individual development plan is prepared yearly by the project manager and the team member and reviewed periodically during the year. **D** is incorrect because formal reviews are usually performed annually.

6. As part of implementing risk responses, you are updating your risk report. You should include:

    A. Any changes to overall risk exposure

    B. Impact of identified risks on achieving project benefits

    C. A change request process for risks that occur that affect project team assignments

    D. A revised list of prioritized issues that affect the project's objectives

    ☑ **A.** The risk report may be updated to include changes to overall project risk exposure that are made because of the Implement Risk Responses process.

    ☒ **B** is incorrect because the risk register already includes the impact of identified risks on achieving project benefits and was being monitored before implementing the risk response. **C** is incorrect because the question does not mention limiting the risk responses to those that affect project team assignments. **D** is incorrect because the issue log includes a revised list of prioritized issues that affect the project's objectives.

7. As part of your Implement Risk Responses process, for a risk you should.

    A. Specify the risk thresholds based on the risk appetite of the sponsor

    B. Encourage risk owners to take necessary action, if required

    C. Document the risk description and impact if it happens

    D. Inform project stakeholders of all ranked risks

    ☑ **B.** Accepting a risk acknowledges its existence, and no proactive action is taken.

    ☒ **A** is incorrect because specifying the risk thresholds based on the risk appetite of the sponsor is part of planning risk management. **C** is incorrect because you document risks in the risk register, and you inform stakeholders in a risk meeting. **D** is incorrect because even if the risk is a low-priority threat, the risk will still be added to the risk register and monitored in risk meetings.

8. You are establishing a Project Management Office (PMO) in your global company. You know you need to set up knowledge management tools. You also have a chief knowledge officer in your company. She is on the project management team and is recommending the project use library services. Why?

    A. To connect every team member so they can share knowledge management

    B. To make reverse shadowing mandatory to build trust

C. To share explicit knowledge for your team

D. To focus the team on organizational learning

☑ **C.** Library services are an information management tool and technique for sharing codified explicit knowledge.

☒ **A** is incorrect because information management tools and techniques connect people to information. **B** is incorrect because reverse shadowing (where a more junior member of staff, who is recognized as one of the organization's lynch pins, shares some of their hard-earned experience with a colleague from the managerial/leadership cadre on how to circumnavigate barriers in order to deliver a key piece of work effectively and efficiently) is a tool and technique used in knowledge management. **D** is incorrect because expert judgment is a tool and technique of the Manage Project Knowledge process and uses an individual's specialized knowledge of organizational learning.

9. Your team is a weak matrix one, and given travel restrictions, you will not have any face-to-face meetings during this two-year project. During this two-year period, you do not want to lose any project members to either other projects or their functional work. To be successful in this environment, you need to:

A. Get commitments in writing that the functional manager will allocate the team member to your project for two years

B. Encourage the project team to collaborate/problem-solve to build consensus and commitment

C. Give certificates of appreciation to the functional team members at key milestone points to influence them to stay on the project

D. Have each team member sign a letter of intent stating that he or she will stay on the project until completion

☑ **B.** Encouraging collaborative problem solving improves consensus and commitment to the team. It also creates a cohesive team culture.

☒ **A** is incorrect because even if the functional manager commits in writing to allocating the team member to your project, there is still no guarantee the commitment would be honored when business/strategy changes. **C** is incorrect because certificates of appreciation will only be effective if they satisfy a need that is valued by that individual. **D** is incorrect because a letter of intent (LOI) is a document outlining the general plans of an agreement between two or more parties before a legal agreement is finalized. A letter of intent is not a contract and cannot be legally enforced; however, it signifies a serious commitment from one involved party to another.

10. Your last assignment before retirement is to design and develop the next-generation handheld device. You have used functional decomposition to create three subprojects in your project: video, audio, and AI. You must consider maintenance and customer support for your new product. Your three teams—one for each subproject—are geographically

located in the United States, Ireland, and Russia. You expect team members to be committed to the success not only of their subproject but also to the overall project. You want to increase team cohesiveness and minimize staff turnover rate. To measure team effectiveness, you should:

A. Use structured interviews and focus group tools

B. Conduct individual team member assessments

C. Evaluate the openness of information sharing and experiences among the team

D. Formally establish a job shadowing program and encourage teams from each country to participate

☑ C. Cohesiveness and staff turnover rate are both based on trust and open communications. Team effectiveness is the capacity of a team to accomplish the goals or objectives of the project. Reducing turnover rate reduces the time teams spend going through the Tuckman ladder and improves productivity.

☒ A is incorrect because structured interviews and focus groups work well in requirements elicitation and do relate to staff turnover rate. B is incorrect because individual assessments can be used to improve understanding and trust. Team performance assessments can be used to improve team interaction. D is incorrect because work shadowing (working with another employee who might have a different job in hand, might have something to teach, or can help the person shadowing him or her to learn new aspects related to the job, organization, certain behaviors or competencies) is a tool and technique used in knowledge management so the team can work together to create new knowledge.

11. Although people may say they can identify, assess, and manage their personal feelings, many teams experience tension and uncooperative behaviors among teammates. You have recognized this on projects where you have been a team member, especially virtual teams. Now that you are a project manager, you want to establish an environment in which teammates can reduce tension and increase cooperation. A best practice to follow is to:

A. Use emotional intelligence to control the sentiments of team members

B. Focus on goals to be served and ask that emotions be left outside the project

C. Emphasize areas of agreement rather than areas of difference

D. Maintain a good relationship with the project sponsor

☑ A. Emotional intelligence (the ability to manage your emotions and others' emotions) leads directly to reducing conflict and making positive decisions.

☒ B is incorrect because focusing only on the goals is too "task" oriented and not enough "relationship" oriented. C is incorrect because this is the definition of the smoothing technique used in conflict resolution. D is incorrect because it is one of the factors that influence conflict resolution methods.

12. You have been working on the SecureAI project for six months. You are scheduled to meet with your steering committee to review project performance next week. You have met individually with each member of the steering committee to better understand their concerns and issues. You found that one person does not believe the project has delivered any benefits to date based on the reports he has received. Another member of the team is concerned because even though you are only in the first six months of this two-year project, already you have had seven change requests. The third steering committee team member was out of the office last week, but her administrative assistant seems to think she is happy—so far. In this meeting you will explain how you are evaluating overall project progress. One approach to use is to:

A. Switch to a critical success factor approach

B. Tell them you are relying on the Project Management Information System (PMIS) as one way to evaluate progress

C. Enable them to have full access to the lessons learned repository

D. Set up a red-amber-green dashboard that emphasizes value and quality rather than the Triple Constraint Triangle

☑ **B.** The PMIS provides access to IT tools as well as corporate knowledge base repositories. Overall project performance can be determined by accessing the Key Performance Indicators (KPIs) in the PMIS.

☒ **A** is incorrect because whether you have a Critical Success Factor (CSF) reporting approach or you use KPIs, the PMIS allows access to the information. **C** is incorrect because the lessons learned repository contains the lessons learned register. The lessons learned register is transferred to the lessons learned repository at the end of a project or phase. **D** is incorrect because a RAG dashboard is commonly used in project status reporting to communicate the level of risk.

13. You are outlining and guiding the selection of resources and assigning them to their respective activities. Which of the following tools and techniques would be least helpful to you?

A. Decision making

B. Resource calendars

C. Negotiation

D. Pre-assignment

☑ **B.** The question asks about tools and techniques of the Acquire Resources process, and resource calendars are a needed input to this process, so would not be designated as "least" important.

☒ **A, C**, and **D** are incorrect because they are the right tools and techniques to use in the Acquire Resources process.

14. You are leading and performing the work defined in the project management plan. Which of the following actions would be least helpful to you?

    A. Allocate available resources

    B. Manage organizational interfaces

    C. Analyze work performance data

    D. Leverage prior organizational knowledge

    ☑ **D.** The question is asking about the Direct and Manage Project Work process. Leveraging prior organizational knowledge is expertise that could be considered in the expert judgment technique.

    ☒ **A, B,** and **C** are incorrect in this case because they are all project activities to complete project deliverables and accomplish established objectives.

15. Leadership and management are about getting things done. In the execution phase, leadership differs from management in that:

    A. Leadership is about demonstrating the value of project management

    B. Management is about delivering better strategic outcomes

    C. Leadership includes making sure the project is delivered on target, on schedule, and on budget

    D. Leadership involves guiding, motivating, and directing the project team

    ☑ **D.** Leadership involves working with others through discussion or debate to guide them from one point to another.

    ☒ **A** is incorrect because management is about demonstrating the value of project management. **B** is incorrect because leadership is about delivering better strategic outcomes. **C** is incorrect because project management is the art and science of getting the project done—on target, on schedule, and on budget.

16. Decision making is the ability to negotiate and influence the project team. A guideline for effective decision making is:

    A. Follow a decision-making process

    B. Seek a compromise/reconcile solution

    C. Improve the efficiency of conflict resolution

    D. Apply both leadership and management techniques

    ☑ **A.** Decision making in this context follows six guidelines. "Follow a decision-making process" is guideline #2.

    ☒ **B** is incorrect because it is one of the five general techniques for solving conflict. **C** is incorrect because it is one of the goals of conflict resolution. **D** is incorrect because applying leadership and management techniques are what you do when performing project management.

17. One of your key stakeholders is upset about the quality of the demo from the last iteration. During the retrospective, one of the developers openly blames the other team members through the entire meeting to the point of hurting people's feelings. You step in and remind the team that the retrospective is a time for them to learn from previous work and make small improvements. Two weeks later, at the next retrospective, the same team member repeats the same "blamestorming" behavior. The team development behavior that you can improve is:

A. Establishing high team performance

B. Encouraging collaborative problem solving

C. Providing "stretch" objectives

D. Setting up a project room

☑ **B.** A servant leader/facilitator encourages collaboration through interactive meetings and knowledge sharing.

☒ **A** is incorrect because high-performing teams are a result of the project manager's skills to motivate and inspire project teams. **C** is incorrect because providing challenges is one way a project manager can create an environment that encourages teamwork. **D** is incorrect because establishing a "war room" is an organizational placement strategy that will improve communications.

18. Translating the quality management plan into executable quality activities during the execution phase is:

A. Execute Quality Management

B. Manage Quality

C. Control Quality

D. Project Quality Management

☑ **B.** This is the definition of the Manage Quality process.

☒ **A** is incorrect because Execute Quality Management is a made-up term. **C** is incorrect because Control Quality is a Monitoring and Controlling process group. **D** is incorrect because Project Quality Management is the name of a knowledge area.

19. A structured, independent process to determine whether project activities comply with project policies, processes, and procedures is called a:

A. Quality inspection

B. Quality audit

C. Retrospective

D. Quality demo

☑ **B.** This is the definition of a quality audit.

☒ **A** is incorrect because a quality inspection involves reviewing the product to see if it meets the defined quality norms. Conducting reviews is an example of inspection. **C** is incorrect because at the end of each sprint, a sprint review meeting is held. During this meeting, the Scrum team shows what they accomplished during the sprint. Typically, this takes the form of a demo of the new features. **D** is incorrect because at the end of each sprint, the team holds a sprint review meeting where the team must demonstrate the user stories completed during the sprint to the product owner and other interested stakeholders.

20. A key benefit of the Manage Team process is that it:

    A. Requires subject matter experts to create sustainable solutions

    B. Selects team members who can deal with high rates of change

    C. Implements a zero-sum reward and recognition system for the team

    D. Influences team behavior to optimize project performance

    ☑ **D.** The Manage Team process influences team behavior, manages conflict, and resolves issues.

    ☒ **A** is incorrect because subject matter experts are used for expert knowledge based on an application area. **B** is incorrect because selecting change-tolerant team members would be useful in an agile environment. **C** is incorrect because project managers should avoid zero-sum awards where only one project team member can win the award, such as project team member of the month. These rewards can damage trust among the project team.

21. Which of the following is a tool and technique of the Manage Communications process?

    A. Reporting performance

    B. Project reporting

    C. Work performance reports

    D. Project communications

    ☑ **B.** Project reporting is the act of collecting and distributing project information in the Manage Communications process.

    ☒ **A** is incorrect because reporting performance is not a tool; it would be an action, and of more specific use would be project reporting. **C** is incorrect because work performance reports are an input to the Manage Communications process. **D** is incorrect because project communications is an output of Manage Communications.

22. Which of the following trends and emerging practices in procurement management could have a negative effect on the success of your project?

    A. Advances in tools

    B. Permanent engagements

C. More advanced risk management

D. Changing contracting processes

☑ **B.** Trial engagements are used to evaluate potential partners.

☒ **A, C,** and **D** are incorrect because all three are recognized as major trends in procurement that positively affect the success rate of projects.

23. An effective way to ensure that no prospective bidders receive preferential treatment is to hold a vendor conference. A vendor conference should be held:

A. Before you prepare the request for quotation (RFQ) so prices can be submitted by prospective sellers

B. Before prospective sellers submit their proposals and after procurement documents have been distributed

C. Before you issue the statement of work to the prospective sellers

D. After the contract is awarded so that unsuccessful vendors can improve their bid packages

☑ **B.** Bidder conferences (contractor conferences/vendor conferences) are meetings between the buyer and prospective sellers prior to submitting proposals.

☒ **A** is incorrect because if the seller is going to submit a price proposal, a good practice is for it to be separate from the technical proposal. **C** is incorrect because the procurement statement of work is developed from the scope baseline and defines what is to be included in the related contract. **D** is incorrect because after the contract is awarded is the time for unsuccessful bidders to meet with procurement to understand the proposal evaluation process.

24. Seller proposals is an input to:

A. Plan Procurement Management

B. Request Procurements

C. Procurement Strategy

D. Conduct Procurements

☑ **D.** Seller proposals are an input to the Conduct Procurements process.

☒ **A** is incorrect because Plan Procurement Management is a process in the Planning process group. **B** is incorrect because request procurements is not an activity of Plan Procurement Management. **C** is incorrect because procurement strategy is the planned approach to cost-effectively purchasing a company's required goods and supplies.

25. You are translating the quality management plan into executable quality activities. Which of the following inputs will be least helpful to you?

A. Quality control measurements

B. Process improvement plan

C. Lessons learned register

D. Risk report

☑ **B.** The process improvement plan details the steps for analyzing project management and product development processes to identify activities that enhance their value.

☒ **A, C,** and **D** are incorrect because they are all inputs to the Conduct Procurements process.

26. Finally, after three months of negotiating with the resource allocation manager, a new business analyst, Sharon, has been added to your current project team. Given the introduction of a new team member, which team development stage might your team fall into?

A. Forming

B. Storming

C. Norming

D. Performing

☑ **B.** Project team members who have worked together in the past might skip a stage; instead of starting with forming, the team could move up the ladder to storming.

☒ **A, C,** and **D** are incorrect because it is common for the Tuckman team stages to occur in order: forming, storming, norming, performing, and adjourning (reforming).

27. Negotiation is a key interpersonal and team skill used in the Conduct Procurements process. The negotiation should be led by:

A. The project manager working on behalf of the project sponsor

B. The senior member of the steering committee

C. A member of the procurement team who is authorized to sign contracts

D. The contracting officer representative assigned to the project

☑ **C.** Procurement negotiation concludes with a signed document that can be executed by both seller and buyer.

☒ **A, B,** and **D** are incorrect because the project manager and other members of the project team may be present during procurement negotiation to help as needed.

28. You are a junior project manager assigned to your first takeover project. The team does not feel confident in their own abilities. In fact, they show feelings of inferiority for assignments. What level of Maslow's hierarchy of needs is not being met?

A. Safety

B. Self-esteem

C. Physiological

D. Love/belonging

☑ **B.** Although not found in the *PMBOK Guide, Sixth Edition,* questions about Maslow's hierarchy of needs may be on your exam. In Maslow's hierarchy of needs, level 3, self-esteem, is the need to have self-esteem and self-respect. Esteem presents the typical human desire to be accepted and valued by others. People often engage in a profession or hobby to gain recognition. These activities give the person a sense of contribution or value. Low self-esteem or an inferiority complex may result from imbalances during this level in the hierarchy.

☒ **A, C,** and **D** are incorrect because they describe the most fundamental needs at the bottom of the hierarchy.

29. You have an optimistic, positive opinion of your project team, and you use a decentralized, participative management style. Douglas McGregor called this:

A. Theory Y

B. Theory X

C. Theory W

D. Theory Z

☑ **A.** Although not found in the *PMBOK Guide, Sixth Edition,* questions about McGregor's Theory X and Theory Y may be on your exam. Theory Y denotes a positive view of human nature and assumes individuals are generally industrious, creative, and able to assume responsibility and exercise self-control in their jobs.

☒ **B** is incorrect because Theory X represents a negative view of human nature that assumes individuals generally dislike work, are irresponsible, and require close supervision to do their jobs. **C** is incorrect because so far, there is no Theory W attributed to anyone in the project management field. **D** is incorrect because Theory Z focuses on increasing employee loyalty to the company by providing a job for life, with a strong focus on the well-being of the employee, both on and off the job.

30. Effective project managers know that resources needed for the project can be acquired internally or externally. Which of the following outputs of the Acquire Resources process documents the material, equipment, and supplies that will be used in the project?

A. Project team assignments

B. Resource management plan

C. Resource breakdown structure

D. Physical resource assignments

☑ **D.** This is the definition of physical resource assignments.

☒ **A** is incorrect because project team assignments record the team members and their roles and responsibilities. **B** is incorrect because the resource management plan is an output of the Plan Resource Management process. **C** is incorrect because a resource breakdown structure is used in the Plan Resource Management process.

31. The Manage Project Knowledge process consists of:

   A. Managing tacit and explicit knowledge

   B. Knowledge sharing and codifying implicit knowledge

   C. Making sure tools and techniques are shared by the stakeholders

   D. Ensuring that all stakeholder knowledge needs are met

   ☑ **A.** Explicit knowledge can be readily codified, and tacit knowledge is personal and difficult to express. The Manage Project Knowledge process is concerned with managing both explicit and tacit knowledge.

   ☒ **B** is incorrect because codifying implicit knowledge is part of work done by a business analyst to create explicit knowledge. Codified explicit knowledge can be used in lessons learned. **C** is incorrect because tools are something tangible used in producing a product or result, and techniques are defined procedures used by a human resource to perform an activity to produce a product or result or deliver a service. **D** is incorrect because knowledge management is about making sure all the skills and expertise of the stakeholders are used throughout the project.

32. Corporate communications requirements are an example of:

   A. Organizational process assets

   B. A best practice in information management

   C. A knowledge requirement for knowledge management

   D. Enterprise environmental factors

   ☑ **A.** Formal and informal communications are used to influence the Manage Project Knowledge process. Both are examples of organizational process assets.

   ☒ **B** is incorrect because the answer is specific to "corporations," whereas communication is not. **C** is incorrect because requirements are not referred to as "knowledge requirements." **D** is incorrect because organizational communication requirements are organizational process assets, not enterprise environmental factors.

33. Design for X (DfX) is a(n):

   A. Set of technical guidelines for the optimization of a specific aspect of the product design

   B. Situational guideline for using agile approaches

   C. Specific design tool that addresses specific aspects of a mature product

   D. Agile tool used by everybody throughout the project

   ☑ **A.** This is the definition of design for X (DfX).

   ☒ **B** is incorrect because DfX is not a situational guideline, but rather a tool/technique of the Manage Quality process. **C** is incorrect because DfX is used in new product development. **D** is incorrect because DfX is not an agile tool.

34. Which of the following inputs for the Develop Team process documents the team values and operating guidelines?

    A. Team charter

    B. Project team assignments

    C. Agile team manifesto

    D. Single-team process framework

    ☑ **A.** The team charter is where the team values and operating guidelines are documented.

    ☒ **B** is incorrect because project team assignments identify the team and member roles and responsibilities. **C** is incorrect because the Agile Manifesto is the original and official definition of agile values and principles. **D** is incorrect because it is a made-up phrase.

35. Two of the common quality improvement tools are:

    A. Define, Measure, Analyze, Improve and Control (DMAIC) and three-point estimating

    B. Design of experiments (DOE) and Mean time between failure (MTBF)

    C. Logical data models and Suppliers, inputs, process, outputs, and customers (SIPOC)

    D. Plan-do-check-act (PDCA) and Six Sigma

    ☑ **D.** Trends and emerging practices in project quality management include PDCA, as defined by Shewhart and implemented by Deming. Six Sigma may improve project management processes and products.

    ☒ **A** is incorrect because DMAIC is an acronym for Define, Measure, Analyze, Improve, and Control and refers to a data-driven improvement cycle used for improving, optimizing, and stabilizing business processes and designs. The DMAIC improvement cycle is the core tool used to drive Six Sigma projects. The three-point estimating technique is used in estimating time and costs. **B** is incorrect because design of experiments (DOE) is a statistical method used in the Plan Quality process, and mean time between failure (MTBF) is a key performance indicator. **C** is incorrect because logical data models are used in data architecture to show a detailed representation of an organization's data, independent of any technology, and is described in business language; the SIPOC (Supplier, Input, Process, Output, Customer) model is a type of flowchart used to map procedures.

36. The least effective way to motivate team members is to ensure there is adequate:

    A. Opportunity to grow

    B. Application of professional skills

    C. Financial reward

    D. Appreciation

☑ **C.** People are motivated when they feel they are valued in the organization. Money is a tangible aspect of a rewards system; intangible rewards could be even more effective.

☒ **A, B,** and **D** are incorrect in this case because most project team members are motivated by an opportunity to grow, accomplish, be appreciated, and apply their professional skills to meet new challenges.

37. Conflict is a reality that project managers face every day. Successful conflict resolution can produce positive results for everyone. When the project manager actively works to increase stakeholder support and minimize resistance, it is an example of which process?

A. Plan Conflict Management

B. Manage Stakeholder Engagement

C. Manage Stakeholder Conflict

D. Manage Communications

☑ **B.** The key benefit of the Manage Stakeholder Engagement process is that it allows the project manager to increase support and minimize resistance from stakeholders.

☒ **A** and **C** are incorrect because they are not the name of recognized processes. **D** is incorrect because the Manage Communications process enables an effective and efficient information flow between the project team and the stakeholders.

38. In David McClelland's needs-based motivational model, this determined results-driven approach is almost invariably present in the character makeup of all successful project managers:

A. People with strong achievement motivation

B. A strong power/authority motivation

C. Strong affiliation motivation

D. Motivational or needs "mix"

☑ **A.** McClelland's research suggests that the n-ach person is "achievement motivated" and therefore seeks achievement, attainment of realistic but challenging goals, and advancement in the job. There is a strong need for feedback as to achievement and progress and a need for a sense of accomplishment.

☒ **B** is incorrect because McClelland theorizes two distinct types of power motivation: socialized power and personal power (n-pow), and this type of person is "authority motivated." This does not indicate a successful project manager. The n-pow driver produces a need to be influential, effective, and make an impact. There is a strong need to lead and for their ideas to prevail. There is also motivation and need for increasing personal status and prestige. **C** is incorrect because the n-affil person is "affiliation motivated" and has a need for friendly relationships and is motivated for interaction with other people. The affiliation driver produces motivation and need to be liked and held in popular regard. These people are team players. **D** is incorrect because McClelland's research did not identify a motivational or needs "mix" that affects working/managing style.

39. Frederick Herzberg's two-factor theory, also known as motivation-hygiene theory or intrinsic vs. extrinsic motivation, concludes that certain factors in the workplace can cause job satisfaction and a separate set of factors can cause dissatisfaction. Which of the following factors would be least effective in increasing motivation?

A. Sense of achievement

B. Job recognition and potential for promotion

C. The work itself and responsibility

D. Lifetime employment

☑ **D.** This is the exception. Top pay and lifetime employment are not motivators; Herzberg called them hygiene factors. Pay means the pay or salary structure should be appropriate and reasonable. It must be equal and competitive to those in the same industry in the same domain. Job security means the organization must provide job security to the employees.

☒ **A, B,** and **C** are incorrect because they are motivators. The motivational factors yield positive satisfaction. These factors are inherent to work and motivate the employees to provide superior performance. These factors are called satisfiers, and employees find them intrinsically rewarding.

40. You are working in an adaptive environment. You want to streamline team member access to information and have transparent decision making. The most effective project reporting technique in this situation would be to:

A. Set up an intranet site

B. Email and fax project status reports

C. Form an online community

D. Use information radiators

☑ **D.** Information radiators are visible, physical displays that provide up-to-the-minute knowledge sharing without having to disturb the team.

☒ **A** is incorrect because setting up a SharePoint site, wiki, or intranet site requires additional resources. **B** is incorrect because electronic communications will be either push or pull methods, and stakeholders will participate based on cost and time constraints. **C** is incorrect because forming an online community gives the opportunity to engage with stakeholders who are members of that community, and stakeholders may not have familiarity with the tools.

41. Which of the following project communications artifacts would be most useful in managing communications?

A. Issue log

B. Schedule progress

C. Risk register

D. Communications management plan

☑ **B.** Schedule progress is monitored in the Control Schedule process.

☒ **A, C,** and **D** are incorrect because they are project documents that may be updated when carrying out the Manage Communications process.

42. You are in the process of implementing agreed-upon risk response plans. Which of the following actions is least likely to occur?

   A. A change request to the cost baseline

   B. A change request to the schedule baseline

   C. A change request to the scope baseline

   D. An update to the project team assignments

   ☑ **C.** A change request to the scope baseline would come from the Control Scope process.

   ☒ **A, B,** and **D** are incorrect because they are most likely to occur during the Implement Risk Responses process.

43. You have been hired by a large organization to apply agile techniques and approaches. Your job is to move the organization from being internally focused to being focused outwardly on the customer experience. The PMO is a stumbling block; their lack of support in establishing an organizational change management (OCM) group is a major concern. You are pushing the PMO to adopt an agile mind-set. Your agile implementation strategy depends on the PMO and the OCM. Addressing this concern is an example of:

   A. Manage Communications

   B. Manage Team Members

   C. Manage Stakeholder Engagement

   D. Direct and Manage Project Work

   ☑ **C.** Manage Stakeholder Engagement is the process of developing approaches to involve stakeholders based on their needs, expectations, interests, and potential impact on the project.

   ☒ **A** is incorrect because the Manage Communications process enables an effective and efficient information flow between the project team and the stakeholders. **B** is incorrect because Manage Team Members is not the name of a process. **D** is incorrect because the Direct and Manage Project Work process is concerned with providing overall management of the project work and implementing approved changes.

44. Your project team is collecting requirements. Sally has proposed interviewing as an elicitation technique to gather information from three system operators working three different shifts to cover their job tasks in a 24-hour period. She anticipates she will need two hours per shift from each person for a three-week period. In the meeting with the system operators' manager, she confirms listening by nodding, eye contact, and asking questions for clarification. Sally summarizes the conversation along the way. What communication skill is being practiced here?

A. Language management

B. Verbal feedback

C. Effective listening

D. Active listening

☑ **D.** Active listening is a communication technique used in conflict resolution. It requires that the listener fully concentrate, understand, respond, and then remember what is being said.

☒ **A** is incorrect because it is a made-up term. **B** is incorrect because verbal feedback is communication that is spoken. Feedback is defined as a return of information about a result or the returned portion of a process. **C** is incorrect because effective listening requires that communication is heard completely and effectively interpreted into meaningful messages. It requires knowledge of the subject being discussed and attention to the speaker.

45. You are obtaining seller responses, selecting a seller, and awarding a contract. Which of the following is an enterprise environmental factor that can influence the Conduct Procurements process?

A. List of preferred sellers that have been prequalified

B. Resource management systems

C. Prior agreements already in place

D. Resource pre-assignment in the project charter

☑ **C.** Prior agreements already in place is an EEF that can influence the Conduct Procurements process.

☒ **A, B,** and **D** are incorrect in this question because they are distracters—made-up words and phrases—not in the PMBOK Guide.

46. Who is primarily responsible for execution of the project management plan?

A. Project manager and project team

B. Project sponsor and project manager

C. Program sponsor and project manager

D. Program manager and project manager

☑ **A.** The project management plan execution is the primary responsibility of the project manager and the project team once the initial planning activities are completed and execution of the project has begun.

☒ **B, C,** and **D** are incorrect because though it involves the project manager, the project team is not present.

47. You will be producing many outputs during the execution phase, such as deliverables, work performance data, and the issue log. You will also be implementing which of the following during the execution phase?

A. Project scope, business case, project charter

B. Project management plan, communications plan, work breakdown structure (WBS)

C. Procurement management plan, contract statement of work, contract management plan

D. Defect repairs, corrective actions, preventive actions

☑ **D.** This question lists deliverables of the Direct and Manage Project Work process. In addition to producing deliverables, this process implements approved change requests, corrective actions, defect repairs, and preventive actions once they have been integrated within the relevant plans.

☒ **A, B,** and **C** are incorrect because each represents deliverables for processes other than the Direct and Manage Project Work process.

48. Key skills are needed to manage project data and the flow of information in and out of project processes. Which of the following is least useful in consolidating project data?

A. Organizing various data metrics

B. Using reporting tools to create and assemble the reports

C. Clarifying requirements

D. Communicating and presenting complex information

☑ **C.** Consolidating project data requires us to use predefined reporting tools and methods to monitor project performance–required skills and organize various data metrics, analyze and evaluate appropriate project data, use reporting tools to create and assemble the reports, and communicate and present complex information.

☒ **A, B,** and **D** are all useful aspects of consolidating project data.

49. A major automotive manufacturer is working hard to adjust to recent legislative changes to the fuel mileage ratings on new vehicles. The government has changed the calculation methods to make the determination for gas mileage more realistic. This has caused the distance ratings to decline and resulted in a decline in sales due to consumer expectations to get better fuel economy. When the project was established, which of the following were most likely involved in developing governance for project tracking and updating?

A. Project board

B. Project managers

C. Project office

D. Project management office (PMO)

☑ **B.** When you are establishing a management infrastructure, you must set up governance for all projects within the organization. This normally includes a project board, project management office, and project teams. Project managers are not normally involved directly with setting up governance for the project. Project managers execute and apply project governance as defined by the project management office.

☒ **A** is incorrect because there is no entity referred to as the project board. **C** and **D** are incorrect because both reference the project management office, which may preexist the project, and the question is asking about governance when the project was first established.

50. Which of the following tool sets will be most useful in facilitating project management activities to deliver the benefits of the project?

    A. Creation of the milestone plan

    B. Measuring project performance

    C. Estimation of task schedule

    D. Estimating resource usage

    ☑ **B.** Measuring project performance is an ongoing task during a project that will ensure you are tracking progress and benefits, measuring project performance, and communicating effectively.

    ☒ **A, C,** and **D** are incorrect because these activities take place during the planning of the project.

51. A new project needs to be chartered to ensure adjustments are made to keep the project work aligned with new strategic goals related to the reductions in fuel economy. Which of the following techniques/notations is least useful in chartering new projects?

    A. The "rich picture" approach

    B. The "context diagram" from structured analysis

    C. Lean manufacturing's "A3"

    D. eXtreme programming (XP) best practice

    ☑ **D.** eXtreme programming is an approach used to code software project solutions and therefore doesn't apply to all types of projects.

    ☒ **A, B,** and **C** are incorrect because each are valid techniques or notations used to charter new projects.

52. Many key resources from other projects in the organization will be needed on the new project you are starting. Which of the following should you apply as constraints when you level the related resources?

   A. Schedule, budget, quality

   B. Schedule, availability, level of expertise

   C. Time, schedule, availability

   D. Availability, level of expertise, commitment

   ☑ **A.** When you charter projects, you assign project managers and allocate appropriate resources to meet project objectives. This requires knowledge of resource leveling and applying resource leveling within the constraints of schedule (time), budget, and quality.

   ☒ **B, C,** and **D** are incorrect because each is missing some aspect of schedule, budget, or quality.

53. Even though your matrix management organization uses projects extensively to bring change to the company, nearly all decisions are made by and are the responsibility of functional managers. Project managers are primarily facilitators for their respective projects. Which of the following will be most useful in managing this circumstance?

   A. Identifying market trends for benefits planning

   B. Negotiating trade-offs with functional managers

   C. Identifying personal aspirations

   D. Identifying tools for resource determination

   ☑ **B.** When you charter projects, you assign project managers and allocate appropriate resources to meet project objectives. This requires knowledge of matrix management and the use of project-perceived benefits as a means of cross-functional negotiation and the use of techniques to negotiate for trade-offs with functional managers.

   ☒ **A, C,** and **D** are incorrect because they do not directly address the aspect of matrix management and the negotiations required.

54. Which of the following processes is focused on creating the project's intended benefits?

   A. Plan Risk Management

   B. Manage Quality

   C. Direct and Manage Project Work

   D. Manage Project Knowledge

   ☑ **C.** The Direct and Manage Project Work process is what delivers the intended benefits.

   ☒ **A** is incorrect because Plan Risk Management is a part of the Planning process group. **B** is incorrect because Manage Quality is a separate process in the Executing process group. **D** is incorrect because Manage Project Knowledge is a separate process in the Executing process group.

55. Most of your staff has been assigned to you temporarily from various functional departments. Even so, you want to motivate them as much as possible and make sure their level of commitment is high. Which of the following will help you manage their career development the most?

   A. Identify career path within available and potential roles

   B. Identify competence assessment techniques

   C. Identify intellectual property

   D. Create team ground rules and techniques

   ☑ **A.** When you charter projects, you assign project managers and allocate appropriate resources to meet project objectives. This requires knowledge of line management and career development, where you identify personnel aspirations, identify career paths within available and potential roles, and communicate personal performance to line managers.

   ☒ **B, C,** and **D** are incorrect because they do not directly reflect the aspect of managing the careers of team members in a matrix management situation.

56. To motivate the team, it is essential to use appropriate tools and techniques to increase commitment to the project objectives. Which of the following skills will be most useful in generating the highest level of commitment?

   A. Conflict resolution between team members

   B. Analyzing data and reports

   C. Scenario analysis

   D. Maintaining work/life balance

   ☑ **D.** Motivating the team using appropriate tools and techniques to increase commitment to the program deliverables requires skills in building a team, balancing discipline and recognition, maintaining work/life balance, mentoring members from the project team, ensuring a safe and secure working environment, allocating resources, conducting resource assessments, demonstrating leadership, demonstrating empathy, demonstrating a sense of integrity and ethics, demonstrating loyalty to the company and customer, facing the issues, collaborating with stakeholders, resource leveling, coaching and mentoring, and empowering.

   ☒ **A, B,** and **C** are incorrect because they are not directly related to a team member's individual commitment but instead are focused on conflict between team members.

57. More and more organizations today are becoming globally diversified. Outsourcing resources from around the world and having staff work remotely are two optimization methods that will increase your need to manage diversity in your project. Awareness of the diverse population in your project will benefit least from which of the following?

   A. Describing the organization's culture

   B. Describing the team structure and individual cultures

C. Maintaining cohesiveness among all teams

D. Establishing workgroups that consist of individual cultural groups

☑ **D.** Motivating the team using appropriate tools and techniques to increase commitment to the project deliverables requires you to have knowledge of diversity awareness and be able to describe the organization's culture, describe the team structure and individual cultures, establish a safe and secure work environment, and maintain cohesiveness among all teams.

☒ **A, B,** and **C** are incorrect because they do not go far enough individually to create an awareness of the diverse population.

58. The project you are managing is complex and challenging. This has resulted in concerns by several of the staff on this project that their performance may be viewed poorly in relation to others on less complex and demanding projects. Which of the reward and recognition policies will assist you in managing this dilemma best?

A. Facilitate coaching and mentoring across the teams

B. Measure resource retention and personal achievement

C. Map results to rewards

D. Complete a skill set inventory

☑ **C.** Motivating the team using appropriate tools and techniques to increase commitment to the project deliverables requires you to have knowledge of rewards and recognition policies and to map results to rewards, design a commensurate incentive program, and demonstrate a sense of integrity and ethics.

☒ **A, B,** and **D** refer to allocating appropriate resources to meet project objectives rather than reward and recognition policies.

59. What Project Resource Management processes do you manage as a part of the Executing process group?

A. Acquire Resources, Develop Team, Manage Team

B. Initiate Team, Develop Team, Close Team

C. Human Resource Planning, Acquire Project Team, Develop Project Team

D. Initiate Team, Acquire Team, Develop Team

☑ **A.** The Project Resource Management processes that map to the Executing process group include Acquire Resources, Develop Team, and Manage Team.

☒ **B, C,** and **D** are incorrect because they each include processes that do not map from Project Resource Management to the Executing process group.

60. A major educational institution is late in developing a project that allows students to attend classes and complete educational requirements online. This has resulted in a 20% reduction in enrollment and led the executive board to establish a project that will increase enrollment in the next year by 10%. Part of your project is delayed pending availability of resources. The programming can start in the next two weeks. The delayed projects will maintain the staff, regardless of changes, because no other resources are available and the budget does not support hiring contractors who have the necessary expertise. Which of the following will be least useful in developing the teams for these projects under these conditions?

A. Training plan

B. Staffing management plan

C. Project preferred-vendor list

D. Training records

☑ **C.** The Develop Team process builds individual and group competencies to enhance project performance. This process supports development of personnel by providing necessary knowledge and skills to the project or to relevant project management competencies. In this situation, key inputs would include the training plan, assign training resources, personnel records, project management plan, role and responsibility assignments, staffing management plan, and training records. These are parts of the Project Procurement Management knowledge area.

☒ **A, B,** and **D** are incorrect because these are useful ways to develop team skills and should be used.

61. Your current project is construction oriented with a variety of subcontractors bidding on various parts of the work. Which of the following will be least useful in assessing potential contractors you will use?

A. Request for proposal (RFP)

B. Request for information (RFI)

C. Return on investment (ROI)

D. Request for quotation (RFQ)

☑ **C.** Return on investment (ROI) is not part of the process of assessing contractors.

☒ **A, B,** and **D** are incorrect because each is involved in assessing potential contracts. The process of issuing a request for information (RFI), request for proposal (RFP), and request for quotation (RFQ) and obtaining the responses is the Conduct Procurements process. These formal documents are used in the initial stages of planning to help evaluate "make vs. buy" decisions, as well as to gain an understanding of seller interest and qualifications. Key inputs include evaluation criteria and preferred-vendor lists, and the key outputs are seller responses to requests.

62. Your construction project has identified four possible vendors who can connect the water and sewer lines to the municipality's main water and sewer trunk. To select a subcontractor for this work, which of the following will be most useful in managing the selection process fairly and equitably?

   A. Request for proposal (RFP)

   B. Source selection criteria

   C. Project budget

   D. Lease agreements

   ☑ **B.** The process for reviewing offers, choosing among potential sellers, and negotiating the details of the contract, including technical terms and conditions, roles and responsibilities, deliverables, and final cost, is part of the Conduct Procurements process and requires source selection criteria to complete. The key inputs for this process include source selection criteria, seller proposals, and bid documents.

   ☒ **A, C,** and **D** are incorrect because they do not help the project manager in the selection process.

63. You establish a formal documented procedure to define how work will be authorized to ensure work is done by the right people at the right time and in the right sequence. Which of the following is this a description of?

   A. Work authorization system

   B. Project management information system

   C. Manage quality

   D. Performance monitoring system

   ☑ **A.** A collection of formal documented procedures defining how the project work will be authorized to ensure work is being done by the right organization, at the right time, and in the right sequence is a work authorization system.

   ☒ **B, C,** and **D** are incorrect because the project management information system, quality assurance system, and performance monitoring system serve purposes unrelated to documenting how work will be authorized.

64. To make sure there is an evaluation of overall project performance, you manage the quality on a regular basis to provide confidence that the project will comply with the quality policy and standards. Which of the following is least useful as an input for managing quality?

   A. Quality control measurements

   B. Quality metrics

   C. Risk report

   D. Resource capabilities and availability

☑ **D.** Resource capabilities and availability are not part of the input to managing quality.

☒ **A, B,** and **C** are incorrect because each is part of the process of evaluating overall project performance on a regular basis to provide confidence that the project will comply with the relevant quality policies and standards. This is the Manage Quality process. Key inputs for this process include the quality management plan, quality control measurements, quality metrics, and the risk report.

65. Several options are available to you in formulating the team on a project. Which of the following is a common method for staffing projects?

   A. Requesting resources from the directors of functional managers through the project management office

   B. Procuring resources from family members

   C. Negotiating with functional managers

   D. Preassigning external resources before internal resources

   ☑ **C.** When performing the Acquire Resources process, you must be able to negotiate with functional managers or other project management teams within the performing organization.

   ☒ **A** is incorrect because requesting resources from directors is a last resort and therefore uncommon. **B** and **D** are incorrect because they are not common occurrences for staffing projects. When performing the Acquire Resources process, you must be able to negotiate with functional managers or other project management teams within the performing organization. This is typically done for internal staff members. You also do pre-assignments when project team members are known in advance. You would not procure resources from family members.

66. A major metropolitan city has lost over 40% of its manufacturing jobs due to outsourcing overseas. Left with a large volume of skilled workers from the manufacturing sector, the city and businesses have combined their efforts to generate a new class of manufacturing jobs building ecofriendly products. The consortium has launched a project that will provide training to existing workers in the area, focusing on currently unemployed members. A consulting firm did a study and found there are currently 1,700 electrical tradesmen in the community that are not employed. One project, already funded, will build a facility to manufacture solar panels. The unemployed tradesmen are skeptical of potentially working at the solar panel plant because their skills are related to other types of electrical products. Which of the following will be most useful in convincing the workers to accept these immediately available jobs?

   A. Change the project scope.

   B. Build trust and establish good working relationships.

   C. Define a process for budget allocation.

   D. Complete a skills inventory.

☑ **B.** As a part of the Develop Team process, you perform team-building activities to build trust and establish good working relationships and to improve team relationships and communications to develop cohesiveness between the team members and other teams.

☒ **A, C,** and **D** are incorrect because they are not directly related to team development.

67. You've been assigned as the replacement project manager for a project that is already in the executing phase. After a brief period of ramping up on the project, you have determined you will need to make changes to the project as you go forward. Which of the following will you need least to manage changes effectively?

   A. Change control board

   B. Stage gates

   C. Change request reviews

   D. Resource leveling

☑ **D.** Resource leveling is a schedule compression technique, not a technique to manage project change.

☒ **A, B,** and **C** are incorrect because each will enable informed project decision making; you need to establish project consistency by deploying uniform standards, resources, infrastructure, tools, and processes. This requires knowledge of change acceptance procedures, which includes establishing a change control board, stage gates, and reviewing change requests.

68. While executing the Solar Panel Retraining project, you need to capture status and store data in the project management information system. To maintain accurate and current information for the diverse set of stakeholders on this project, you will need to consolidate the approach to information and decide on a set of data points that matter to a large cross-section of the stakeholders. Which of the following steps will benefit you least as you consolidate the information?

   A. Demonstrating the benefits of the project

   B. Applying resource-leveling techniques

   C. Developing a project data retrieval process

   D. Applying the data retrieval process

☑ **B.** Applying resource leveling is not related to consolidating information, but rather is a schedule compression technique.

☒ **A, C,** and **D** are incorrect because each will help maintain accurate and current project information for the use of stakeholders. You need to capture program status and data by ensuring the population of the project management information system. This requires you to consolidate information, which includes three steps: 1) demonstrate the benefits of project data consolidation, 2) develop a project data consolidation process, and 3) apply the data consolidation process.

69. You are managing project communications and are wondering what tools to use as part of the PMIS. The least effective tool to use so that stakeholders can easily retrieve the information they need in a timely manner is:

A. Work performance reports

B. Social media

C. Web conferencing

D. Blogs

☑ **A.** Work performance reports represent information that can be retrieved, but this is not a tool for retrieval.

☒ **B, C,** and **D** are incorrect because all are instances of organizational process assets that provide stakeholders with access to information that they can retrieve themselves.

70. As you execute a project, you use appropriate project plans to ensure all facets of the project are managed and carried out consistent with the project governance criteria you established. Which plan do you review and adjust to reflect needed changes to personnel that are moved from project to project based on skill sets needed to support technical activities?

A. Risk management plan

B. Human resource management plan

C. Communications management plan

D. Staffing management plan

☑ **D.** Staffing information (found in the staffing management plan) should be reviewed prior to making personnel changes during the executing phase.

☒ **A, B,** and **C** are incorrect because project plans are used in the planning phase; by auditing the results of the use of these plans, you ensure that the project outcomes meet stakeholder expectations and standards.

71. You plan to staff your project using internal company staff and to avoid the use of consultants and contractors. Which of the following will be least useful to you in trying to staff internally?

A. Identifying existing personnel qualified for open positions

B. Negotiating for existing personnel with their functional management

C. Balancing the needs of the individual with the individual's career path

D. Transitioning them to their project positions

☑ **C.** Balancing the needs of the individual with the individual's career path is a part of developing the project team and is least useful to performing the staffing requirement.

☒ **A, B,** and **D** are incorrect because each relates to activities helpful in staffing a project internally. The Acquire Resources process addresses the provision of resources for the project through selection of internal or external candidates. In this case, because they are staffing with internal resources, identifying existing personnel qualified for open positions, negotiating for existing personnel with their functional management, and transitioning them to their project positions are relevant activities.

72. You are focused on creating new knowledge that helps achieve the project's objectives while simultaneously contributing to organizational learning for the company and the project team. Which of the following is the most important part of knowledge management?

    A. Reporting project data

    B. Creating an atmosphere of trust

    C. Coaching and mentoring members of the project team

    D. Analyzing appropriate project data

    ☑ **B.** Knowledge exists within people, and sharing that information is best established by creating an atmosphere of trust that encourages safe sharing of information.

    ☒ **A** and **D** are incorrect because they are related to specific types of knowledge rather than the big picture of sharing information. **C** is incorrect because coaching and mentoring may help team members share, but the sharing will still not take place without the atmosphere of trust being present first.

73. One technique you can use to develop a project team is to place the team members in the same physical location. This technique enhances the team's ability to perform and is commonly referred to as:

    A. Co-location

    B. Geographic leveling

    C. Remote staffing

    D. Peer transfer

    ☑ **A.** Co-location places project team members in the same physical location.

    ☒ **B, C,** and **D** are incorrect because although many tools and techniques are used to develop a project team, geographic leveling, remote staff, and peer transfer are not among them.

74. There are many methods for communicating key information within the project team. Which of the following methods is most useful for collecting, sharing, and distributing timely information to stakeholders?

    A. Written reports distributed through a channeling system

    B. Meetings and conferences with all the key players

    C. Electronic communications and conferencing tools

    D. Monthly or quarterly reviews

☑ **C.** Electronic communication and conferencing tools help with information distribution and allow you to collect, share, and distribute timely information to stakeholders.

☒ **A, B,** and **D** are incorrect because each tends to be costly and includes inherent time delays that are adverse to project progress.

75. What are the key outputs of the Conduct Procurements process?

   A. Evaluation criteria, proposals, and qualified sellers lists

   B. Evaluation criteria and project preferred-vendor lists

   C. RFIs, RFPs, and RFQs

   D. Procurement statement of work, selected sellers, and change requests

   ☑ **D.** The key outputs of the Conduct Procurements process include procurement statement of work, selected sellers, and change requests. The process for reviewing offers, choosing among potential sellers, and negotiating the details of the contract—including technical terms and conditions, roles and responsibilities, deliverables, and final cost—is the Conduct Procurements process.

   ☒ **A, B,** and **C** are incorrect because all are involved in conducting procurements as inputs or tasks, but not as outputs.

76. As a project manager, you are assuring that benefits management and stakeholder engagement are carried out according to established policies and plans. Where in the project life cycle do these activities occur?

   A. Pre-project setup

   B. Initiation

   C. Project planning

   D. Execution

   ☑ **D.** It is in the execution phase that projects deliver the incremental benefits focused on carrying out the work of the project and assuring benefits are occurring, stakeholders are engaged, and governance is performed.

   ☒ **A, B,** and **C** are incorrect because these aspects take place before carrying out plans.

77. You are a project manager and are periodically verifying that team leaders are adhering to established project management methodologies and delivering products that meet business and technical requirements. What major project management theme do these activities most support?

   A. Manage quality

   B. Stakeholder engagement

   C. Project governance

   D. Benefits delivery

☑ **C.** Project governance focuses on oversight of the project. This is carried out through phase gate reviews to aid in project control and provides an objective check against exit criteria.

☒ **A, B,** and **D** are incorrect because each is unrelated to verifying that team leaders are following project management methodologies.

78. Samantha is the newly assigned project manager for a proposed project to provide basic cable service to retirement facilities nationwide. She establishes a formal documented procedure to define how work will be authorized to ensure work is done by the right organization, at the right time, and in the right sequence. This is a description of:

A. Work authorization system

B. Project management information system

C. Quality assurance system

D. Performance monitoring system

☑ **A.** A collection of formal documented procedures defining how project work will be authorized to ensure work is being done by the right organization, at the right time, and in the right sequence is a work authorization system.

☒ **B, C,** and **D** are incorrect because the project management information system, quality assurance system, and performance monitoring system serve purposes unrelated to authorizing project work.

79. Samantha is performing an evaluation of her project using the Manage Quality process to provide confidence that the project will comply with the quality policy and standards. Which of the following is least useful as an input for performing the Manage Quality process?

A. Quality management plan

B. Quality metrics

C. Resource availability

D. Lessons learned register

☑ **C.** Resource availability is not an input into the Manage Quality process.

☒ **A, B,** and **D** are incorrect because each is part of the process of evaluating overall project performance on a regular basis to provide confidence that the project will comply with the relevant quality policies and standards, which are part of the Manage Quality process. Key inputs for this process include the quality management plan, quality metrics, and lessons learned register.

80. Gary is using appropriate project plans to ensure all phases of his project are managed and carried out according to criteria that have been established. Which plan will he review and adjust to reflect needed changes to personnel based on skill sets and the need to be moved from one project to another?

A. Human resource management plan

B. Quality management plan

C. Personnel assignment plan

D. Resource management plan

☑ **D.** As a project manager, you execute appropriate project plans, including the risk management plan, quality management plan, communications management plan, resource management plan, and other applicable plans in the project management plan. You use the tools identified in the planning phase, and by auditing the results of the use of these plans, you ensure that the project outcomes meet stakeholder expectations and standards. The plan with staffing information in it is the resource management plan.

☒ **A, B,** and **C** are incorrect because none are the specific plans that will be updated for staff changes.

81. You have just been appointed as the project manager for a new project at Smart Planes, Inc., and are responsible for the development of a new innovative unmanned aerial vehicle. This is your first large-scale project, and you know that the project management plan execution is your primary responsibility once the initial planning activities are completed and execution of the project has begun. Who else is primarily responsible for the project management plan execution?

A. Business analyst

B. Project team

C. Project managers

D. PMO

☑ **B.** Executing the project management plan becomes the primary responsibility of the project manager, together with the project team, once the initial planning activities are completed and execution of the project has begun.

☒ **A, C,** and **D** are incorrect because all are a part of or associated with the project team, but are not the same as the project team being responsible for carrying out the work.

82. In addition to producing deliverables, the Direct and Manage Project Work process implements which of the following the least?

A. Approved change requests

B. Corrective actions

C. Key performance indicators

D. Preventive actions

☑ **C.** Key performance indicators are planned before project execution and tracked in the PMIS.

☒ **A, B,** and **D** are incorrect because in addition to producing deliverables, the Direct and Manage Project Work process implements approved change requests, corrective actions, and preventive actions once they have been integrated with the relevant plans.

83. Which project management processes in the Executing process group provide change requests as an input to the Perform Integrated Change Control process?

A. Direct and Manage Project Execution, Schedule Control

B. Manage Quality, Project Contract Administration

C. Direct and Manage Project Work, Perform Quality Control

D. Implement Risk Responses, Manage Quality, Direct and Manage Project Work

☑ **D.** The Executing processes provide change requests as an input to the Perform Integrated Change Control processes of Implement Risk Responses, Manage Quality, and Direct and Manage Project Work.

☒ **A, B,** and **C** are incorrect because each contains a variation of processes but not the exact inputs to the Perform Integrated Change Control process.

84. A household appliance company has established a major project to upgrade numerous products using projects for each product. The director of research and development will oversee all the projects, and the CFO will ensure that the benefits are realized from these upgrades by conducting independent reviews. The director of research and development is managing a:

A. Large project

B. Program

C. Operation

D. Functional area

☑ **A.** Although the large project is split into smaller, more manageable projects, taken together the director is managing a large project.

☒ **B, C,** and **D** are incorrect because the director is not managing a project, an operation, or a functional area in the company.

85. A major filmmaker has established a large project to enhance the technologies for special effects development for several upcoming productions. Several teams are working on the project, and resources are shared between the project and ongoing operations. To develop some of your project team, you decide to have your team work in pairs, with experienced members working side by side with less experienced members. Which tool or technique of developing a team have you implemented?

A. Centralized staffing

B. Remote staffing

C. Co-location

D. Peer transfer

☑ **C.** Co-location will be necessary to place staff members side by side to work.

☒ **A, B,** and **D** are incorrect because none will result in placing team members side by side to work.

86. A large defense contractor has an established safety project to support manufacturing operations. Recent regulatory changes from government regulators and increased risks related to new work have increased operational cost substantially. You have instituted a process to provide timely and accurate information to project stakeholders and to use formats and media that are useful to the clients, sponsors, and the project team. Which of the following tools is most consistent with these actions?

   A. Meetings

   B. RACI (responsible, accountable, inform, consult) chart

   C. Project management information system

   D. Resource breakdown structure

   ☑ **C.** A project management information system (PMIS) will help provide timely and accurate project information to stakeholders. Information distribution is the process of providing timely and accurate information to project stakeholders in useful formats and appropriate media. It includes administration of three major communication channels: the client, the sponsors, and the project team.

   ☒ **A, B,** and **D** are incorrect because none will result in information being distributed to the project team.

87. Outsourcing resources from around the world and having staff resources work remotely are two resource optimization methods that will increase your need to manage diversity in your project. Given the global nature of team resourcing present in your company, awareness of the diverse population in your project will benefit least from which of the following?

   A. Establishing work groups that consist of individual cultural groups

   B. Identifying and understanding the organization's culture

   C. Describing the team structure and individual cultures

   D. Maintaining cohesiveness among all cross-divisional teams

   ☑ **A.** Establishing workgroups that consist of individual cultural groups is averse to these ideals. To increase commitment to the project deliverables, you need to motivate the team using appropriate tools and techniques. This requires you to have knowledge of diversity awareness and be able to describe the organization's culture, describe the team structure and individual cultures, establish a safe and secure work environment, and maintain cohesiveness among all teams.

   ☒ **B, C,** and **D** are incorrect because each will help establish an awareness of the diversity in your team.

88. You sent out RFPs to three vendors and received their offers. Currently you are reviewing the offers to choose potential vendors and negotiate contract conditions and are involved in the Conduct Procurements process. Which of the following are you expected to have to complete this process?

A. Seller responses

B. Executed seller risk plans

C. Selected sellers

D. Planned project contracting

☑ **C.** Sellers are selected in the Conduct Procurements process where a project manager reviews offers, chooses among potential sellers, and negotiates the details of the contract, including technical terms and conditions, roles and responsibilities, deliverables, and final cost.

☒ **A, B,** and **D** are incorrect because these are not needed to complete the Conduct Procurements process.

89. A large defense contractor has an established safety project to support manufacturing operations. Recent regulatory changes from government regulators and increased risks related to new work have increased operational cost substantially. You need to select contractors. Which of the following will be most useful in managing the selection process fairly and equitably?

A. Evaluation criteria

B. Request for proposal (RFP)

C. Project budget

D. Lease agreements

☑ **A.** Evaluation criteria will be helpful in being fair and equitable when choosing a contractor. The process for reviewing offers, choosing among potential sellers, and negotiating the details of the contract, including technical terms and conditions, roles and responsibilities, deliverables, and final cost, is the Conduct Procurements process. The key inputs for this process include source selection criteria, seller proposals, and bid documents.

☒ **B, C,** and **D** are incorrect because the RFP is sent to the sellers, and project budget and lease agreements are part of other processes.

90. The specific technique for evaluating sellers' proposals that involves evaluation of the proposals by a multidiscipline team containing members with specialist knowledge in each of the areas covered by the proposed contract is called a(n):

A. Seller rating system

B. Expert judgment

C. Screening system

D. Bidder conference

☑ **B.** Expert judgment is the specific technique for evaluating sellers' proposals that involves evaluation of the proposals by a multidiscipline team containing members with specialist knowledge in each of the areas covered by the proposed contract.

☒ **A, C,** and **D** are incorrect. Having proposals evaluated by a multidiscipline team containing members with specialist knowledge in each of the areas covered by the proposed contract is known as using expert judgment. Seller rating systems are based on past performance. Screening systems are based on predefined minimum levels of compliance to requirements. Bidder conferences are used to ensure that all prospective sellers have a clear and mutual understanding of the procurement.

91. Within the Conduct Procurements process, the procurement management plan, seller proposals, and source selection criteria are examples of:

A. Contract types

B. Tools and techniques

C. Inputs

D. Outputs

☑ **C.** The procurement management plan, seller proposals, and source selection criteria are examples of inputs to the Conduct Procurements process.

☒ **A, B,** and **D** are incorrect. They are not contract types, tools and techniques, or outputs.

92. The project sponsor asks you to be certain that you ensure that all prospective sellers have a clear and collective understanding of the procurement you require. He suggests you have a structured meeting to do this. What type of meeting is being suggested?

A. Request seller responses

B. Contract status meeting

C. Project progress meeting

D. Bidder conference

☑ **D.** A structured meeting to ensure that all prospective sellers have a clear and mutual understanding of the procurement you require is called a bidder conference.

☒ **A, B,** and **C** are incorrect. Request seller responses occurs after this conference takes place and is not a common meeting. A contract status meeting may be internal or with a single seller. A project progress meeting may discuss the potential sellers, and this is not generally an open meeting.

93. The part of the procurement process involving obtaining seller responses, selecting a seller, and awarding a contract is called:

A. Qualified sellers list

B. Bidder conference

C. Conduct procurements

D. Selected sellers

☑ **C.** The part of the procurement process involving obtaining seller responses, selecting a seller, and awarding a contract is called Conduct Procurements.

☒ **A, B,** and **D** are incorrect. A qualified sellers list is an input to this process, bidder conferences are tools and techniques used within this process, and selected sellers is an output of the process.

94. You are part of a team running a complex project spanning several years and involving several subcontractors. The contracts signed for this project might or will end during:

A. Any phase of the project

B. The completion phase

C. The execution phase

D. The acceptance phase

☑ **A.** In a complex project involving many contracts and subcontractors, each contract life cycle can end during any phase of the project as and when the deliverables are accepted.

☒ **B, C,** and **D** are incorrect. In a complex project involving many contracts and subcontractors, each contract life cycle can end during any phase of the project as and when the deliverables are accepted, not only at the end of one phase.

95. Documenting the effectiveness of risk responses in dealing with identified risks and the root causes and of the effectiveness of managing risk is called (a):

A. Implement risk responses

B. Risk identification

C. Risk analysis

D. Risk audit

☑ **D.** The actions of documenting the effectiveness of risk responses in dealing with identified risks and the root causes, and of the effectiveness of the risk management process, are known as a risk audit.

☒ **A, B,** and **C** are incorrect. Risk mitigation is a specific set of alternatives to manage risk. Risk identification and risk analysis are processes used to build a risk management plan.

96. When engaging project stakeholders, you may use many different techniques, including written and oral and both giving and receiving. These techniques are examples of what type of skills?

A. Influence

B. Negotiating

C. Delegation

D. Communications

☑ **D.** Written and oral communication techniques are a part of communications skills.

☒ **A, B,** and **C** are incorrect. Influence skills, negotiating skills, and delegation skills are different attributes of the soft skills set that a project manager should have.

97. You have completed an end-of-phase review meeting. Several actions and suggestions have been given to you as the project manager. You must document these and ensure that they become part of the project and organizational process assets (OPAs) from this point on. These actions and suggestions are called (the):

A. Project issues list

B. Lessons learned

C. Risk register items

D. Project documentation

☑ **B.** Actions and suggestions that are documented and become part of the project and organization processes from this point on are called lessons learned.

☒ **A, C,** and **D** are incorrect because project issues may become lessons learned; a risk register is for actions that may also become lessons learned. Project documentation is a broad topic for the whole project and does include lessons learned.

98. Which of the following is the recommended way of reporting on project progress to stakeholders?

A. Regularly at preset times

B. Comprehensively at the end of the project

C. Regularly and on exception

D. On exception and at the end of the project

☑ **C.** Generally, regular reports are required by stakeholders, and exception reports should be issued as appropriate.

☒ **A, B,** and **D** are incorrect. Generally regular reports are required by stakeholders, and exception reports should be issued as appropriate.

99. You have been asked to collect and provide performance information to the project stakeholders. This action is called:

A. Baselining the schedule

B. Stakeholder management

C. Performance analysis

D. Performance reporting

☑ **D.** Performance reporting is the act of collecting and distributing performance information, including status reports, progress measurements, and forecasts.

☒ **A, B,** and **C** are incorrect. Baselining the project is a specific action to record the planned schedule, budget, etc. Stakeholder management is analyzing and communicating with the stakeholders. Performance analysis may be a part of the input to performance reporting.

100. Work performance reports on the status of deliverables and what has been accomplished in the project is part of which process group?

A. Initiating

B. Executing

C. Closing

D. Planning

☑ **B.** Work performance reports on the status of deliverables and what has been accomplished in the project are part of the Executing process group.

☒ **A, C,** and **D** are incorrect. Work performance reports on the status of deliverables and what has been accomplished in the project are part of the Executing process group.

101. You have many reports, including analysis of project forecasts, status of issues and risks, and work completed during the Manage Communications process. The collective name for this information is:

A. Performance measurements

B. Forecast completion

C. Performance reports

D. Deliverables status reports

☑ **C.** Information that includes bar charts, S-curves, histograms, and tables for the data analyzed against the project baseline is known as performance reports.

☒ **A, B,** and **D** are incorrect. Performance measurements, forecast completion, and deliverables status are all inputs to the performance reporting process.

102. You have been asked to give details of how you propose to develop the project team. What description best describes what you should be doing?

A. Improve the competencies of team members

B. Document the resource calendars of team members

C. Assign the appropriate people to activities on the project

D. Finalize roles and responsibilities in the project plan

☑ **A.** The Develop Team process includes activities such as improving the competencies of team members.

☒ **B, C,** and **D** are incorrect. Document the resource calendars of team members, assign the appropriate people to activities on the project, and finalize roles and responsibilities in the project plan are outputs of the Acquire Resources process.

103. You are discussing the work that you have been doing with a colleague. The activities include assisting others when the workload is unbalanced, sharing information, and communicating in diverse ways to suit individual team members. This group of activities is related to:

   A. Communications planning

   B. Effective team working

   C. Improving team competencies

   D. Management by objectives (MBO)

   ☑ **B.** Activities including assisting others when the workload is unbalanced, sharing information, and communicating in diverse ways to suit the individual team members are related to effective team work.

   ☒ **A, C,** and **D** are incorrect. Communications planning is a planning activity. Improving team competencies is related to developing the project team. Management by objectives is related to objective setting and measurement and is not mentioned in the question.

104. At your personal performance review, your line manager suggests many areas in which you can improve. These include understanding better the sentiments of the project team members and acknowledging their concerns. These skills are most related to:

   A. Effective team working

   B. Communication planning

   C. Interpersonal skills

   D. Negotiating techniques

   ☑ **C.** Understanding better the sentiments of the project team members and acknowledging their concerns are examples of interpersonal skills.

   ☒ **A, B,** and **D** are incorrect. Effective team work includes assisting others when the workload is unbalanced, sharing information, and communicating in diverse ways. Communication planning is about planning how to communicate to the team. Negotiation techniques are not as described in the question.

105. You are required to develop a recognition and reward system for your project office. Which of the following is an appropriate basis for this system?

   A. Reward only desirable behavior

   B. Reward the team member of the month

   C. Reward all team members who work overtime

   D. Reward individualism, regardless of culture

☑ **A.** Only desirable behavior should be rewarded in a recognition and reward system.

☒ **B, C,** and **D** are incorrect. Rewarding the team member of the month and rewarding all team members who work overtime will damage the team. Rewarding individualism, regardless of culture, may not always be appropriate.

106. Which type of organization complicates the management of the project team?

    A. Functional

    B. Matrix

    C. Projectized

    D. Hierarchical

☑ **B.** Management of the project team is complicated when team members are accountable to both a functional and a project manager, as in a matrix organization.

☒ **A, C,** and **D** are incorrect. Functional and project organizations have clear accountability. Hierarchical organizations are the norm.

107. Tracking team performance, providing feedback, resolving issues, and coordinating changes to enhance project performance are all part of which process?

    A. Develop Team

    B. Perform Team

    C. Manage Team

    D. Build Team

☑ **C.** Tracking team performance, providing feedback, resolving issues, and coordinating changes to enhance project performance are all part of the Manage Team process.

☒ **A, B,** and **D** are incorrect. Recognition and reward systems, team performance assessment, and team-building activities are all part of developing the project team process.

108. Checking skills improvements, recording current competencies, and monitoring reduction in team turnover rates are related to:

    A. Project staff assignments

    B. Project team building activities

    C. Recognition and reward systems

    D. Team performance assessment

☑ **D.** Checking skills improvements, recording current competencies, and monitoring reduction in team turnover rates are part of project team performance assessment.

☒ **A, B,** and **C** are incorrect. Project staff assignments are an input to developing the project team. Recognition and reward systems, as well as team-building activities, are part of developing the project team process.

109. To help you manage the project team, you are using a system that documents who is responsible for resolving a specific problem by a target date. This system is called using (a):

A. Project risk register

B. Change control

C. Project issue log

D. Performance reports

☑ **D.** Performance reports are related to staff management.

☒ **A, B,** and **C** are incorrect. A system that documents who is responsible for resolving a specific problem by a target date is known as using a project issue log. A project risk register is a specific tool for identifying, tracking, and resolving risks. Change control is the process that supports changes to any item or process within the project.

110. You meet with the project sponsor, and the conversation covers the following topics: availability, competencies, experience, interests, and costs of the potential project team. A list or chart of these items is known as a(n):

A. Enterprise environmental factor (EEF)

B. Project resource histogram

C. Responsibility assignment matrix (RAM)

D. Organizational hierarchy chart

☑ **B.** The project resource histogram shows use of resources on a time base.

☒ **A, C,** and **D** are incorrect. Acquiring the project team has the following inputs to the enterprise environmental factors: availability, competencies, experience, interests, and costs of the potential project team. The responsibility assignment matrix is done once the issues in the question have been defined. The organization hierarchy chart does not include the topics in the question.

111. Which of the following is an input to the Manage Quality process?

A. Quality metrics

B. Project requirements

C. Change requests

D. Validated deliverables

☑ **A.** Quality metrics are an input to the Manage Quality process.

☒ **B, C,** and **D** are incorrect. Project requirements are not usually quality inputs. Change requests are an output of Manage Quality. Verified deliverables are an output of Control Quality.

112. A project manager is reviewing a project that is in progress. She is trying to identify the best project practices being used and gaps between best practices and current practices, as well as sharing the best practices introduced or implemented in similar projects in the organization. This is known as:

A. Developing the quality metrics

B. Performing a quality audit

C. Setting the quality baseline

D. Building quality checklists

☑ **B.** Identifying the good/best practices being implemented, identifying gaps/shortcomings, sharing the good practices introduced or implemented in similar projects in the organization and/or industry, proactively improving process implementation, and highlighting the results in the lessons learned repository is known as performing a quality audit.

☒ **A, C,** and **D** are incorrect. Quality metrics are an input to quality assurance and define the quality control measurements. The quality baseline records the quality objectives for the project. Quality checklists are component specific.

113. You are coaching a new team member in your project. One of her functions is to recommend corrective actions to increase the effectiveness and efficiency of the organization. This falls under the Manage Quality process ITTOs (inputs, tools and techniques, and outputs). This list of actions is documented as:

A. Change requests

B. Organizational process assets (OPAs) updates

C. Project management plan updates

D. Recommended preventive actions

☑ **C.** Project management plan updates are related to changes to the quality management plan.

☒ **A, B,** and **D** are incorrect. Actions that have been recommended to increase the effectiveness and efficiency of the organization are documented as change requests. Change requests can be used to take corrective or preventive action or to perform defect repair. Process assets updates are changes to the processes.

114. As a project manager you must audit the quality requirements and the results from quality control measurements to ensure that appropriate quality standards and operational definitions are used. This is part of which of the following processes?

A. Improve Quality Standards

B. Manage Quality

C. Plan Quality

D. Plan Quality Improvement

☑ **B.** Manage Quality process ensures that appropriate quality standards are used.

☒ **A, C,** and **D** are incorrect. Plan Quality is related to establishing the quality requirements and/or standards for the project. Monitoring and recording results of executing quality activities to assess performance and recommend necessary changes is Control Quality. Quality improvement is an organizational development process.

115. You are managing the execution stage of a project. Your responsibilities include gathering data on actual start and finish dates of activities, along with remaining durations for work in progress. The work you are doing is involved with:

   A. Cost variance analysis

   B. Performance measurement

   C. Performance reviews

   D. Critical path analysis

   ☑ **C.** Gathering actual start and finish dates of activities, along with remaining durations for work in progress, is known as performance reviews.

   ☒ **A, B,** and **D** are incorrect. Cost variance analysis compares baseline to actual data. Performance measurement is a specific earned value technique. Critical path analysis is a planning tool.

116. You are managing a project that is running late. You have proposed corrective actions that will affect the schedule baseline. These actions are called:

   A. Change requests

   B. Action change control

   C. Schedule baseline updates

   D. Project scope updates

   ☑ **A.** Schedule variance analysis, along with project report reviews and performance measure results, can result in change requests to the schedule baseline.

   ☒ **B, C,** and **D** are incorrect. Action change control does not itself constitute corrective actions. Schedule baseline updates may not be a result of the activity described. Project scope updates are not necessarily implied.

117. You are managing the execution of a project in your organization. You work with many people and groups regularly during this stage of a project. With whom do you work closely to direct, manage, and execute the project?

   A. The project initiator and sponsor

   B. The business unit as the customer

   C. No one; as project manager, you assume full responsibility

   D. The project management team

☑ **D.** The project manager cannot do it all. She needs to work with the team to execute the range of activities to be performed.

☒ **A, B,** and **C** are incorrect. The project manager, in conjunction with the project management team, directs, manages, and executes the project. The project sponsor or initiator does not manage the day-to-day activities of the project. The business unit/customer receives the deliverables from the project.

118. You are asked by your line manager to describe your current activities as a project manager. You list the activities as "obtain, manage, and use resources to accomplish the project objectives." In what process group is this project?

A. Initiating

B. Executing

C. Planning

D. Monitoring and Controlling

☑ **B.** The definition of the Executing process group is "obtain, manage, and use resources to accomplish the project objectives."

☒ **A, C,** and **D** are incorrect. The other stages do not match the description given of the activities.

119. During the execution of a project, many influences drive a project manager's activities. Which of the following is an input to this process?

A. Outstanding defects and faults

B. Administrative procedure edits

C. Approved change requests

D. Postponed change requests

☑ **C.** The execution process has many inputs defined. These are approved documents or actions. The correct answer is "approved change requests."

☒ **A, B,** and **D** are incorrect. The answers are not inputs to the execution process.

120. You are managing a project that is time critical and essential for the survival of the business. You have many changes on this project. Which of the following do you spend your time scheduling into the work for the project team?

A. Likely changes to the schedule

B. Change requests to the scope

C. Requested changes to the budget

D. Approved change requests

☑ **D.** Only approved changes should be scheduled into the project activities.

☒ **A, B,** and **C** are incorrect. Likely changes have not been approved and should not be scheduled into the project workload. Requests for change are approved only through the formal change control process.

121. A new team member has joined your project team and asks you what is a project deliverable from a generic perspective rather than for your project. Which of the following is the best answer to this question?

   A. All items consumed in the project during the execution

   B. The goods that are delivered to the shipping dock and are signed for

   C. A product purchased according to the procurement plan

   D. Something that is produced to complete the project

   ☑ **D.** Deliverables are produced as outputs from the processes described in the project management plan.

   ☒ **A, B,** and **C** are incorrect. Not all tasks produce project deliverables, and not all WBS elements produce project deliverables. The initial project scope document does not list project deliverables.

122. A quantitative standard of measurement typically used in projects to measure performance and progress is a:

   A. Metric

   B. Process

   C. Tool

   D. Technique

   ☑ **A.** A metric is a description of a project or product attribute and how to measure it. An example of a quality metric is the number of defects identified per day.

   ☒ **B** is incorrect because a process is a systematic series of activities directed toward causing a result. **C** is incorrect because a tool is something tangible, such as a template or software program. **D** is incorrect because a technique is a defined systematic procedure employed by a human resource.

123. Which of the following tool sets will be most useful in facilitating project management activities to deliver the benefits of the project?

   A. Creating the milestone plan

   B. Estimating the task schedule

   C. Estimating resource usage

   D. Measuring project performance

☑ **D.** Projects are initiated to realize business opportunities and deliver business benefits. The success of the project is measured against the project objectives, and the most useful tool set in facilitating project management activities to deliver the benefits of the project is to measure and monitor project performance.

☒ **A** is incorrect because the milestone plan is frequently used to monitor project progress, but there are limitations to its effectiveness. The milestone plan usually shows progress only on the critical path and ignores noncritical activities. **B** is incorrect because estimating the schedule's tasks and activities will provide the amount of time each activity will take to complete—not tell you how the work is progressing. **C** is incorrect because estimating resource usage will tell you the type, quantity, and characteristics of resources required to complete the project.

124. What Project Integration Management processes do you manage as a part of the Executing process group?

    A. Integrate Team, Develop Team, Close Team

    B. Project Integration Planning, Acquire Project Team, Integrate Team

    C. Direct and Manage Project Work, Manage Project Knowledge

    D. Acquire Project Team, Develop Project Team, Manage Project Team

☑ **C.** The two processes in the Executing process group that are in the Project Integration Management knowledge area are Direct and Manage Project Work and Manage Project Knowledge.

☒ **A** and **B** are incorrect because these processes are made-up terms. **D** is incorrect because these three processes are the Executing processes in the Project Resource Management knowledge area.

CHAPTER 5

The Monitoring and Controlling Domain

This chapter includes questions from the following tasks:

- **Task 1**   Measure project performance using appropriate tools and techniques in order to identify and quantify any variances and corrective actions.
- **Task 2**   Manage changes to the project by following the change management plan in order to ensure that project goals remain aligned with business needs.
- **Task 3**   Verify that project deliverables conform to the quality standards established in the quality management plan by using appropriate tools and techniques to meet project requirements and business needs.
- **Task 4**   Monitor and assess risk by determining whether exposure has changed and evaluating the effectiveness of response strategies in order to manage the impact of risks and opportunities on the project.
- **Task 5**   Review the issue log, update if necessary, and determine corrective actions by using appropriate tools and techniques in order to minimize the impact on the project.
- **Task 6**   Capture, analyze, and manage lessons learned, using lessons learned management techniques, in order to enable continuous improvement.
- **Task 7**   Monitor procurement activities according to the procurement plan in order to verify compliance with project objectives.

The Monitoring and Controlling process group consists of those processes required to measure and correct the progress and performance of the project; identify any areas in which changes to the plan are required; and trigger change requests. The 12 processes in Monitoring and Controlling are essential to maintaining an efficient and effective workflow throughout the project.

The Monitoring and Controlling domain accounts for 25% (50) of the questions on the PMP exam. The *PMBOK Guide, Sixth Edition,* Sections 4.5, 4.6, 5.5, 5.6, 6.6, 7.4, 8.3, 9.6, 10.3, 11.7, 12.3, and 13.4, cover the 24 tasks in the Monitoring and Controlling domain.

The 100 practice questions in this chapter are mapped to the style and frequency of question types you will see on the PMP exam.

1. On your project, a configuration audit has been scheduled. Your best C++ programmer, Radhika, asks you what this process entails. Your response should indicate that:

   A. Configuration audits involve reviewing deliverables with the customer or sponsor to ensure they are completed satisfactorily and obtaining formal acceptance by the customer or sponsor

   B. Configuration audits ensure that the composition of a project's configuration items is correct and that corresponding changes are registered, approved, tracked, and correctly implemented

   C. Configuration auditing is the process of monitoring and recording results of executing quality activities to assess performance and recommend necessary changes, and it is done throughout the project

   D. Configuration audits include the process of tracking, reviewing, and regulating the progress to meet the performance objectives defined in the project management plan, and they are done throughout the project

2. Your company, Stay Home Shopping Network (SHSN), a creative and fluid family business that sells products using television network combined with a data streaming service, is about to be bought out by a corporate conglomerate that already owns 18% of the company stock, Home Quality Value Convenience (HQVC). This takeover will affect your project, and all the other projects in the organization's portfolio. You understand how risky this is. While you are performing the Implement Risk Responses process, you may identify new risks. What document might be updated now, to help you later, with identifying overall project risk?

   A. PESTLE framework

   B. Prompt list

   C. VUCA list

   D. TECOP log

3. You are the project manager for a small project team for a project that has a set of approved functional requirements. In one of the regular meetings, your software developer team member, Patty, proposes an additional feature to the system. As project manager, you remind the team that they must concentrate on completing only the work approved. Your statement was guided by your adherence to:

A. Quality management

B. Change management

C. Scope management

D. Configuration management

4. You have been assigned as the project manager on a project focused on developing a new process for your organization called configuration management. Which of the following identifies the functions this process performs?

A. Identifying, submitting, approving, tracking, and validating changes

B. Submitting, approving, tracking, measuring, and validating changes

C. Identifying, requesting, assessing, validating, and communicating changes

D. Reviewing, approving, tracking, validating, and proving changes

5. You are managing a project that is in progress. Many tasks have been completed, some are in progress, and others are yet to start. You are reviewing your work load related to the work performance monitoring of the activities in the project. When is the best time to collect this information?

A. At the start of the activity

B. Routinely and regularly

C. At the end of the task only

D. Monthly for progress reports

6. When running a project, the project manager must manage the project work. Which of the following is part of effectively monitoring and controlling the project progress?

A. Email the team the schedule according to the plan.

B. Record the actual progress on tasks daily.

C. Compare actual activity performance against the plan.

D. Report only completed activities, schedules, and costs.

7. One of the tools you use during project management is the "earned value technique." Which of the following best explains why you are using the earned value technique?

A. Future performance can be made to exactly meet the plan.

B. Past performance can be measured to an accuracy of less than 5%.

C. Future performance can be predicted to within 10% of the budget.

D. Future performance can be forecasted based on past performance.

8. Which of the following statements best describes the purpose of using preventive actions in a project?

   A. It reduces the probability of negative consequences related to risks.

   B. It reduces the impact of negative consequences related to risks.

   C. It increases the project budget to allow for some cost overruns.

   D. It increases the reporting frequency on activities that are critical.

9. You are planning a project and wish to introduce the concept of integrated change control to your team. What is the best way to describe the use of integrated change control to the team?

   A. Change control applies to the inception stage to define the scope only.

   B. Change control applies from the beginning of the project to the end.

   C. Change control is used only when there are substantial changes to the budget.

   D. Change control is used at the execution stage to control schedule creep.

10. You are managing a section of a large project and have adopted an integrated change control system for the constant flow of changes from the project team. Which of the following describes how you would act on changes?

    A. Approve changes that cost less than 10% of the budget.

    B. Automatically approve all changes to the schedule.

    C. Review, then approve or reject project changes.

    D. Reject all changes to the budget, scope, or deliverables.

11. You are asked to describe why you are using the Perform Integrated Change Control process in your projects. You refer to the systems and processes that are in place in your workplace. Which of the following best describes your reasons for using change control?

    A. We have a form that we always use on every project.

    B. We always use change control to limit budget overspending.

    C. It is required on our project because of legislation.

    D. It is part of our project management methodology.

12. A project that is using the Perform Integrated Change Control process will have many outputs. A member of your team suggests that the project management plan is an output of this process. What should your answer be?

    A. Disagree because project management plan updates are outputs.

    B. Disagree because the project management plan is not an output.

    C. Agree that the project management plan is an output.

    D. Disagree because the project management plan is not used in this process.

13. The project team you are working with is doing the work of obtaining formal stakeholders' acceptance of the completed project and associated deliverables. Each deliverable is reviewed to check that it has been completed satisfactorily. What is this process called?

    A. Validate Scope

    B. Define Scope

    C. Control Scope

    D. Plan Scope Management

14. You are discussing your project roles with a colleague. She states that she is working on developing a process that ensures all scope changes make use of the company-wide change control system. What project work is she performing?

    A. Defining change control

    B. Validating configuration management

    C. Developing a risk register

    D. Validating scope

15. The project team is involved in the following tasks: measuring, examining, and verifying that the work and deliverables meet the product and acceptance criteria. Which of the following is a summary description of the work your team is doing?

    A. Define Scope: Inputs

    B. Validate Scope: Outputs

    C. Validate Scope: Inspection

    D. Plan Scope Management: Inputs

16. You have been working on defining the procedures by which the project scope and product scope can be changed. In which process is your team engaged?

    A. Validate Scope

    B. Plan Configuration Management

    C. Initial Scope Definition

    D. Control Scope

17. You are writing a procedure for ensuring that changes to product scope and project scope are considered and documented. These artifacts will be processed through Perform Integrated Change Control. What title should you put on this process?

    A. Configuration management

    B. Scope validation

    C. Integrated change control

    D. Project Scope Management

18. Many changes to the project schedule and requirements have been suggested by the project team and the customer. These are urgent, and all affect the resources you are using. What is the next step to take?

   A. Submit the changes to Perform Integrated Change Control for review.

   B. Notify the project sponsor that the work on the changes will start immediately.

   C. Ignore the changes to eliminate the risk to the project schedule.

   D. Reschedule resources to begin the changes immediately.

19. What does the term variance analysis mean for a project manager?

   A. Recording the actual start date of critical activities in the project

   B. Analyzing the calendar contract start date and finish date

   C. Calculating the difference between total slack and free slack

   D. Comparing activity target start date with actual start date

20. The project archives you are reviewing show that the project has had several changes to the start and finish dates of the approved baseline schedule. These changes are known as:

   A. Schedule variance analysis

   B. Schedule baseline updates

   C. Approved change requests

   D. Performance measurement

21. What factors are needed to calculate the ETC for a project?

   A. EAC and PV

   B. BAC, AC, and PV

   C. BAC, EV, and AC

   D. ECA and AC

22. You have been asked to report to the project sponsor on project performance. She asks you for an estimate of the project completion date. Which of the following would help you to provide this estimate?

   A. CPI

   B. SPI

   C. ETC

   D. EAC

23. The values for CV, SV, CPI, and SPI for the activities in a project are used to calculate:

   A. Schedule estimates

   B. Cost estimates

C. Earned value

   D. Corrective actions

24. A new team member is monitoring and recording results of executing quality activities to assess performance and recommend necessary changes. He asks for clarification on what his activities are related to. Which of the following is the best answer to his question?

   A. Control Quality

   B. Manage Quality

   C. Plan Quality Management

   D. Quality Improvement

25. In the process of Control Quality, when is time normally allocated to do this work?

   A. At every project milestone

   B. At termination of the project

   C. At the initiation stage only

   D. Throughout the project

26. The project you are managing has a fundamental problem that will compromise the delivery of a key component. Your team is trying to find the reasons for the failure of the system, using a tool consisting of a diagram that shows how several factors might be linked to the problem or the effects. This diagram is called:

   A. Variable scatter diagram

   B. Cause-and-effect diagram

   C. Process control chart

   D. Statistical sampling matrix

27. Your mentor suggests that you use a chart that shows, by frequency of occurrence, events and defects in the project. The common name for this chart is:

   A. Scatter diagram

   B. Flowchart

   C. Pareto chart

   D. Control chart

28. A common tool used in analyzing problems on a project is a diagram that shows the relationship between two variables. This is called a:

   A. Control chart

   B. Pareto chart

   C. Run chart

   D. Scatter diagram

29. Your team has proposed that a resource optimization strategy should be adopted for the project schedule from this point on. Which of the following best describes what they are suggesting?

A. No change to the resources and reducing the project schedule

B. Adding resources and reducing the project schedule

C. Reducing resources but not changing the project schedule

D. Adding more resources or modifying the project schedule

30. The document that covers the topics of identifying project successes and failures, and making recommendations on how to improve future performance on other projects, is referred to as the:

A. Lessons learned documentation

B. Project management plan

C. Issue log

D. Change log

31. As part of your role as project manager, you must frequently update and reissue work performance information as the project proceeds. This information concerns how the project's past performance could affect the project in the future. This information is called:

A. Performance reports

B. Corrective actions

C. Change requests

D. Variance analysis

32. One of the tools a project manager uses to help document and monitor the resolution of issues in the project is a(n):

A. Risk register

B. Issue log

C. Change requests

D. Corrective actions

33. Sally is reviewing the risk management plan for the current project. How often should she monitor the project work for new and changing risks?

A. At the beginning of project planning

B. Continuously throughout the project life cycle

C. At the beginning of each project phase

D. At the end of each project phase

34. A consultant has been reviewing your Monitor Risks process outputs. She lists many actions that are required to bring the project into compliance with the project management plan. What are these actions called?

A. Recommended preventive actions

B. Risk register updates

C. Recommended corrective actions

D. Project management plan updates

35. You have been asked by the project sponsor to ensure that the seller's performance meets the contractual requirements and that your organization, as the buyer, performs according to the contract. What best describes your efforts?

A. Control Procurements

B. Plan Procurement Management

C. Conduct Procurements

D. Selected Sellers

36. The project you are managing has a problem that requires the contract with a seller to be modified. The alteration to the contract is in accordance with the change control terms of the contract and project. The best time to make this change to the contract is:

A. Never; the contract cannot be modified at any time

B. At any time, regardless of the response from the seller

C. At any time prior to the contract being awarded to the seller

D. At any time prior to contract closure by mutual consent

37. You are managing a system that includes the following information: contract documentation, tracking systems, dispute resolution procedures, and approved levels of authority for changes. What is this system called?

A. Short-listing the qualified sellers

B. Change control system

C. Procurement management plan

D. Contract change control system

38. As part of the Control Procurements process, contested changes will arise where the buyer and seller cannot reach an agreement on compensation for the change, or cannot agree that a change has occurred. These are called claims, disputes, or appeals. If the parties cannot resolve a claim by themselves, it may need to be resolved using what method?

A. Alternative dispute resolution (ADR)

B. Compromising technique

C. Integrated change control

D. Economic price adjustment

39. A document produced by the contract manager that rates how well each seller is performing the project work is called a:

   A. Seller selection criteria

   B. Seller performance evaluation

   C. Procurement management plan

   D. Work performance information

40. In a project, the seller is performing below the contracted level of work consistently. What is the most appropriate procedure to follow?

   A. Continue until the seller provides an explanation.

   B. Add time to the project schedule.

   C. Terminate the seller's contract early.

   D. Increase the budget allocated to the contract.

41. The project management office wants to do a structured review on your project of the Project Procurement Management knowledge area from Plan Procurement Management to Control Procurements. This review is called:

   A. Performance reporting

   B. Contract management

   C. Procurement audit

   D. Claims administration

42. What is the objective of the use of a procurement audit on a project when conducted in the Close Project or Phase process?

   A. Identify when legal action should be started.

   B. Terminate the nonperforming suppliers' contracts.

   C. Identify who signed the nonperforming contracts.

   D. Identify success and failure for use in future contracts.

43. What is the most common logical relationship in a PDM?

   A. Finish-to-start (FS)

   B. Start-to-finish (SF)

   C. Finish-to-finish (FF)

   D. Start-to-start (SS)

44. The ADM is visually the opposite of _____:

   A. MDA

   B. PDM

   C. AON

   D. AOA

45. As the project manager for a major shipyard, you are responsible for ensuring that safety regulations and quality standards are complied with for all activities. Your project involves nuclear work. Last month a nuclear incident occurred. The root cause was an uncertified technician being tasked to work on a shift without the change being reviewed and approved. Which of the following control processes is most related to preventing the unauthorized worker from being assigned and most likely would have prevented the incident?

    A. Control Schedule

    B. Control Costs

    C. Manage Quality

    D. Perform Integrated Change Control

46. After the incident, a thorough review of the work packages to perform nuclear repair work was conducted to make sure each repair plan included specific instructions to follow the procedures for reassignment of personnel. Which of the following is least related to this action?

    A. Perform quality audit

    B. Evaluate additional training and resourcing needs

    C. Apply earned value techniques

    D. Apply change management tools and techniques

47. You are managing a project for the new nuclear power facility due to go live in the next six months. In nuclear repair work, changes must be controlled without error to prevent risk to the health and welfare of the workers and possibly the public. These risks demand careful attention to change control and management through which framework of the project life cycle?

    A. Starting the project, organizing and preparing, carrying out the work, and ending the project

    B. Initiating, planning, executing, monitoring and controlling, and closing

    C. Feasibility study, requirements, analysis, design, coding, and testing

    D. Goal, plan, status

48. Which of the following processes is most needed to monitor and measure resources to ensure the committed resources are made available to the project consistent with commitments and to ensure resources are allocated to the project according to the project management plan?

    A. Control Staffing

    B. Control Team

    C. Control Scope

    D. Control Resources

49. In preparation for a major political election, your political party has tasked you with increasing voter participation by 10% nationwide for the primary elections. You have established a separate polling group to perform polls in various geographic areas and determine the effectiveness of your project. As the poll results are received, you need to change the scope of your project to improve the project results and better accomplish the benefits delivery and achieve the strategic goals for your party. Which of the following tasks will be least useful in changing the scope of the project?

   A. Ensuring a project manager is assigned to the CCB

   B. Evaluating each requested change

   C. Deciding the disposition of each change

   D. Archiving change requests and the supporting detail for them

50. You assign one of your junior staff to track the actual start and finish of activities and milestones to ensure they are being performed against the planned timeline. They report regularly any deviations and keep the plan updated as changes occur. Which of the following processes is most consistent with these activities?

   A. Control Scope

   B. Control Schedule

   C. Monitor Communications

   D. Monitor Risks

51. From your experience with other projects, you know that the Control Schedule process results in people focusing on slippage and many times forgetting to look for:

   A. Lag

   B. Slack

   C. Opportunities

   D. Critical tasks

52. Which of the following documents is least useful in managing your program scope?

   A. Scope management plan

   B. Scope baseline

   C. Change management plan

   D. Procurement management plan

53. As a part of your quality control efforts, you are required to monitor repetitive activities to make sure they are operating inside three standard deviations of the mean. Which tool are you required to understand and use?

   A. Scatter diagrams

   B. Pareto diagrams

   C. Control chart

   D. Failure mode effects analysis (FMEA)

54. As a part of your quality control efforts, you are required to use a procedure to test ways in which components fail and determine the impact of the failures. Which tool should you be required to understand and use?

A. Mean time between failure (MTBF)

B. Pareto diagrams

C. Control chart

D. Failure mode effects analysis (FMEA)

55. It is imperative that you keep your budget in control. Project governance has been established to keep budgets within 10% of what was planned and report weekly when costs are more or less than this threshold. Which of the following facets of cost control is least useful in controlling your budget?

A. Contracting outsource services vs. using capable in-house staff

B. Holding down costs so the project remains on budget

C. Bringing the project back on budget when an overrun occurs

D. Identifying opportunities to return project funding to the enterprise

56. The project management plan directs monitoring and controlling of specific project deliverables and reviewing results to determine if the deliverables fulfill specified requirements. Which process ensures this best?

A. Control Project Work

B. Risk Monitoring and Control

C. Control Quality

D. Schedule Control

57. It was identified during project planning that a strong potential of going over budget might exist. What process did you put into place to identify this possibility, define how to react to it, and evaluate how effective your response to its occurrence was?

A. Monitor Risks

B. Plan Risk Management

C. Validate Scope

D. Manage Risk

58. Which process group or process provides the most primary interface with the project governance structure?

A. Executing

B. Monitoring and Controlling

C. Direct and Manage Project Work

D. Monitor and Control Project Work

59. As a newly assigned project manager, you find that your stakeholder list contains every functional manager and all executive managers, as well as users of the future solution. You send scope, schedule, cost, quality, and value reports to several key stakeholders. No one seems to agree on the expectations from your project. You check with stakeholders' involvement as you proceed through your project's life cycle and focus on strategies and plans with all stakeholders. You are performing:

    A. Plan Stakeholder Management

    B. Monitor Stakeholder Engagement

    C. Develop Project Life Cycle

    D. Maintain Project Management Plan

60. You are a project manager documenting corrective actions that have been taken on your project and their associated outcomes. In performing this activity across your project life cycle, what document would you use to best log this information for subsequent analysis and archiving?

    A. Historical information

    B. Supporting details

    C. Lessons learned

    D. Risk log

61. You are a project manager reviewing the benefits management plan with a key member of the organization's executive staff to determine effort and cost for a set of current tasks. What term best describes the technique you are applying?

    A. Walkthrough

    B. Performance review

    C. Root cause analysis

    D. Expert judgment

62. You are a new project manager attempting to understand what is expected of you when you are managing the relationships with sellers and buyers. What process best describes what work activities are required?

    A. Control Procurements

    B. Perform Qualitative Risk Analysis

    C. Identify Stakeholders

    D. Develop Team

63. For the last nine months you have been the project manager for the Rio Grande railroad upgrade project. Several of the activities are on track, but some have started to derail. During project planning, a strong potential of going off the tracks (over budget) was identified. What process should be in place to identify this possibility, define how to react to it, and evaluate how effective your response to its occurrence has been?

A. Control Quality

B. Control Costs

C. Control Resources

D. Monitor Risks

64. In one of the project status meetings, you find several team members have conflicts between tasks for the functional manager and the project team. Which control process is most related to preventing unauthorized or conflicting assignments to prevent future occurrences of these incidents?

A. Monitor and Control Project Work

B. Perform Integrated Change Control

C. Control Resources

D. Monitor Human Resources

65. As a part of your efforts to ensure quality, you require each project manager to monitor repetitive activities to make sure they are operating inside three standard deviations of the mean. Which tool should they be required to understand and use?

A. Control chart

B. Scatter diagram

C. Mind mapping

D. Failure mode effects analysis (FMEA)

66. Which of the following processes is most related to managing the project's staff and supplies correctly and the associated costs related to them in accordance with the project management plan?

A. Perform Integrated Change Control

B. Control Resources

C. Monitor Stakeholder Engagement

D. Develop Staff Release Plan

67. A pharmaceutical company is developing three new drugs. Each one is a part of a line of products. One of the drugs is used over the counter. The second is a prescription for retail purchase. The third is used exclusively in hospitals during critical operations as a router point for small businesses to provide broadband capability to customers. You are over budget by 20% and your schedule for the project has slipped by several weeks. To compound your problems, marketing is recommending releasing the products simultaneously to the market at least three weeks earlier than planned. Your budget is thin, and your sponsor has informed you that no additional funding is available at this time. In this case, to deliver ahead of schedule, which of the following constraint adjustments will be most useful in resolving this challenge?

    A. Scope

    B. Budget

    C. Schedule

    D. Quality

68. Joyce is a senior project manager. Her team successfully completed the SellMe project. The collection of all SellMe documents are archived into a SharePoint repository and full text indexed for easy searching for reusability downstream. Joyce's company is about to be bought out by a corporate conglomerate that already owns 18% of the company stock. Semaj, the CIO, asks Joyce to "protect the cost baseline." What is a key to effective cost control (managing the approved cost baseline)?

    A. Monitoring cost performance to isolate and understand variances from the approved cost baseline

    B. Controlling the work performance data, information, and reports

    C. Updating the cost management plan using earned value analysis

    D. Preventing approved change requests from being included in the reported cost or resource usage

69. As a project manager, you gather final values of work and compare them to planned values for quality, cost, schedule, and resource usage to determine project performance and generate performance reports for the project. Which of the following skills is least related to these tasks?

    A. Communicating results of project performance

    B. Managing stakeholder expectations

    C. Organizing cost, resource, and schedule data

    D. Rebudgeting and financial modeling

70. A pharmaceutical company is developing three new drugs. Each one is a part of a line of products. One of the drugs is used over the counter. The second is a prescription for retail purchase. The third is used exclusively in hospitals during critical operations as a router point for small businesses to provide broadband capability to customers.

You are over budget by 20% and your schedule for the project has slipped by several weeks. To compound your problems, marketing is recommending releasing the products simultaneously to the market at least three weeks earlier than planned. In your performance report on the drug project, you note a change because there is new technology that can add features to the router point for small businesses. This technology was not included in the project management plan. You have issued a change request, but because it requires corrective action beyond your approval level, your next step is to:

A. Schedule a meeting with your PMO.

B. Receive governance approval to proceed.

C. Set up a change control board to see if the change should be implemented.

D. Use your project management information system.

71. As the project manager in your drug company, you know you are over budget by 20% and your schedule for the project has slipped by several weeks. You have set up a system of regularly reporting on progress to:

A. Forecast completion because you are using earned value management (EVM)

B. Describe each task/activity benefit and when it is scheduled for completion

C. Provide stakeholders with metrics to show the benefits realized

D. Provide stakeholders with overall customer and sponsor feedback

72. The work on the drug project has not gone according to plan. Even though you are tracking its progress, it appears to be missing its due dates. On Friday, you meet with your project steering committee. Many issues have resulted because of lack of resources. The first thing to do is:

A. Tell the steering committee you have analyzed the work performance data, and the work performance reports are wrong

B. Start with general and background information about the project's performance

C. The problems from lack of resources have been noted in variance and trend analysis reports, which you are bringing to the project steering committee to justify more resources

D. You now need to rebaseline the project's schedule because of the resource shortage

73. Finally, on your drug project, you have a meeting with your project management team tomorrow. While you will discuss the resource problem, you also should include in your meeting:

A. Your scope management plan

B. A discussion of the schedule management plan

C. An analysis of the BAC, VAC, and ETC

D. Feedback from customers

74. When you met with the steering committee, given the difficulties with the schedule slippages, the committee members felt you should inform your stakeholders about what was happening. What is the most likely action to take in this situation?

    A. Assign a member of your team to meet individually with each stakeholder.

    B. Use the information management system to distribute information between the project team and the stakeholders.

    C. Submit a change request to the CCB.

    D. Rebaseline your schedule so your stakeholders have a collective understanding of when deliverables will be due.

75. Recently, your drug company conducted an OPM3 assessment and found that it had 349 of the 488 best practices in place. The resulting improvement report showed little work needed to be done in stakeholder engagement, while more emphasis was required in project cost management. As you continue your work on the drug project, you consequently:

    A. Should be adept at keeping costs under control

    B. Need to regularly meet with the financial auditors and other stakeholders and show them your progress in cost-controlling techniques

    C. Need to redefine your budget because of the size of the project

    D. Will not need regular status reviews of the cost status of your project's activities

76. Your program manager says you should use earned value management (EVM) on your drug project. You decide to implement the milestone method of tracking project progress. This means that:

    A. You can also use other methods such as CCM and CPM

    B. Stakeholders must be kept fully informed to establish realistic expectations

    C. You will not need to use EAC, ETC, or BAC

    D. You will need to consider dependency types and integration

77. The PMO has suggested that you use the EAC as your principal means of forecasting costs for your drug project. You should:

    A. Also calculate the CV, SV, SPI, and CPI

    B. Communicate the cost forecasts to the key stakeholders according to the cost forecast plan

    C. Follow the cost forecast strategy in the stakeholder management plan

    D. Know that you can use three common methods to calculate EAC values

78. As the project manager for the AISecure project, you have awarded two contracts. Every two weeks you receive performance reports from both contractors. Contractor 1 is not achieving its objectives and had made no progress in the last two 2 weeks. This contractor's work is important because it affects three major components of the AISecure product. As the project manager, the next thing to do is:

    A. Schedule a contract performance review

    B. Ask the procurement department to conduct an audit of Contractor 1

    C. Update the seller-developed technical documentation

    D. Ask the contracts department to begin alternative dispute resolution (ADR) procedures

79. You recognize the importance of monitoring contract performance and closing out contracts in your drug project. As the project manager, it is important to focus on:

    A. Including contractors in the project governance process

    B. Ensuring contractors understand the benefits management plan

    C. Prequalified seller lists updates

    D. Setting up a lessons learned repository for ease of archiving

80. The major focus of the drug project is on value and quality. You also want to focus on benefits delivery because of the competition you face in the market. You decide to conduct inspections. A key purpose is to:

    A. Ensure the process improvement plan is being followed

    B. Decrease the payback period as described in the business case

    C. Avoid the need for walkthroughs, reviews, and audits

    D. Promote fitness for use

81. You are conducting these inspections on your project so you can focus on:

    A. Taking corrective actions

    B. The need for issue resolution

    C. Inspecting the correctness of deliverables resulting in verified deliverables

    D. Overall project deliverable validity

82. A senior project manager recommends that you use checklists in the Control Quality process on your project. A best practice is to:

    A. Ensure completed checklists are documented and archived

    B. Rely on the senior project manager's judgment in determining whether a checklist fits your project

    C. Use them as part of walkthroughs for works in progress

    D. Use a corporate-approved template

83. Many quality control measurements can be used, but given the nature of this drug project, the most effective is:

    A. Root cause analysis (RCA) versus design for X (DfX)

    B. Planned versus actual project performance reviews

    C. Customer satisfaction surveys

    D. Retrospectives/lessons learned

84. In the early phases of your drug project, you prepared a resource management plan, which included a project organization chart and a recognition plan. Now, because of a rise in interest rates, resource cuts are going to result in a 12% reduction in force throughout the company. As the project manager, your next step is to:

   A. Carefully monitor and control the scarce resources

   B. Request a preassigned contractor for needed resources

   C. Suggest that a contractor officer representative (COR) be used for all project procurements

   D. Use MoSCoW to reprioritize the work in your project

85. Recognizing the resource capacity constraints that now affect your project, you built a responsibility assignment matrix (RAM) to determine if any resources were underallocated. Several team members work in a weak matrix structure, and another is in a strong matrix. A best practice is to:

   A. Prepare a RACI chart to show an overall picture of project resource requirements

   B. Release resources back to their functional managers when they are not required

   C. Work with other project managers to share scarce resources

   D. Update your resource management plan and present it to the sponsor to determine alternative approaches

86. You realize that a key part of your sphere of influence is to establish relationships with subject matter experts (SMEs). You have three SMEs "on loan" to your project. Two of the SMEs are overallocated on your project, and other project managers need them, too. You may be required to assign alternative resources. Your best course of action is to:

   A. Meet with the project sponsor to show the impact on benefit delivery if you cannot keep the three SMEs

   B. Meet with the change control board and plead your case that your project deserves the necessary resources to meet the strategic goals

   C. Reprioritize each work package in your WBS and the milestone due dates and present this information to your steering committee

   D. Use resource leveling in your schedule to show overallocation

87. You are a PMI-RMP. You know that risk management planning takes a considerable amount of time in a project. Risk identification is an agenda item at your project status meetings, and you include risk analysis as part of the status reports you submit on a biweekly basis to the project management team. You and your team work actively to perform the Monitor Risks process. An example is:

   A. Unresolved project risks that require resolution by the risk management department

   B. Identifying and analyzing new risks at the work package level

   C. Time and cost contingency reserves allocated to each work package in the project

   D. Fallback plans in the risk register

88. Having been a project manager for over 20 years and passed the PMI-RMP exam, you recognize the importance of preparing a risk management plan early on in projects and then monitoring and controlling the risks throughout the project. You also had the opportunity to work as a risk management officer on your last project. You realize a key action to reduce the risk that may affect the delivery of the project's benefits is to:

A. Use communication as a risk mitigation strategy

B. Focus on maximizing business value delivery

C. Make sure the right team members are chosen for the project team

D. Decompose and progressively elaborate project risks

89. The measure used to forecast the final project completion estimates is:

A. CPI

B. ETC

C. EAC

D. BAC

90. A project was estimated to cost $1.5 million and scheduled to last six months. Halfway through the project, the earned value analysis shows the following:

EV = $650,000

PV = $750,000

AC = $800,000

What are the schedule and cost variances?

A. SV= +$100,000 / CV= +$150,000

B. SV= +$150,000 / CV= –$100,000

C. SV= –$50,000 / CV= +$150,000

D. SV= –$100,000 / CV= –$150,000

91. Configuration management is a technique for:

A. Overall change control

B. Project plan execution

C. Project scope

D. Perform qualitative risk analysis

92. In anticipation of a corporate merger completion, your business analyst team has been tasked with the business process and software system integration effort with an emphasis on determining which processes and systems should be absorbed into the new company and which aren't needed, what data is important to migrate, and how much integration is needed before the companies are technically joined. You anticipate that your new project, the actual integration work, will be a matter of extracting the data from one system and putting in another. Throughout the project, you will verify that project deliverables and work meet the requirements specified by key stakeholders for final acceptance. What process are you performing?

    A. Manage Quality

    B. Validate Scope

    C. Control Scope

    D. Control Quality

93. Reviewing work products and results to ensure that all were completed satisfactorily and formally accepted is part of:

    A. Plan Risk Acceptance

    B. Control Quality

    C. Perform Integrated Change Control

    D. Validate Scope

94. Through no fault of your own, your project has been canceled. The Validate Scope process:

    A. Will be delayed until the project is continued

    B. Should determine the correctness of the work results

    C. Should establish and document the level and extent of completion

    D. Will form the basis of the project management audit

95. If the CPI is expected to be the same for the remainder of the project, you should calculate the project's estimate at completion (EAC) by using the following formula:

    A. AC + ETC

    B. BAC / CPI

    C. AC + (Remaining PV / CPI)

    D. AC + BAC − EV

96. You are halfway through a 12-month project. Your BAC is $12,000. The contractor's performance to date is PV = $8,000, EV = $7,000, and AC = $9,000. Your SPI = 0.87, and CPI = 0.77. The contractor tells you this is okay because the project still has six months to go, and they can make it up in the last half of the project. This is the first time you have worked with this contractor, so you have no history of past performance. For the contractor to get back to the original due date, the performance level must be:

    A. 60%

    B. 80%

    C. −133%

    D. 167%

97. If you feel your initial plan is no longer valid for your project, you should calculate your estimate at completion (EAC) using the following formula:

A. AC + EV

B. AC + Bottom-up ETC

C. AC + (BAC – EV)

D. AC + [(BAC – EV / (CPI * SPI)])

98. According to your schedule baseline, you should have completed $2,000 worth of work by this date. The latest status report says you have completed $1,500 worth of work. This means you are:

A. Behind schedule by $500

B. Ahead of schedule by $500

C. Behind schedule by $750

D. Ahead of schedule by $750

99. On the AISecure project, you have completed $30,000 worth of work. The value of the work scheduled is $25,000. Your schedule performance index (SPI) is:

A. 0.33

B. 1.2

C. 5,000

D. –5,000

100. As recommended by your PMO, you are using the earned value technique on your AISecure project. Your project is 25% complete, your cost performance index (CPI) is 0.75, and your schedule performance index (SPI) is 0.80. How do you interpret these results?

A. You cannot complete your project without the use of additional resources.

B. It seems that your CPI and SPI will never reach 1.0.

C. You need to control costs and improve the project progress.

D. A risk officer should be appointed immediately.

1. B	26. B	51. C	76. B
2. B	27. C	52. D	77. D
3. C	28. D	53. C	78. A
4. C	29. D	54. D	79. C
5. B	30. A	55. A	80. D
6. C	31. A	56. C	81. C
7. D	32. B	57. A	82. A
8. A	33. B	58. B	83. C
9. B	34. A	59. B	84. A
10. C	35. A	60. C	85. B
11. D	36. D	61. D	86. A
12. A	37. D	62. A	87. B
13. A	38. A	63. D	88. B
14. B	39. B	64. C	89. A
15. C	40. C	65. A	90. D
16. D	41. C	66. B	91. A
17. A	42. D	67. A	92. D
18. A	43. A	68. A	93. D
19. D	44. B	69. D	94. C
20. B	45. D	70. B	95. B
21. C	46. C	71. C	96. D
22. B	47. A	72. B	97. B
23. C	48. D	73. D	98. A
24. A	49. A	74. B	99. B
25. D	50. B	75. A	100. C

1. On your project, a configuration audit has been scheduled. Your best C++ programmer, Radhika, asks you what this process entails. Your response should indicate that:

   A. Configuration audits involve reviewing deliverables with the customer or sponsor to ensure they are completed satisfactorily and obtaining formal acceptance by the customer or sponsor

   B. Configuration audits ensure that the composition of a project's configuration items is correct and that corresponding changes are registered, approved, tracked, and correctly implemented

   C. Configuration auditing is the process of monitoring and recording results of executing quality activities to assess performance and recommend necessary changes, and it is done throughout the project

   D. Configuration audits include the process of tracking, reviewing, and regulating the progress to meet the performance objectives defined in the project management plan, and they are done throughout the project

   ☑ **B.** Configuration audits ensure that the composition of a project's configuration items is correct. This audit also confirms that corresponding changes are registered, approved, tracked, and correctly implemented to ensure that the functional requirements defined in the configuration document have been met.

   ☒ **A** is incorrect because it refers to Validate Scope. **C** is the definition of Control Quality. **D** describes Monitor and Control Project Work.

2. Your company, Stay Home Shopping Network (SHSN), a creative and fluid family business that sells products using television network combined with a data streaming service, is about to be bought out by a corporate conglomerate that already owns 18% of the company stock, Home Quality Value Convenience (HQVC). This takeover will affect your project, and all the other projects in the organization's portfolio. You understand how risky this is. While you are performing the Implement Risk Responses process, you may identify new risks. What document might be updated now, to help you later, with identifying overall project risk?

   A. PESTLE framework

   B. Prompt list

   C. VUCA list

   D. TECOP log

   ☑ **B.** A prompt list is a predetermined list of risk categories that might give rise to individual project risks and that could also act as sources of overall project risk. The prompt list can be used as a framework to aid the project team in idea generation when using risk identification techniques.

   ☒ **A, C,** and **D** are incorrect. PESTLE framework, VUCA list, and TECOP log are made-up terms. And, PESTLE, VUCA, and TECOP are common strategic frameworks for identifying sources of overall risks.

3. You are the project manager for a small project team for a project that has a set of approved functional requirements. In one of the regular meetings, your software developer team member, Patty, proposes an additional feature to the system. As project manager, you remind the team that they must concentrate on completing only the work approved. Your statement was guided by your adherence to:

A. Quality management

B. Change management

C. Scope management

D. Configuration management

☑ **C.** Approved project scope defines the approved work that the project delivers, and only this work should be done. Any changes are managed by reference to the project scope.

☒ **A, B,** and **D** are incorrect. The Quality management, change management, and configuration management processes are control processes used to implement or approve changes to the project scope.

4. You have been assigned as the project manager on a project focused on developing a new process for your organization called configuration management. Which of the following identifies the functions this process performs?

A. Identifying, submitting, approving, tracking, and validating changes

B. Submitting, approving, tracking, measuring, and validating changes

C. Identifying, requesting, assessing, validating, and communicating changes

D. Reviewing, approving, tracking, validating, and proving changes

☑ **C.** Configuration management is the process of identifying, requesting, assessing, validating, and communicating changes to the project management plan.

☒ **A, B,** and **D** are incorrect. Configuration management does not include measuring and does not include proving.

5. You are managing a project that is in progress. Many tasks have been completed, some are in progress, and others are yet to start. You are reviewing your work load related to the work performance monitoring of the activities in the project. When is the best time to collect this information?

A. At the start of the activity

B. Routinely and regularly

C. At the end of the task only

D. Monthly for progress reports

☑ **B.** Work performance measurement should be done routinely and regularly as part of the execution of the project management plan.

☒ **A, C,** and **D** are incorrect. "At the start of the activity" does not give progress information. "At the end of the task only" does not give start or variance information. "Monthly for progress reports" is possible but not advised, and it does not allow for short activities (less than one month in duration).

6. When running a project, the project manager must manage the project work. Which of the following is part of effectively monitoring and controlling the project progress?

   A. Email the team the schedule according to the plan.

   B. Record the actual progress on tasks daily.

   C. Compare actual activity performance against the plan.

   D. Report only completed activities, schedules, and costs.

   ☑ **C.** Comparing actual activity performance against the project management plan identifies deviations and problems early.

   ☒ **A, B,** and **D** are incorrect. Broadcasting the plan does not measure progress. Recording progress does not refer to the plan or commitment of the project. Completed activity does not refer to the plan.

7. One of the tools you use during project management is the "earned value technique." Which of the following best explains why you are using the earned value technique?

   A. Future performance can be made to exactly meet the plan.

   B. Past performance can be measured to an accuracy of less than 5%.

   C. Future performance can be predicted to within 10% of the budget.

   D. Future performance can be forecasted based on past performance.

   ☑ **D.** The earned value technique is used to predict future performance based on past performance.

   ☒ **A, B,** and **C** are incorrect. Future performance cannot be manipulated to exactly match the plan, past performance can be measured only as closely as actual data allow and earned value cannot predict absolutely to 10%.

8. Which of the following statements best describes the purpose of using preventive actions in a project?

   A. It reduces the probability of negative consequences related to risks.

   B. It reduces the impact of negative consequences related to risks.

   C. It increases the project budget to allow for some cost overruns.

   D. It increases the reporting frequency on activities that are critical.

   ☑ **A.** Preventive actions are documented actions that aim to reduce the probability of negative consequences associated with project risks.

   ☒ **B, C,** and **D** are incorrect. Preventive actions do not reduce the impact. Increasing the project budget to allow for some cost overrun or increasing the reporting frequency on activities that are critical could be considered preventive actions, but they are not considered an output of the Monitoring and Controlling processes.

9. You are planning a project and wish to introduce the concept of integrated change control to your team. What is the best way to describe the use of integrated change control to the team?

A. Change control applies to the inception stage to define the scope only.

B. Change control applies from the beginning of the project to the end.

C. Change control is used only when there are substantial changes to the budget.

D. Change control is used at the execution stage to control schedule creep.

☑ **B.** In the Monitoring and Controlling process group, the Perform Integrated Change Control process applies from the beginning to the end of the project.

☒ **A, C,** and **D** are incorrect. The use of change control at one stage only is not recommended because many items may change and could be missed at other stages of the project.

10. You are managing a section of a large project and have adopted an integrated change control system for the constant flow of changes from the project team. Which of the following describes how you would act on changes?

A. Approve changes that cost less than 10% of the budget.

B. Automatically approve all changes to the schedule.

C. Review, then approve or reject project changes.

D. Reject all changes to the budget, scope, or deliverables.

☑ **C.** An integrated change control system must have a review step that results in approval, rejection, or deferral of changes to the project.

☒ **A, B,** and **D** are incorrect. This is applied not only to budgets or to schedules, and it does not mean that all changes should be rejected or accepted.

11. You are asked to describe why you are using the Perform Integrated Change Control process in your projects. You refer to the systems and processes that are in place in your workplace. Which of the following best describes your reasons for using change control?

A. We have a form that we always use on every project.

B. We always use change control to limit budget overspending.

C. It is required on our project because of legislation.

D. It is part of our project management methodology.

☑ **D.** Perform Integrated Change Control is part of the project management methodology that aids the project team in managing changes to the project.

☒ **A** is incorrect because "a form" is too generic. **B** is incorrect because change control is not a guaranteed way to limit budget overspending. **C** is incorrect because external factors (e.g., legislation) cannot mandate how a project is carried out; however, it can influence it.

12. A project that is using the Perform Integrated Change Control process will have many outputs. A member of your team suggests that the project management plan is an output of this process. What should your answer be?

   A. Disagree because project management plan updates are outputs.

   B. Disagree because the project management plan is not an output.

   C. Agree that the project management plan is an output.

   D. Disagree because the project management plan is not used in this process.

   ☑ **A.** The Perform Integrated Change Control process has several outputs, among which is project management plan updates.

   ☒ **B, C,** and **D** are incorrect. The project management plan is used in Perform Integrated Change Control as an input to this process and not as an output.

13. The project team you are working with is doing the work of obtaining formal stakeholders' acceptance of the completed project and associated deliverables. Each deliverable is reviewed to check that it has been completed satisfactorily. What is this process called?

   A. Validate Scope

   B. Define Scope

   C. Control Scope

   D. Plan Scope Management

   ☑ **A.** Validate Scope is the process of obtaining stakeholders' formal acceptance of the project and associated deliverables. This process is performed at project closure or termination to determine if the project has delivered the contracted scope.

   ☒ **B, C,** and **D** are incorrect. Define Scope is the process of defining what the project will deliver. Control Scope is the process of managing changes to the scope. Plan Scope Management is the overall process, defined in the project management plan, of how the team will manage scope.

14. You are discussing your project roles with a colleague. She states that she is working on developing a process that ensures all scope changes make use of the company-wide change control system. What project work is she performing?

   A. Defining change control

   B. Validating configuration management

   C. Developing a risk register

   D. Validating scope

   ☑ **B.** Defining or developing a process that ensures all scope changes go through integrated change control in a project is part of Control Scope.

   ☒ **A, C,** and **D** are incorrect. The change control process supports scope control. A risk register does not ensure all changes go through change control. Validate Scope occurs at the end of a project to confirm that deliverables cover the contracted scope.

15. The project team is involved in the following tasks: measuring, examining, and verifying that the work and deliverables meet the product and acceptance criteria. Which of the following is a summary description of the work your team is doing?

   A. Define Scope: Inputs

   B. Validate Scope: Outputs

   C. Validate Scope: Inspection

   D. Plan Scope Management: Inputs

   ☑ **C.** The process of Validate Scope uses many techniques, including inspection. Inspection is a process of measuring, examining, and verifying that the work and deliverables meet the product and acceptance criteria.

   ☒ **A, B,** and **D** are incorrect. This is not a definition of inputs for Define Scope. Validate Scope outputs are not as described, and they include accepted deliverables. Plan Scope Management inputs are documents such as a scope statement and a list of deliverables.

16. You have been working on defining the procedures by which the project scope and product scope can be changed. In which process is your team engaged?

   A. Validate Scope

   B. Plan Configuration Management

   C. Initial Scope Definition

   D. Control Scope

   ☑ **D.** Defining the procedures by which the project scope and product scope can be changed is known as Control Scope.

   ☒ **A, B,** and **C** are incorrect. Validate Scope is done at the end of a project or phase to confirm the deliverables are as contracted. Configuration management is the process of considering changes before they are put into change control. Initial scope definition is not about Control Scope.

17. You are writing a procedure for ensuring that changes to product scope and project scope are considered and documented. These artifacts will be processed through Perform Integrated Change Control. What title should you put on this process?

   A. Configuration management

   B. Scope validation

   C. Integrated change control

   D. Project Scope Management

☑ **A.** The procedures for ensuring that changes to product scope and project scope are considered and documented are known as configuration management.

☒ **B, C,** and **D** are incorrect. Scope validation is related to deliverables. Integrated Change Control is a support process after the stated process. Project Scope Management is a superset of the process described.

18. Many changes to the project schedule and requirements have been suggested by the project team and the customer. These are urgent, and all affect the resources you are using. What is the next step to take?

    A. Submit the changes to Perform Integrated Change Control for review.

    B. Notify the project sponsor that the work on the changes will start immediately.

    C. Ignore the changes to eliminate the risk to the project schedule.

    D. Reschedule resources to begin the changes immediately.

    ☑ **A.** Changes to project scope or requirements must be passed to Perform Integrated Change Control for review and then disposition according to the change control system.

    ☒ **B, C,** and **D** are incorrect. No work should start until it is approved by the change control board. Ignoring the change requests can lessen the probability of success for the project.

19. What does the term variance analysis mean for a project manager?

    A. Recording the actual start date of critical activities in the project

    B. Analyzing the calendar contract start date and finish date

    C. Calculating the difference between total slack and free slack

    D. Comparing activity target start date with actual start date

    ☑ **D.** Variance analysis looks at the difference between the planned and actual performance; in this case, the target start date is the planned and the actual start date is the actual.

    ☒ **A, B,** and **C** are incorrect. Recording dates does not compare planned to actual. Calendar contract dates do not directly give variance analysis because they do not compare to the planned dates. The difference between total and free slack is not the variance that is analyzed in variance analysis.

20. The project archives you are reviewing show that the project has had several changes to the start and finish dates of the approved baseline schedule. These changes are known as:

    A. Schedule variance analysis

    B. Schedule baseline updates

    C. Approved change requests

    D. Performance measurement

☑ **B.** Changes to the start and finish dates of the approved baseline schedule for the project are known as schedule baseline updates.

☒ **A, C,** and **D** are incorrect. Variance analysis compares planned to actual dates, and performance measurement implies making the same kind of comparison. The description is not of a list of approved change requests.

21. What factors are needed to calculate the ETC for a project?

   A. EAC and PV

   B. BAC, AC, and PV

   C. BAC, EV, and AC

   D. ECA and AC

   ☑ **C.** Calculating the Estimate to Completion (ETC) requires the Budget at Completion (BAC), Earned Value (EV) to date, and Actual Costs (AC) to date.

   ☒ **A** and **B** are incorrect because EAC and PV, and BAC, AC and PV are used to calculate other earned value measurements. **D** is incorrect because ECA is not an acronym used in the PMBOK.

22. You have been asked to report to the project sponsor on project performance. She asks you for an estimate of the project completion date. Which of the following would help you to provide this estimate?

   A. CPI

   B. SPI

   C. ETC

   D. EAC

   ☑ **B.** The Schedule Performance Index (SPI) is the only indicator that would help to predict the schedule.

   ☒ **A, C,** and **D** are incorrect. They are related to costs.

23. The values for CV, SV, CPI, and SPI for the activities in a project are used to calculate:

   A. Schedule estimates

   B. Cost estimates

   C. Earned value

   D. Corrective actions

   ☑ **C.** The use of the calculations for CV, SV, CPI, and SPI for the activities in the project is the basis for earned value management.

   ☒ **A, B,** and **D** are incorrect. Schedule estimates and cost estimates are the results of specific calculations on only two of the given parameters. Corrective actions are not directly driven by the parameters given.

24. A new team member is monitoring and recording results of executing quality activities to assess performance and recommend necessary changes. He asks for clarification on what his activities are related to. Which of the following is the best answer to his question?

A. Control Quality

B. Manage Quality

C. Plan Quality Management

D. Quality Improvement

    ☑ **A.** Monitoring and recording results of executing quality activities to assess performance and recommend necessary changes is Control Quality.

    ☒ **B, C,** and **D** are incorrect. Manage Quality is ensuring that appropriate quality standards are used. Plan Quality Management is related to establishing the requirements and/or standards for the project. Quality improvement is an organizational development process.

25. In the process of Control Quality, when is time normally allocated to do this work?

A. At every project milestone

B. At termination of the project

C. At the initiation stage only

D. Throughout the project

    ☑ **D.** Managing quality should be done throughout the project.

    ☒ **A, B,** and **C** are incorrect because implementing quality control only at milestones or when a project begins, or ends is not as effective as managing quality throughout the project.

26. The project you are managing has a fundamental problem that will compromise the delivery of a key component. Your team is trying to find the reasons for the failure of the system, using a tool consisting of a diagram that shows how several factors might be linked to the problem or the effects. This diagram is called:

A. Variable scatter diagram

B. Cause-and-effect diagram

C. Process control chart

D. Statistical sampling matrix

    ☑ **B.** A diagram that shows how numerous factors might be linked to the problem or the effects is known as a cause-and-effect diagram.

    ☒ **A, C,** and **D** are incorrect. A variable scatter diagram shows the relationship between two variables only. A process control chart is used to determine the stability of a system. Statistical sampling is related to population sampling of components.

27. Your mentor suggests that you use a chart that shows, by frequency of occurrence, events and defects in the project. The common name for this chart is:

   A. Scatter diagram

   B. Flowchart

   C. Pareto chart

   D. Control chart

   ☑ **C.** A chart that shows, by frequency of occurrence, events and defects in the project is known as a Pareto chart.

   ☒ **A, B,** and **D** are incorrect. A scatter diagram shows the relationship between two variables only. A flowchart is a graphical representation of a process. A control chart relates to stability of processes.

28. A common tool used in analyzing problems on a project is a diagram that shows the relationship between two variables. This is called a:

   A. Control chart

   B. Pareto chart

   C. Run chart

   D. Scatter diagram

   ☑ **D.** A scatter diagram shows the relationship between two variables in a process.

   ☒ **A, B,** and **C** are incorrect. A control chart relates to stability of processes. A Pareto chart shows, by frequency of occurrence, events and defects in the project. A run chart shows the history of the occurrence of a variation in a process.

29. Your team has proposed that a resource optimization strategy should be adopted for the project schedule from this point on. Which of the following best describes what they are suggesting?

   A. No change to the resources and reducing the project schedule

   B. Adding resources and reducing the project schedule

   C. Reducing resources but not changing the project schedule

   D. Adding more resources or modifying the project schedule

   ☑ **D.** Adding more resources or modifying the project schedule is a commonly used resource optimization strategy.

   ☒ **A, B,** and **C** are incorrect. None of the other strategies listed is a resource optimization strategy in and of itself.

30. The document that covers the topics of identifying project successes and failures, and making recommendations on how to improve future performance on other projects, is referred to as the:

    A. Lessons learned documentation

    B. Project management plan

    C. Issue log

    D. Change log

    ☑ **A.** Identifying project successes and failures, and making recommendations on how to improve future performance on other projects, is part of the lessons learned documentation.

    ☒ **B, C,** and **D** are incorrect. The other choices are all inputs to the Manage Stakeholder Engagement process.

31. As part of your role as project manager, you must frequently update and reissue work performance information as the project proceeds. This information concerns how the project's past performance could affect the project in the future. This information is called:

    A. Performance reports

    B. Corrective actions

    C. Change requests

    D. Variance analysis

    ☑ **A.** Performance reports are issued periodically and may range from simple status reports to more elaborate reports. More elaborate reports may contain analysis of past performance, forecasted project completion, status of risks and issues, and results of variance analysis, among other information.

    ☒ **B, C,** and **D** are incorrect. Variance analysis, corrective actions, and change requests are not related to impact to the project in the future.

32. One of the tools a project manager uses to help document and monitor the resolution of issues in the project is a(n):

    A. Risk register

    B. Issue log

    C. Change requests

    D. Corrective actions

    ☑ **B.** One of the tools used to help document and monitor the resolution of issues in a project is known as the issue log.

    ☒ **A, C,** and **D** are incorrect. The risk register contains all issues identified as risks. Change requests are actions required because of issues or risks identified. Corrective actions refer to changes made when executing the project.

33. Sally is reviewing the risk management plan for the current project. How often should she monitor the project work for new and changing risks?

A. At the beginning of project planning

B. Continuously throughout the project life cycle

C. At the beginning of each project phase

D. At the end of each project phase

☑ **B.** The project team should monitor the project work for new and changing risks continuously throughout the project life cycle.

☒ **A, C,** and **D** are incorrect. The Monitoring and Controlling process should be defined in the risk management plan, and it should specify continuous monitoring for new and changing risks.

34. A consultant has been reviewing your Monitor Risks process outputs. She lists many actions that are required to bring the project into compliance with the project management plan. What are these actions called?

A. Recommended preventive actions

B. Risk register updates

C. Recommended corrective actions

D. Project management plan updates

☑ **A.** Actions that are required to bring the project into compliance with the project management plan are known as recommended preventive actions.

☒ **B, C,** and **D** are incorrect. Recommended corrective actions include contingency plans and work-around plans. Risk register updates and project management plan updates are also outputs of the Monitor Risks process, but do not fit the question posed.

35. You have been asked by the project sponsor to ensure that the seller's performance meets the contractual requirements and that your organization, as the buyer, performs according to the contract. What best describes your efforts?

A. Control Procurements

B. Plan Procurement Management

C. Conduct Procurements

D. Selected Sellers

☑ **A.** The activity of ensuring that the seller's performance meets the contractual requirements and that the buying organization performs according to the contract is called Control Procurements.

☒ **B, C,** and **D** are incorrect. Plan Procurement Management and Conduct Procurements are steps prior to Control Procurements. Selected sellers is an output of Conduct Procurements.

36. The project you are managing has a problem that requires the contract with a seller to be modified. The alteration to the contract is in accordance with the change control terms of the contract and project. The best time to make this change to the contract is:

A. Never; the contract cannot be modified at any time

B. At any time, regardless of the response from the seller

C. At any time prior to the contract being awarded to the seller

D. At any time prior to contract closure by mutual consent

☑ **D.** The contract with a seller can be modified at any time, in accordance with the change control terms of the contract and project.

☒ **A, B,** and **C** are incorrect. Contracts usually are varied or modified during a project for practical reasons. The contract is not in place until it has been awarded.

37. You are managing a system that includes the following information: contract documentation, tracking systems, dispute resolution procedures, and approved levels of authority for changes. What is this system called?

A. Short-listing the qualified sellers

B. Change control system

C. Procurement management plan

D. Contract change control system

☑ **D.** A contract change control system includes contract documentation, tracking systems, dispute resolution procedures, and approved levels of authority for changes.

☒ **A, B,** and **C** are incorrect. This is a subset of the change control system. The short list of qualified sellers is part of the general procurement process. The procurement management plan refers to how the procurement processes will be managed.

38. As part of the Control Procurements process, contested changes will arise where the buyer and seller cannot reach an agreement on compensation for the change, or cannot agree that a change has occurred. These are called claims, disputes, or appeals. If the parties cannot resolve a claim by themselves, it may need to be resolved using what method?

A. Alternative dispute resolution (ADR)

B. Compromising technique

C. Integrated change control

D. Economic price adjustment

☑ **A.** If the parties cannot resolve a claim by themselves, it may need to be handled in accordance with alternative dispute resolution (ADR), usually following procedures established in the contract.

☒ **B, C,** and **D** are incorrect. Compromising is a technique for conflict resolution within project teams; integrated change control is the process for handling changes, not claims; and economic price adjustment is a form of contract.

39. A document produced by the contract manager that rates how well each seller is performing the project work is called a:

A. Seller selection criteria

B. Seller performance evaluation

C. Procurement management plan

D. Work performance information

   ☑ **B.** A document that rates how well each seller is performing the project work is known as a seller performance evaluation.

   ☒ **A, C,** and **D** are incorrect. Seller selection criteria is an input to contract documentation. The procurement management plan refers to how the procurement processes will be managed. Work performance management is raw data to the seller performance evaluation.

40. In a project, the seller is performing below the contracted level of work consistently. What is the most appropriate procedure to follow?

A. Continue until the seller provides an explanation.

B. Add time to the project schedule.

C. Terminate the seller's contract early.

D. Increase the budget allocated to the contract.

   ☑ **C.** Although all the solutions are possible, the consistent underperformance can help to indicate early termination of the seller contract.

   ☒ **A, B,** and **D** are incorrect. Although all the solutions are possible, the consistent underperformance can help to indicate early termination of the seller contract.

41. The project management office wants to do a structured review on your project of the Project Procurement Management knowledge area from Plan Procurement Management to Control Procurements. This review is called:

A. Performance reporting

B. Contract management

C. Procurement audit

D. Claims administration

   ☑ **C.** A structured review of the procurement process from planning, through acquiring, then to contract administration is called a procurement audit.

   ☒ **A, B,** and **D** are incorrect. Contract management is the generic term for the overall process. Performance reporting and claims administration are other subsets of contract management.

42. What is the objective of the use of a procurement audit on a project when conducted in the Close Project or Phase process?

   A. Identify when legal action should be started.

   B. Terminate the nonperforming suppliers' contracts.

   C. Identify who signed the nonperforming contracts.

   D. Identify success and failure for use in future contracts.

   ☑ **D.** The objective of the use of the procurement audit process is to identify success and failure for use in future contracts on this or other projects. This is performed as part of the project closure process.

   ☒ **A, B,** and **C** are incorrect. Identifying when legal action should be started, terminating the nonperforming suppliers' contracts, and identifying who signed the nonperforming contracts are part of contract administration.

43. What is the most common logical relationship in a PDM?

   A. Finish-to-start (FS)

   B. Start-to-finish (SF)

   C. Finish-to-finish (FF)

   D. Start-to-start (SS)

   ☑ **A.** The most commonly used dependency in a precedence diagramming method (PDM) is finish-to-start (FS). The predecessor must finish before the successor can start. Land must be purchased before road building can start.

   ☒ **B** is incorrect because start-to-finish (SF) means the predecessor must start before the successor can finish. Road excavating must start before line painting can be completed. **C** is incorrect because finish-to-finish (FF) means the predecessor must finish before the successor can finish. Laying asphalt must be complete before line painting can be completed. **D** is incorrect because start-to-start (SS) means the predecessor must start before the successor can start. Road excavating must start before asphalt can be laid.

44. The ADM is visually the opposite of _____:

   A. MDA

   B. PDM

   C. AON

   D. AOA

   ☑ **B.** The arrow diagramming method (ADM) is visually the opposite of the PDM.

   ☒ **A** is incorrect because it is a distracter. **C** is incorrect because the activity-on-node (AON) method is a type of PDM. Activity-on-node uses boxes to denote schedule activities. These various boxes, or "nodes," are connected from beginning to end, with arrows to depict a logical progression of the dependencies between the schedule activities. Each node is coded with a letter or number that correlates to an activity on the project schedule. **D** is incorrect because AOA is a type of ADM. The ADM refers to a schedule network diagramming technique in which the schedule activities within a given project are represented using arrows.

45. As the project manager for a major shipyard, you are responsible for ensuring that safety regulations and quality standards are complied with for all activities. Your project involves nuclear work. Last month a nuclear incident occurred. The root cause was an uncertified technician being tasked to work on a shift without the change being reviewed and approved. Which of the following control processes is most related to preventing the unauthorized worker from being assigned and most likely would have prevented the incident?

   A. Control Schedule

   B. Control Costs

   C. Manage Quality

   D. Perform Integrated Change Control

   ☑ **D.** The process of coordinating changes in the project—including changes to cost, quality, schedule, and scope—is the Perform Integrated Change Control process. This process controls the approval and refusal of requests for change and makes sure those changes are beneficial and agreed upon. Measures in integrated change control would help ensure this replacement was made more capably.

   ☒ **A, B,** and **C** are incorrect because controlling the schedule and costs and managing quality are processes that can initiate change requests.

46. After the incident, a thorough review of the work packages to perform nuclear repair work was conducted to make sure each repair plan included specific instructions to follow the procedures for reassignment of personnel. Which of the following is least related to this action?

   A. Perform quality audit

   B. Evaluate additional training and resourcing needs

   C. Apply earned value techniques

   D. Apply change management tools and techniques

   ☑ **C.** This is the exception. A common technique to assess cost variance is called the earned value technique (EVT), also called earned value management (EVM). Applying earned value techniques is part of the Control Costs process and is not directly related to change control.

   ☒ **A, B,** and **D** are incorrect because you are responsible for analyzing variances of cost, schedules, quality, and risk by comparing actual values to planned values from the project plan, trends, and extrapolation to identify corrective actions necessary.

47. You are managing a project for the new nuclear power facility due to go live in the next six months. In nuclear repair work, changes must be controlled without error to prevent risk to the health and welfare of the workers and possibly the public. These risks demand careful attention to change control and management through which framework of the project life cycle?

- **A.** Starting the project, organizing and preparing, carrying out the work, and ending the project
- **B.** Initiating, planning, executing, monitoring and controlling, and closing
- **C.** Feasibility study, requirements, analysis, design, coding, and testing
- **D.** Goal, plan, status

☑ **A.** Integrated change control is performed throughout the entire project life cycle, from starting the project, organizing and planning, carrying out the work, to closing the project.

☒ **B** is incorrect because these are names of process groups. **C** is incorrect because these are names of phases in a project life cycle. **D** is incorrect because goal, plan, status is a distracter.

48. Which of the following processes is most needed to monitor and measure resources to ensure the committed resources are made available to the project consistent with commitments and to ensure resources are allocated to the project according to the project management plan?

- **A.** Control Staffing
- **B.** Control Team
- **C.** Control Scope
- **D.** Control Resources

☑ **D.** Control Resources is the process of measuring and monitoring all project resources, and their associated costs, according to the project management plan. It is the process of managing resources to ensure the committed resources are made available to the project consistent with the commitments, resources are allocated within the project according to the plan, and resources are released from the project as dictated by the plan.

☒ **A** and **B** are incorrect because Control Staffing and Control Team are made-up terms. **C** is incorrect because Control Scope monitors project and product status and maps changes to the scope baseline.

49. In preparation for a major political election, your political party has tasked you with increasing voter participation by 10% nationwide for the primary elections. You have established a separate polling group to perform polls in various geographic areas and determine the effectiveness of your project. As the poll results are received, you need to change the scope of your project to improve the project results and better accomplish the benefits delivery and achieve the strategic goals for your party. Which of the following tasks will be least useful in changing the scope of the project?

A. Ensuring a project manager is assigned to the CCB

B. Evaluating each requested change

C. Deciding the disposition of each change

D. Archiving change requests and the supporting detail for them

☑ **A.** This is the least useful task. Ensuring the project manager is assigned to the change control board (CCB) is a part of Control Resources and is least applicable to controlling scope.

☒ **B, C,** and **D** are incorrect because Control Scope is a process for controlling changes to the project scope. This is a formal process for accomplishing the following tasks: capturing requested changes, evaluating each requested change, deciding the disposition of each requested change, communicating a decision to affected stakeholders, archiving the change request and its supporting detail, and, when a request is accepted, initiating the activities required to have the change incorporated into the project management plan.

50. You assign one of your junior staff to track the actual start and finish of activities and milestones to ensure they are being performed against the planned timeline. They report regularly any deviations and keep the plan updated as changes occur. Which of the following processes is most consistent with these activities?

A. Control Scope

B. Control Schedule

C. Monitor Communications

D. Monitor Risks

☑ **B.** Control Schedule is the process of ensuring that the project will produce its required deliverables and solutions on time. The activities in this process include tracking the actual start and finish of activities and milestones against the planned timeline and updating the plan so that the comparison to the plan is always current.

☒ **A, C,** and **D** are incorrect because Control Scope, Monitor Communications, and Monitor Risks include other activities to support their respective processes.

51. From your experience with other projects, you know that the Control Schedule process results in people focusing on slippage and many times forgetting to look for:

A. Lag

B. Slack

C. Opportunities

D. Critical tasks

☑ **C.** Control Schedule is the process of ensuring that the project will produce its required deliverables and solutions on time. The activities in this process include tracking the actual start and finish of activities and milestones against the planned timeline and updating the plan so that the comparison to the plan is always current.

☒ **A, B,** and **D** are incorrect because Control Schedule works closely with the other project control processes. It involves identifying not only slippages, but also opportunities.

52. Which of the following documents is least useful in managing your program scope?

    A. Scope management plan

    B. Scope baseline

    C. Change management plan

    D. Procurement management plan

    ☑ **D.** This is the exception. Control Scope is a process for controlling changes to the project scope. This is a formal process for accomplishing the following tasks: capturing requested changes, evaluating each requested change, deciding the disposition of each requested change, communicating a decision to affected stakeholders, archiving the change request and its supporting detail, and, when a request is accepted, initiating the activities required to have the changes incorporated into the project management plan.

    ☒ **A, B,** and **C** are incorrect because key inputs to the Control Scope process include three scope-related project documents: scope management plan, scope baseline, and change management plan.

53. As a part of your quality control efforts, you are required to monitor repetitive activities to make sure they are operating inside three standard deviations of the mean. Which tool are you required to understand and use?

    A. Scatter diagrams

    B. Pareto diagrams

    C. Control chart

    D. Failure mode effects analysis (FMEA)

    ☑ **C.** The control chart monitors repetitive activities, where activities are in control if they are operating within three standard deviations of the mean.

    ☒ **A** is incorrect because the possible relationships between two variables are identified using scatter diagrams. To understand data, it is important to understand the relationships among data elements. **B** is incorrect because a Pareto diagram is a vertical bar graph in which values are plotted in decreasing order of relative frequency from left to right. **D** is incorrect because FMEA helps to identify potential failure modes and the consequences of those failures and to formulate improvement solutions.

54. As a part of your quality control efforts, you are required to use a procedure to test ways in which components fail and determine the impact of the failures. Which tool should you be required to understand and use?

A. Mean time between failure (MTBF)

B. Pareto diagrams

C. Control chart

D. Failure mode effects analysis (FMEA)

☑ **D.** Failure mode effects analysis is a procedure for testing the ways in which a component may fail and determining the effect of each failure on product reliability.

☒ **A** is incorrect because mean time between failures (MTBF) is a measure of how reliable a hardware product or component is. **B** is incorrect because a Pareto diagram is a vertical bar graph in which values are plotted in decreasing order of relative frequency from left to right. **C** is incorrect because the control chart monitors repetitive activities, where activities are in control if they are operating within three standard deviations of the mean.

55. It is imperative that you keep your budget in control. Project governance has been established to keep budgets within 10% of what was planned and report weekly when costs are more or less than this threshold. Which of the following facets of cost control is least useful in controlling your budget?

A. Contracting outsource services vs. using capable in-house staff

B. Holding down costs so the project remains on budget

C. Bringing the project back on budget when an overrun occurs

D. Identifying opportunities to return project funding to the enterprise

☑ **A.** This is least helpful, given the importance of staff in any effort to add value to an organization; however, project managers should keep the focus on long-term impact, not short-term costs.

☒ **B, C,** and **D** are incorrect; these are the most helpful because there are three facets to controlling costs: holding down costs so the project remains on budget, bringing the project back on budget when an overrun occurs, and identifying opportunities to return project funding to the organization.

56. The project management plan directs monitoring and controlling of specific project deliverables and reviewing results to determine if the deliverables fulfill specified requirements. Which process ensures this best?

A. Control Project Work

B. Risk Monitoring and Control

C. Control Quality

D. Schedule Control

☑ **C.** Control Quality is the process of monitoring specific program deliverables and results to determine if they fulfill quality requirements. This process identifies faulty outcomes and allows the elimination of causes of unsatisfactory performance at all stages of the quality loop, from the identification of needs to the assessment of whether the identified needs have been satisfied.

☒ **A** is incorrect because the proper name is Monitor and Control Project Work. Control Project Work is a distracter. **B** is incorrect because Risk Monitoring and Control is not the name of a process. **D** is incorrect because the proper name is Control Schedule not Schedule Control.

57. It was identified during project planning that a strong potential of going over budget might exist. What process did you put into place to identify this possibility, define how to react to it, and evaluate how effective your response to its occurrence was?

   A. Monitor Risks

   B. Plan Risk Management

   C. Validate Scope

   D. Manage Risk

   ☑ **A.** Monitor Risks is the process of tracking identified project risk, identifying new risk to the project, executing risk response plans, and evaluating their effectiveness in reducing risk throughout the project life cycle. Monitor Risks involves tracking risk currently identified in the risk response plan and identifying new risk that emerged during the execution of the project.

   ☒ **B** is incorrect because Plan Risk Management is the process of identifying, analyzing, and responding to risk factors throughout the life of a project and in the best interests of its objectives. **C** is incorrect because Validate Scope is a project management process that is used to formally accept completed project deliverables. **D** is incorrect because Manage Risk is a distracter.

58. Which process group or process provides the most primary interface with the project governance structure?

   A. Executing

   B. Monitoring and Controlling

   C. Direct and Manage Project Work

   D. Monitor and Control Project Work

   ☑ **B.** The Monitoring and Controlling process group is where the project manager obtains and consolidates status and progress data from project work packages, interfaces with the project governance structure, and reports on project performance.

   ☒ **A** is incorrect because project governance is most prevalent in the Monitoring and Controlling process group. **C** is incorrect because Direct and Manage Project Work is the process of leading and performing the work defined in the project management plan and implementing approved changes to achieve the project's objectives. **D** is incorrect because the proper name is Monitor and Control Project Work.

59. As a newly assigned project manager, you find that your stakeholder list contains every functional manager and all executive managers, as well as users of the future solution. You send scope, schedule, cost, quality, and value reports to several key stakeholders. No one seems to agree on the expectations from your project. You check with stakeholders' involvement as you proceed through your project's life cycle and focus on strategies and plans with all stakeholders. You are performing:

A. Plan Stakeholder Management

B. Monitor Stakeholder Engagement

C. Develop Project Life Cycle

D. Maintain Project Management Plan

☑ **B.** Monitor Stakeholder Engagement is the process of monitoring stakeholder relationships and tailoring strategies for keeping them engaged.

☒ **A** is incorrect because stakeholder management includes considering interesting concerns of stakeholders relative to your project's success. This spans the entire project life cycle. New stakeholders will be identified and need to be added to your project, and some may go away. It's important to identify stakeholders as early as possible, manage their expectations as they change, and ensure stakeholders have necessary support. **C** and **D** are incorrect because a project life cycle is already in place, and maintaining the project management plan, while required, is not the focus of stakeholder interactions.

60. You are a project manager documenting corrective actions that have been taken on your project and their associated outcomes. In performing this activity across your project life cycle, what document would you use to best log this information for subsequent analysis and archiving?

A. Historical information

B. Supporting details

C. Lessons learned

D. Risk log

☑ **C.** Lessons learned are documented in the lessons learned register; it is updated as an output in many processes throughout the project. They may document such things as causes of variance from the project management plan; corrective actions taken; and their outcomes, risk mitigations, and other information. They are identified and documented throughout the project management processes and ultimately flow to the Close Project or Phase process for analysis and archiving.

☒ **A** is incorrect because historical information includes documents and data on prior projects. **B** is incorrect because the term "supporting details" can be defined as additional information that explains, defines, or proves an idea. **D** is incorrect because lessons learned are transferred to the lessons learned repository at the end of a project or phase, not the risk log.

61. You are a project manager reviewing the benefits management plan with a key member of the organization's executive staff to determine effort and cost for a set of current tasks. What term best describes the technique you are applying?

    A. Walkthrough

    B. Performance review

    C. Root cause analysis

    D. Expert judgment

      ☑ **D.** Expert judgment is a common project management tool and technique that includes functional and technical area specialists, external consultants, professional and technical organizations, and government or industry bodies. These people may be internal or external to the project. Examples of expert judgment in the Control Costs process include financial analysis.

      ☒ **A** and **B** are incorrect because they are tools and techniques of Control Quality. **C** is incorrect because root cost analysis is a technique used to determine underlying causes for an occurring problem and is used in the control processes.

62. You are a new project manager attempting to understand what is expected of you when you are managing the relationships with sellers and buyers. What process best describes what work activities are required?

    A. Control Procurements

    B. Perform Qualitative Risk Analysis

    C. Identify Stakeholders

    D. Develop Team

      ☑ **A.** The Control Procurements process manages procurement relationships (the relationship with sellers and buyers).

      ☒ **B, C,** and **D** are incorrect because the question relates to relationships between sellers and buyers, not risks, stakeholders, or teams.

63. For the last nine months you have been the project manager for the Rio Grande railroad upgrade project. Several of the activities are on track, but some have started to derail. During project planning, a strong potential of going off the tracks (over budget) was identified. What process should be in place to identify this possibility, define how to react to it, and evaluate how effective your response to its occurrence has been?

    A. Control Quality

    B. Control Costs

    C. Control Resources

    D. Monitor Risks

☑ **D.** Monitor Risks is the process of monitoring the implementation of agreed-upon risk responses throughout the project life cycle. Risk monitoring involves tracking risks currently identified in the risk response plan and identifying new risks that emerge during the execution of the project.

☒ **A** is incorrect because the Control Quality process is performed to measure the completeness of a product, service, or result prior to user acceptance. **B** is incorrect because Control Costs is performed to maintain the cost baseline throughout the project. **C** in incorrect because the Control Resources process is performed to ensure that the physical resources assigned and allocated to the project are available as planned, as well as monitoring the planned versus actual use of resources, and performing corrective action as necessary.

64. In one of the project status meetings, you find several team members have conflicts between tasks for the functional manager and the project team. Which control process is most related to preventing unauthorized or conflicting assignments to prevent future occurrences of these incidents?

   A. Monitor and Control Project Work

   B. Perform Integrated Change Control

   C. Control Resources

   D. Monitor Human Resources

   ☑ **C.** Ensuring that the assigned resources are available to the project at the right time and in the right place is a key benefit of the Control Resources process.

   ☒ **A** is incorrect because the Monitor and Control Project Work process is concerned with comparing actual project performance against the project management plan. **B** is incorrect because the process of coordinating changes across the entire project, including changes to cost, quality, schedule, and scope, is the Perform Integrated Change Control process. **D** is incorrect because there is no process called Monitor Human Resources in the PMBOK.

65. As a part of your efforts to ensure quality, you require each project manager to monitor repetitive activities to make sure they are operating inside three standard deviations of the mean. Which tool should they be required to understand and use?

   A. Control chart

   B. Scatter diagram

   C. Mind mapping

   D. Failure mode effects analysis (FMEA)

   ☑ **A.** The control chart monitors repetitive activities where activities are in control if they are operating within three standard deviations of the mean.

☒ **B** is incorrect because a scatter diagram is used in the Manage Quality process to show the relationship between two variables. **C** is incorrect because mind mapping is a diagrammatic method used to visually organize information. **D** is incorrect because failure mode effects analysis (FMEA) is a step-by-step approach for identifying all possible failures in a design, a manufacturing or assembly process, or a product or service.

66. Which of the following processes is most related to managing the project's staff and supplies correctly and the associated costs related to them in accordance with the project management plan?

    A. Perform Integrated Change Control

    B. Control Resources

    C. Monitor Stakeholder Engagement

    D. Develop Staff Release Plan

    ☑ **B.** The process of managing and measuring all project resources and their associated costs according to the project management plan is the Control Resources process.

    ☒ **A** is incorrect because the process of coordinating changes across the entire project, including changes to cost, quality, schedule, and scope, is the Perform Integrated Change Control process. **C** is incorrect because Monitor Stakeholder Engagement is the process of monitoring stakeholder relationships and tailoring strategies for keeping them engaged. **D** is incorrect because the Develop Staff Release Plan process is not a task in the PMBOK.

67. A pharmaceutical company is developing three new drugs. Each one is a part of a line of products. One of the drugs is used over the counter. The second is a prescription for retail purchase. The third is used exclusively in hospitals during critical operations as a router point for small businesses to provide broadband capability to customers. You are over budget by 20% and your schedule for the project has slipped by several weeks. To compound your problems, marketing is recommending releasing the products simultaneously to the market at least three weeks earlier than planned. Your budget is thin, and your sponsor has informed you that no additional funding is available at this time. In this case, to deliver ahead of schedule, which of the following constraint adjustments will be most useful in resolving this challenge?

    A. Scope

    B. Budget

    C. Schedule

    D. Quality

    ☑ **A.** Based on the triad of constraints—scope, budget, and schedule—the most probable option would be modifying the scope; your budget is tight and you now have to deliver early with no additional costs.

☒ **B** is incorrect because the question clearly states that you have no additional funding currently. **C** is incorrect because your schedule has been moved up by "at least three weeks earlier than planned." **D** is incorrect because quality matters most; ignore quality, and you shorten the life of your product, not to mention its usefulness.

68. Joyce is a senior project manager. Her team successfully completed the SellMe project. The collection of all SellMe documents are archived into a SharePoint repository and full text indexed for easy searching for reusability downstream. Joyce's company is about to be bought out by a corporate conglomerate that already owns 18% of the company stock. Semaj, the CIO, asks Joyce to "protect the cost baseline." What is a key to effective cost control (managing the approved cost baseline)?

    A. Monitoring cost performance to isolate and understand variances from the approved cost baseline

    B. Controlling the work performance data, information, and reports

    C. Updating the cost management plan using earned value analysis

    D. Preventing approved change requests from being included in the reported cost or resource usage

    ☑ **A.** Much of the effort of cost control involves analyzing the relationship between the consumption of project funds and the work being accomplished for such expenditures.

    ☒ **B** is incorrect because throughout the project data is collected, analyzed, and transformed to become project information. The information is communicated verbally or stored and distributed in various formats as reports. You would not want to control the data, information, or reports. **C** is incorrect because the cost management plan is an output of the Control Costs process and is updated when control thresholds and levels of accuracy required in managing the project's costs change. Earned value analysis information is documented in work performance reports. **D** is incorrect because you want to prevent "unapproved" change requests from being included in the reported cost or resource usage. Caution, read carefully.

69. As a project manager, you gather final values of work and compare them to planned values for quality, cost, schedule, and resource usage to determine project performance and generate performance reports for the project. Which of the following skills is least related to these tasks?

    A. Communicating results of project performance

    B. Managing stakeholder expectations

    C. Organizing cost, resource, and schedule data

    D. Rebudgeting and financial modeling

☑ **D.** Rebudgeting and financial modeling can be used in monitoring and controlling the project. It is a skill used in analyzing variances in costs, schedules, quality, and risks.

☒ **A, B,** and **C** are incorrect because communicating results of project performance; managing stakeholder expectations; and organizing cost, resource, and schedule data cover some of the key aspects of the role of the project manager in monitoring and controlling the project.

70. A pharmaceutical company is developing three new drugs. Each one is a part of a line of products. One of the drugs is used over the counter. The second is a prescription for retail purchase. The third is used exclusively in hospitals during critical operations as a router point for small businesses to provide broadband capability to customers. You are over budget by 20% and your schedule for the project has slipped by several weeks. To compound your problems, marketing is recommending releasing the products simultaneously to the market at least three weeks earlier than planned. In your performance report on the drug project, you note a change because there is new technology that can add features to the router point for small businesses. This technology was not included in the project management plan. You have issued a change request, but because it requires corrective action beyond your approval level, your next step is to:

A. Schedule a meeting with your PMO.

B. Receive governance approval to proceed.

C. Set up a change control board to see if the change should be implemented.

D. Use your project management information system.

☑ **B.** Governance is the framework within which authority is exercised in organizations. This framework includes policies, procedures, and approval levels.

☒ **A** is incorrect because the PMO standardizes the project-related governance processes. **C** is incorrect because the change control board is responsible for deciding what to do with change requests. **D** is incorrect because the PMIS is used for the outputs of project management processes.

71. As the project manager in your drug company, you know you are over budget by 20% and your schedule for the project has slipped by several weeks. You have set up a system of regularly reporting on progress to:

A. Forecast completion because you are using earned value management (EVM)

B. Describe each task/activity benefit and when it is scheduled for completion

C. Provide stakeholders with metrics to show the benefits realized

D. Provide stakeholders with overall customer and sponsor feedback

☑ **C.** The benefits management plan describes when the benefits of the project will be delivered. Metrics are the direct and indirect measurements used to show the benefits realized.

☒ **A** is incorrect because EVM uses scope and schedule measurements to assess project progress, not forecast completion. **B** is incorrect because project benefits are an outcome of actions and behaviors that provide value to the sponsoring organization. Describing the benefit of each task/activity and when it is scheduled for completion is too much detail. **D** is incorrect because providing stakeholders with overall customer and sponsor feedback is part of trends in project quality management.

72. The work on the drug project has not gone according to plan. Even though you are tracking its progress, it appears to be missing its due dates. On Friday, you meet with your project steering committee. Many issues have resulted because of lack of resources. The first thing to do is:

    A. Tell the steering committee you have analyzed the work performance data, and the work performance reports are wrong

    B. Start with general and background information about the project's performance

    C. The problems from lack of resources have been noted in variance and trend analysis reports, which you are bringing to the project steering committee to justify more resources

    D. You now need to rebaseline the project's schedule because of the resource shortage

    ☑ **B.** Presenting a chart of the project's performance over time will show how the performance is deteriorating because of scarce resources.

    ☒ **A** is incorrect because work performance data are the raw measurements of start and finish dates of schedule activities. Work performance information—for example, status of deliverables—is represented in work performance reports. You may use the documents to raise awareness of the resource problem—after you show the impact, over time, of the resource problem. **C** is incorrect because the responsibilities of a project steering committee (PSC) in a project management setting include project priority setting and resource allocation, which is usually done after the PSC understands the resource allocation situation. **D** is incorrect because you have rebaselined the project's schedule and identified the corrective or preventive action required each time a due date is missed.

73. Finally, on your drug project, you have a meeting with your project management team tomorrow. While you will discuss the resource problem, you also should include in your meeting:

    A. Your scope management plan

    B. A discussion of the schedule management plan

    C. An analysis of the BAC, VAC, and ETC

    D. Feedback from customers

☑ **D.** Customer satisfaction is measured by meeting customer expectations. If the products are not conforming to requirements and being delivered on time, customers are dissatisfied; then, every aspect of your project should be marked with a red light.

☒ **A** is incorrect because your scope management plan describes how the scope will be defined, developed, monitored, controlled, and validated. **B** is incorrect because the schedule management plan establishes the criteria and activities for developing, monitoring, and controlling the schedule. **C** is incorrect because BAC, VAC, and ETC are EVM computations for performance measurement.

74. When you met with the steering committee, given the difficulties with the schedule slippages, the committee members felt you should inform your stakeholders about what was happening. What is the most likely action to take in this situation?

   A. Assign a member of your team to meet individually with each stakeholder.

   B. Use the information management system to distribute information between the project team and the stakeholders.

   C. Submit a change request to the CCB.

   D. Rebaseline your schedule so your stakeholders have a collective understanding of when deliverables will be due.

   ☑ **B.** Providing accurate, timely, and relevant information is essential to the decision-making process of a project. Relying on an inadequate information system puts a project at risk. Information is a valuable resource for project managers. The information management system can deliver the types of information needed to ensure project success.

   ☒ **A** is incorrect because assigning a member of your team to meet individually with each stakeholder is time consuming and costly. **C** is incorrect because the CCB is a committee that makes decisions regarding whether proposed changes to a project should be implemented. **D** is incorrect because a best practice is to rebaseline the project if you have missed over half your scheduled targets in the last six months.

75. Recently, your drug company conducted an OPM3 assessment and found that it had 349 of the 488 best practices in place. The resulting improvement report showed little work needed to be done in stakeholder engagement, while more emphasis was required in project cost management. As you continue your work on the drug project, you consequently:

   A. Should be adept at keeping costs under control

   B. Need to regularly meet with the financial auditors and other stakeholders and show them your progress in cost-controlling techniques

   C. Need to redefine your budget because of the size of the project

   D. Will not need regular status reviews of the cost status of your project's activities

   ☑ **A.** Cost is one of the key performance indicators for projects. Involved in controlling costs are processes centered around planning, estimating, budgeting, financing, funding, and managing costs so that the project can be completed within the approved budget.

☒ **B** is incorrect because financial audits evaluate financial statements and provide third-party opinions on the truthfulness of these statements. Project audits examine the true status of project cost, schedule, scope, and quality. **C** is incorrect because the concerns about cost control may or may not involve changes in the cost of materials and labor and resource availability—which can alter the budget. **D** is incorrect because regular status reviews of the cost status of your project's activities are described in the cost management plan. Specifically, the cost management plan identifies how to measure project costs, the cost reporting format, and cost variance response processes.

76. Your program manager says you should use earned value management (EVM) on your drug project. You decide to implement the milestone method of tracking project progress. This means that:

    A. You can also use other methods such as CCM and CPM

    B. Stakeholders must be kept fully informed to establish realistic expectations

    C. You will not need to use EAC, ETC, or BAC

    D. You will need to consider dependency types and integration

    ☑ **B.** Project milestones provide actionable goalposts to manage by. When stakeholders are fully informed, you can obtain important feedback to solve problems and/or renegotiate previously established priorities.

    ☒ **A** is incorrect because CCM and CPM are tools and techniques of the Develop Schedule process. **C** is incorrect because EAC, ETC, and BAC are data analysis techniques that can be used to control costs. **D** is incorrect because dependency types are tools and techniques used in the Sequence Activities process.

77. The PMO has suggested that you use the EAC as your principal means of forecasting costs for your drug project. You should:

    A. Also calculate the CV, SV, SPI, and CPI

    B. Communicate the cost forecasts to the key stakeholders according to the cost forecast plan

    C. Follow the cost forecast strategy in the stakeholder management plan

    D. Know that you can use three common methods to calculate EAC values

    ☑ **D.** Three common methods to calculate EAC values are 1) EAC = BAC/Cumulative CPI; 2) EAC = AC + (BAC − EV); and 3) EAC = AC + [BAC − EV / (Cumulative CPI × Cumulative SPI)].

    ☒ **A** is incorrect because CV, SV, SPI, and CPI are types of variance analysis used in the Control Costs process. **B** is incorrect because the cost forecast plan is a distracter. **C** is incorrect because the stakeholder management plan does not include a cost forecast strategy.

78. As the project manager for the AISecure project, you have awarded two contracts. Every two weeks you receive performance reports from both contractors. Contractor 1 is not achieving its objectives and had made no progress in the last two 2 weeks. This

contractor's work is important because it affects three major components of the AISecure product. As the project manager, the next thing to do is:

A. Schedule a contract performance review

B. Ask the procurement department to conduct an audit of Contractor 1

C. Update the seller-developed technical documentation

D. Ask the contracts department to begin alternative dispute resolution (ADR) procedures

☑ **A.** Performance reviews for contracts measure schedule performance against the contract.

☒ **B** is incorrect because an audit is performed to confirm the rights and obligations as described in the procurement contract. **C** is incorrect because updating the seller-developed technical documentation is part of procurement documentation updates and would be done after the performance review. **D** is incorrect because if there is a claim after the performance review and the procurement documentation is updated, any claims administration would be handled in accordance with ADR.

79. You recognize the importance of monitoring contract performance and closing out contracts in your drug project. As the project manager, it is important to focus on:

A. Including contractors in the project governance process

B. Ensuring contractors understand the benefits management plan

C. Prequalified seller lists updates

D. Setting up a lessons learned repository for ease of archiving

☑ **C.** Sellers could be disqualified and removed from the lists based on deficient performance.

☒ **A** is incorrect because the project governance process provides a way for directors and senior management to exercise effective oversight and ensure their strategies are implemented and their benefits realized. Project governance sits above and outside of the project management domain. **B** is incorrect because the responsibility for delivering benefits lies primarily with the project manager. The sponsor has overall responsibility for achieving the benefits in the business case. **D** is incorrect because setting up a lessons learned repository for ease of archiving is an output of Close Project or Phase.

80. The major focus of the drug project is on value and quality. You also want to focus on benefits delivery because of the competition you face in the market. You decide to conduct inspections. A key purpose is to:

A. Ensure the process improvement plan is being followed

B. Decrease the payback period as described in the business case

C. Avoid the need for walkthroughs, reviews, and audits

D. Promote fitness for use

☑ **D.** According to Joseph Juran, fitness for use is "effectiveness of a design, manufacturing method, and support process employed in delivering a good, system, or service that fits a customer's defined purpose, under anticipated or specified operational conditions." An inspection determines if the product, process, and project meet the requirements and the result is used and useful.

☒ **A** is incorrect because the process improvement plan frames a project for improving such PM issues as metrics, quality, issue management, change control, project tracking, and status reporting. **B** is incorrect because when making a decision regarding an initiative, companies can compute the payback period to find out how long it will take to recover their initial investment. Decreasing the payback period as described in the business case will not promote value and quality. **C** is incorrect because walkthroughs, reviews, and audits are types of inspections.

81. You are conducting these inspections on your project so you can focus on:

    A. Taking corrective actions

    B. The need for issue resolution

    C. Inspecting the correctness of deliverables resulting in verified deliverables

    D. Overall project deliverable validity

    ☑ **C.** Inspections can be used to meet the goal of control quality, which is to determine the correctness of deliverables that become an input to the Validate Scope process.

    ☒ **A** is incorrect because corrective action refers to any type of action that is instituted, the point of which is to alter the course of a specific task or project that may have lost focus or somehow deviated from the prespecified direction it was intended to take. **B** is incorrect because issues are any request, complaint, or unexpected condition that leads to unplanned, but in scope, work that must be accomplished on a project. They normally result in the need to implement a workaround to resolve them. **D** is incorrect because the purpose of the Validate Scope process is to formally accept completed project deliverables. Its main advantage is that it provides objectivity to the acceptance process, as well as improve the finished product, service, or result by validating the deliverables.

82. A senior project manager recommends that you use checklists in the Control Quality process on your project. A best practice is to:

    A. Ensure completed checklists are documented and archived

    B. Rely on the senior project manager's judgment in determining whether a checklist fits your project

    C. Use them as part of walkthroughs for works in progress

    D. Use a corporate-approved template

    ☑ **A.** A project quality checklist is a tool used to aid the project team in ensuring they consider all aspects of project and/or process quality. To help achieve consistency, completed checklists can be documented and archived as part of lessons learned.

☒ **B** is incorrect because quality will mean different things to different stakeholders. For every project the quality targets will be different. It is more effective to work through each quality aspect of a checklist to select your own quality indicators. **C** is incorrect because walkthroughs are informal reviews conducted on works in progress. **D** is incorrect because it is more effective to start with a customized template rather than a standard template.

83. Many quality control measurements can be used, but given the nature of this drug project, the most effective is:

    A. Root cause analysis (RCA) versus design for X (DfX)

    B. Planned versus actual project performance reviews

    C. Customer satisfaction surveys

    D. Retrospectives/lessons learned

    ☑ **C.** An effective customer satisfaction survey has 5 to 10 questions that relate to the service delivery, customer experience, and overall satisfaction. The purpose of this type of survey is to gauge how satisfied your customers are.

    ☒ **A** is incorrect because RCA and DfX are tools and techniques of Manage Quality. **B** is incorrect because project performance reviews are a technique that is used to measure actual work in progress against the baseline. **D** is incorrect because retrospectives/lessons learned are types of meetings held as part of the Control Quality process.

84. In the early phases of your drug project, you prepared a resource management plan, which included a project organization chart and a recognition plan. Now, because of a rise in interest rates, resource cuts are going to result in a 12% reduction in force throughout the company. As the project manager, your next step is to:

    A. Carefully monitor and control the scarce resources

    B. Request a preassigned contractor for needed resources

    C. Suggest that a contractor officer representative (COR) be used for all project procurements

    D. Use MoSCoW to reprioritize the work in your project

    ☑ **A.** Projects need resources, and in this question resources are scarce. The task therefore lies with the project manager to determine the proper timing of those resources within the project schedule.

    ☒ **B** is incorrect because pre-assignment allows you to select team members in advance, before the project starts. Team members may be assigned in the Develop Project Charter process. **C** is incorrect because not every project has a COR. **D** is incorrect because the MoSCoW method is not the only technique for prioritizing work in a project. MoSCoW = Must-have, Should-have, Could-have, and Won't have.

85. Recognizing the resource capacity constraints that now affect your project, you built a responsibility assignment matrix (RAM) to determine if any resources were underallocated. Several team members work in a weak matrix structure, and another is in a strong matrix. A best practice is to:

A. Prepare a RACI chart to show an overall picture of project resource requirements

B. Release resources back to their functional managers when they are not required

C. Work with other project managers to share scarce resources

D. Update your resource management plan and present it to the sponsor to determine alternative approaches

☑ **B.** Whenever two project managers are competing for resources, there is potential for conflict. In project work conflict is inevitable; releasing resources back to their functional managers when they are not required can keep conflict constructive and help overcome problems in matrix management.

☒ **A** is incorrect because a RACI chart is an example of a responsibility assignment matrix. It shows the expense at the lowest level of work for managing cost and duration. With a RACI chart, you map out who is Responsible, Accountable, must be Consulted with, and shall stay Informed. **C** is incorrect because in a matrix organization the major disadvantage is that project team members are working for two bosses. In a scarce resource situation, the functional manager, not other project managers, determines work assignments. **D** is incorrect because one of the PMO's primary functions is to facilitate the sharing of resources.

86. You realize that a key part of your sphere of influence is to establish relationships with subject matter experts (SMEs). You have three SMEs "on loan" to your project. Two of the SMEs are overallocated on your project, and other project managers need them, too. You may be required to assign alternative resources. Your best course of action is to:

A. Meet with the project sponsor to show the impact on benefit delivery if you cannot keep the three SMEs

B. Meet with the change control board and plead your case that your project deserves the necessary resources to meet the strategic goals

C. Reprioritize each work package in your WBS and the milestone due dates and present this information to your steering committee

D. Use resource leveling in your schedule to show overallocation

☑ **A.** The project sponsor is generally accountable for the maintenance of the business case document that establishes the validity of the benefits of the project.

☒ **B** is incorrect because the CCB is a committee that makes decisions regarding whether proposed changes to a project should be implemented. **C** is incorrect because meeting with the CCB is for analyzing change requests, not working with SMEs. **D** is incorrect because resource allocation, also called resource loading, commits certain resources to project plan activities. After using the resource allocation process to define project resource needs, resource leveling is used to relate the needs to available resources.

87. You are a PMI-RMP. You know that risk management planning takes a considerable amount of time in a project. Risk identification is an agenda item at your project status meetings, and you include risk analysis as part of the status reports you submit on a biweekly basis to the project management team. You and your team work actively to perform the Monitor Risks process. An example is:

A. Unresolved project risks that require resolution by the risk management department

B. Identifying and analyzing new risks at the work package level

C. Time and cost contingency reserves allocated to each work package in the project

D. Fallback plans in the risk register

☑ **B.** Identifying and analyzing new risks at the work package level is the definition of the Monitor Risks process.

☒ **A** is incorrect because unresolved risks are assigned to a risk owner, who may or may not be in the risk management department. **C** is incorrect because time and cost contingency reserves are allocated to known risks—they are not allocated to each work package in the project. **D** is incorrect because a contingency plan is associated with risk management in a project; in case a risk occurs, these actions must be taken to control/mitigate the risk. A fallback plan is an alternative in case a certain approach fails. Fallback plans are not in the risk register.

88. Having been a project manager for over 20 years and passed the PMI-RMP exam, you recognize the importance of preparing a risk management plan early on in projects and then monitoring and controlling the risks throughout the project. You also had the opportunity to work as a risk management officer on your last project. You realize a key action to reduce the risk that may affect the delivery of the project's benefits is to:

A. Use communication as a risk mitigation strategy

B. Focus on maximizing business value delivery

C. Make sure the right team members are chosen for the project team

D. Decompose and progressively elaborate project risks

☑ **B.** For IT investments to deliver business value in today's complex landscape, IT must 1) be more tightly aligned with business objectives than ever before and 2) carefully control risks, both strategic and operational.

☒ **A** is incorrect because communication as a risk mitigation strategy is one of the greatest tools that you have to reduce conflict in your organization. Reducing conflict does not necessarily maximize the delivery of business benefits. **C** is incorrect because you don't get to choose the right mix of skills and personalities to ensure the project gets done with the minimum friction and the maximum effectiveness. **D** is incorrect because decomposition and progressive elaboration are tools and techniques of Define Activities.

89. The measure used to forecast the final project completion estimates is:

   A. CPI
   B. ETC
   C. EAC
   D. BAC

   ☑ **A.** CPI along with SPI is sometimes used to forecast the final project completion estimates.

   ☒ **B, C,** and **D** are incorrect because ETC is estimate to complete, which is the amount of money required to complete the remaining work from a given date. EAC is estimate at completion, which is the total cost of the project at the end. BAC is budget at completion, which is the total budget allocated to the project.

90. A project was estimated to cost $1.5 million and scheduled to last six months. Halfway through the project, the earned value analysis shows the following:

   EV = $650,000
   PV = $750,000
   AC = $800,000

   What are the schedule and cost variances?

   A. SV= +$100,000 / CV= +$150,000
   B. SV= +$150,000 / CV= –$100,000
   C. SV= –$50,000 / CV= +$150,000
   D. SV= –$100,000 / CV= –$150,000

   ☑ **D.** SV = EV – PV; SV= –$100,000. CV = EV – AC; CV= –$150,000

   ☒ **A, B,** and **C** are incorrect because these answers do not come from using the formulas SV = EV – PV and CV = EV – AC.

91. Configuration management is a technique for:

   A. Overall change control
   B. Project plan execution
   C. Project scope
   D. Perform qualitative risk analysis

   ☑ **A.** Configuration management is a process for establishing and maintaining consistency of a product's performance, functional, and physical attributes with its requirements, design, and operational information throughout its life.

   ☒ **B** is incorrect because the Executing process group is the place where all the project work takes place. It involves carrying out all the work that was planned during the Planning process group. **C** is incorrect because project scope is the part of project planning that involves determining and documenting a list of specific project goals, deliverables, tasks, costs, and deadlines. **D** is incorrect because the Perform Qualitative Risk Analysis process is used in risk management.

92. In anticipation of a corporate merger completion, your business analyst team has been tasked with the business process and software system integration effort with an emphasis on determining which processes and systems should be absorbed into the new company and which aren't needed, what data is important to migrate, and how much integration is needed before the companies are technically joined. You anticipate that your new project, the actual integration work, will be a matter of extracting the data from one system and putting in another. Throughout the project, you will verify that project deliverables and work meet the requirements specified by key stakeholders for final acceptance. What process are you performing?

   A. Manage Quality

   B. Validate Scope

   C. Control Scope

   D. Control Quality

   ☑ **D** is correct because this is the benefit of Control Quality.

   ☒ **A** is incorrect because the Manage Quality process increases the probability of meeting the quality objectives as wells as identifying ineffective processes and causes of inferior quality. **B** is incorrect because the Validate Scope process brings objectivity to the acceptance process and increases the probability of final product, service, or result acceptance by validating (proving) each deliverable. **C** is incorrect because the key benefit of the Control Scope process is that the scope baseline is maintained throughout the project.

93. Reviewing work products and results to ensure that all were completed satisfactorily and formally accepted is part of:

   A. Plan Risk Acceptance

   B. Control Quality

   C. Perform Integrated Change Control

   D. Validate Scope

   ☑ **D.** Validate Scope is the process in which validated deliverables are compared against scope baseline to decide whether the team has produced what was planned and documented. This is a process of formal acceptance of completed delivery by the customer.

   ☒ **A** is incorrect because it is a made-up term. **B** is incorrect because the Control Quality process determines if the project outputs do what they were intended to do. **C** is incorrect because Perform Integrated Change Control is the process of reviewing all change requests; approving changes and managing changes to deliverables, organizational process assets, project documents, and the project management plan; and communicating their disposition.

94. Through no fault of your own, your project has been canceled. The Validate Scope process:

    A. Will be delayed until the project is continued

    B. Should determine the correctness of the work results

    C. Should establish and document the level and extent of completion

    D. Will form the basis of the project management audit

    ☑ **C.** When a project is terminated, you should establish and document the level and extent of completion. It is vital to run the regular project closure procedures for a project that is canceled. Adequate project termination marks successful project management.

    ☒ **A** is incorrect because when a project is terminated, it may never be started up again. **B** is incorrect because the correctness of the work results is performed in the Control Quality process. **D** is incorrect because a project management audit is an examination designed to determine the true status of work performed on a project and its conformance with the project statement of work, including schedule and budget constraints.

95. If the CPI is expected to be the same for the remainder of the project, you should calculate the project's estimate at completion (EAC) by using the following formula:

    A. AC + ETC

    B. BAC / CPI

    C. AC + (Remaining PV / CPI)

    D. AC + BAC – EV

    ☑ **B.** When variances are typical of future variances, you should calculate the project's estimate at completion (EAC) by using BAC / CPI.

    ☒ **A** is incorrect because AC (Actual Cost) + ETC (Estimate to Complete) is a made-up formula. **C** is incorrect because it is a made-up formula. **D** is incorrect because it is the formula for calculating EAC if the future work will be accomplished at the planned rate.

96. You are halfway through a 12-month project. Your BAC is $12,000. The contractor's performance to date is PV = $8,000, EV = $7,000, and AC = $9,000. Your SPI = 0.87, and CPI = 0.77. The contractor tells you this is okay because the project still has six months to go, and they can make it up in the last half of the project. This is the first time you have worked with this contractor, so you have no history of past performance. For the contractor to get back to the original due date, the performance level must be:

    A. 60%

    B. 80%

    C. –133%

    D. 167%

☑ **D.** Using the formula TCPI = (BAC – EV)/(BAC – AC). The To-Complete Performance Index (TCPI) is the estimate of the future cost performance that you may need to complete the project within the approved budget.

☒ **A, B,** and **C** are incorrect because the formula TCPI = (BAC – EV)/(BAC – AC) is used to calculate the efficiency that must be maintained to complete the plan.

97. If you feel your initial plan is no longer valid for your project, you should calculate your estimate at completion (EAC) using the following formula:

    A. AC + EV

    B. AC + Bottom-up ETC

    C. AC + (BAC – EV)

    D. AC + [(BAC – EV / (CPI * SPI)])

☑ **B.** If you feel your original estimating assumptions are no longer appropriate for your project, you calculate your estimate at completion (EAC) using the formula EAC = AC + Bottom-up ETC.

☒ **A** is incorrect because the calculation for EAC should not use EV at this point. **C** is incorrect because it is the formula for calculating EAC when the future work will be accomplished at the planned rate. **D** is incorrect because it is the formula for EAC if both the CPI and SPI influence the remaining work.

98. According to your schedule baseline, you should have completed $2,000 worth of work by this date. The latest status report says you have completed $1,500 worth of work. This means you are:

    A. Behind schedule by $500

    B. Ahead of schedule by $500

    C. Behind schedule by $750

    D. Ahead of schedule by $750

☑ **A.** SV = EV – PV. In this example, EV = $1,500 and PV = $2,000. So, SV = $1,500 – $2,000 = –$500. A negative SV indicates a behind-schedule situation.

☒ **B, C,** and **D** are incorrect because these answers do not come from using the formula SV = EV – PV.

99. On the AISecure project, you have completed $30,000 worth of work. The value of the work scheduled is $25,000. Your schedule performance index (SPI) is:

    A. 0.33

    B. 1.2

    C. 5,000

    D. –5,000

☑ **B.** SPI = EV / PV. Given the amounts of EV = $30,000 and PV = $25,000, then SPI = $30,000 / $25,000 = 1.2.

☒ **A, C,** and **D** are incorrect because these answers do not come from using the formula SPI = EV / PV.

100. As recommended by your PMO, you are using the earned value technique on your AISecure project. Your project is 25% complete, your cost performance index (CPI) is 0.75, and your schedule performance index (SPI) is 0.80. How do you interpret these results?

A. You cannot complete your project without the use of additional resources.

B. It seems that your CPI and SPI will never reach 1.0.

C. You need to control costs and improve the project progress.

D. A risk officer should be appointed immediately.

☑ **C.** When the CPI is less than 1.0, you are over planned cost. An SPI of 0.80 means you are behind schedule. You need to control costs and improve the project progress.

☒ **A** is incorrect because you may use overtime or additional resources to improve your CPI and SPI numbers. **B** is incorrect because you can calculate TCPI to calculate the work that must be achieved with the remaining resources to meet the management goal. **D** is incorrect because the project manager holds responsibility for keeping the project on schedule and on budget. Appointing a separate team member as risk officer can improve interpersonal relations while avoiding groupthink. In this question, we do not know that a risk officer can lead to schedule and cost improvements.

CHAPTER 6

The Closing Domain

This chapter includes questions from the following tasks:

- **Task 1**   Obtain final acceptance of the project deliverables from relevant stakeholders in order to confirm that project scope and deliverables were achieved.
- **Task 2**   Transfer the ownership of deliverables to the assigned stakeholders in accordance with the project plan in order to facilitate project closure.
- **Task 3**   Obtain financial, legal, and administrative closure using generally accepted practices and policies in order to communicate formal project closure and ensure transfer of liability.
- **Task 4**   Prepare and share the final project report according to the communications management plan in order to document and convey project performance and assist in project evaluation.
- **Task 5**   Collate lessons learned that were documented throughout the project and conduct a comprehensive project review in order to update the organization's knowledge base.
- **Task 6**   Archive project documents and materials using generally accepted practices in order to comply with statutory requirements and for potential use in future projects and audits.
- **Task 7**   Obtain feedback from relevant stakeholders using appropriate tools and techniques and based on the stakeholder management plan in order to evaluate their satisfaction.

The Closing domain accounts for 7% (14) of the questions on the PMP exam. The *PMBOK Guide, Sixth Edition,* Section 4.7, covers the seven tasks in the Closing domain. The Close Procurements process present in previous versions of the PMBOK has been deleted; PMI determined that project managers usually do not have the power to close contracts or procurements. The tasks/activities formerly in the Close Procurements process have been rolled into the Close Project or Phase process in the Project Integration Management knowledge area for concluding all tasks/activities for the project, phase, or contract. The 28 practice questions in this chapter are mapped to the style and frequency of question types you will see on the PMP exam.

1. You are at the end of a project that has been successfully delivered. One of the processes that you must manage is called the Close Project or Phase process. You are not certain what this entails. Which project document would you refer to for guidance on the process to help you close the project?

    A. The procurement management plan

    B. The project scope management plan

    C. The project management plan

    D. The quality management plan

2. You are responsible for the Close Project or Phase process on a large project. You are asked to report the activities you are performing. These activities include defining how the project will transfer the services produced to the operational division of the organization. What term describes these activities?

    A. Contract closure

    B. The project management plan

    C. Administrative closure

    D. Deliverable acceptance

3. You have been managing a project for some time and have been asked to identify the current stage of the project. You are reviewing a document that formally indicates that the sponsor has officially accepted the project deliverables. Which document are you reviewing?

    A. Administrative closure documents

    B. Contract closure documents

    C. Project closure documents

    D. Organizational process assets

4. Your multiyear project to build the 2nd Avenue subway system is now complete. Because of your splendid work, your company has won a similar contract to build a subway extension in Toronto, Canada. As you close out the 2nd Avenue project, you should focus on:

A. Keeping your core project team intact for the Canadian project

B. Shutting down your project contractors

C. Information on benefits management

D. Holding a preliminary meeting with those involved in your project to plan the closure meeting

5. As the 2nd Avenue subway project comes to a close, as the project manager, you need to associate a time frame with the realization of benefits. Why is this important?

A. To demonstrate that benefits can be realized by phase: short term, long term, and ongoing

B. To provide evidence that benefits stated in the project charter have been met

C. To provide documentation to the support group during project transition

D. So that stakeholders can see the results of the work of your project

6. Unfortunately, your project to develop the next generation of electric bicycles was canceled because a competitor released its product before your project was scheduled to be complete. Your competitor is already selling their product. Your senior management is determining what product to pursue next. What should you do next?

A. Document the current state of contractual obligations.

B. Focus on the lessons learned from this project.

C. Show the scope of work that was completed.

D. Decide to dispose of all resources.

7. You have completed your project in the SecureAI program. Your project's deliverables are complete and have been accepted by all stakeholders. Your next step is to:

A. Ensure lessons learned from team members are part of the project's organizational process assets

B. Hand over the product to the production support team

C. Ensure you have archived the project documentation

D. Finalize the best practices report for the PMO

8. Your company has a new CEO and she believes in "Go Green!" You have been chosen to manage a project to replace the documentation management system as part of this paperless initiative. Requirements have been elicited, captured, and documented. Now that this phase is complete, your next step is to:

A. Call a meeting with the transition team

B. Reassign contractors to other phases in your project

C. Take a meeting with the key stakeholders

D. Request a preliminary design review

9. On your "Go Green!" project, you have received a request for final payment on a contract. You want to make sure that there are no performance deficiencies to resolve with the contractor. This is especially important because it is the first time your organization has worked with this contractor. Your next step is to:

   A. Consult with the procurement department about adding the contractor to the prequalified sellers list

   B. Check the seller performance evaluation documentation

   C. Review the project management plan

   D. Reread the procurement management plan

10. You are concerned that all the contracted deliverables on your project may not be complete though the contractor has submitted a final payment request. If you are correct, you then need to:

    A. Terminate the contract for lack of performance

    B. Note any unaccounted variations and deviations for follow-up activities

    C. Balance your budget accordingly

    D. Notify your key stakeholders and especially the project management office

11. Because your budget and accounting systems are not integrated with your project management information system, it is difficult to relate expenditures, especially between different project phases. What action should you take in the best interest of your project?

    A. Assign a member of the accounting department to your project team to assist with closing all procurements.

    B. Follow your contract closure procedure as detailed in the procurement management plan.

    C. Cross-reference any differences and explain them with notes.

    D. Conduct a supplier performance review.

12. After two years, your "Go Green!" project has completed all of its multiple phases. It is time to release your project team members. What should you do first?

    A. Return staff members to their functional departments.

    B. Refer to the resource management plan.

    C. Work with the human resource department to reassign each member of your team to a new project.

    D. Notify the project management office so resources are available for other projects.

13. You are preparing your final report on the "Go Green!" project. A key item to include in this report is:

    A. Unresolved schedule issues

    B. Unforeseen risks

C. Resource utilization management

D. A graph of the benefits realization by phase

14. As the project manager for the "Go Green!" project, you have prepared your final project report, which includes your lessons learned. You then had a meeting with as many members of your project team that were available to review them. Your next step is to:

A. Add items as appropriate to the final report

B. Prepare your knowledge management repository

C. Promulgate meeting minutes to the members of the steering committee

D. Ask attendees if they can remain with the project as needed so closure can occur according to organizational policies

15. Your project is ready to be closed: all deliverables have been met, and you have met the planned benefits as described in the benefits management plan. As you are preparing the project final report, you should emphasize:

A. Benefits realized by phase

B. Transition steps to ongoing operations

C. Quality objectives—product and project

D. Scope management—actual versus baseline

16. You are part of a National Health Services that has been delivering benefits to stakeholders during the last seven months. Fourteen projects are in progress, and you are managing one of them. Three will be finishing up in the next week, ten will be completing in the month following, and your project will finish six weeks from now. There have been a variety of visible results during the NHS to date. Four project managers have performed poorly, but have been able to make up for the related losses by adjusting the scope, schedule, and budgets in other projects and nonproject-related operations. Your project has met all major milestones. In your efforts to formalize acceptance of the project, you need to accomplish several activities and present the results to the stakeholder or customers. Which of the following will be least useful for this task?

A. Analyze and document lessons learned.

B. Capture and archive information and records.

C. Level resources for the project.

D. Obtain sponsor sign-off.

17. You will need documentation to justify closing requirements as you shut down the various phases of your project. Which of the following is most needed to commence closure proceedings for the phase?

A. Change requests

B. Performance reports

C. Variance reports

D. Lessons learned

18. As project manager for an international training company, you are responsible for new product development and maintenance of existing training products. Ninety percent of the development is outsourced to contract professionals. A system of processes is in place to consistently manage product development, and several contracts are used to control the work and ensure acceptable work is performed. After a contractor reports completion of a phase and the transfer of the completed deliverables to others, what is your next step?

   A. Update the training certifications.

   B. Review customer acceptance documentation.

   C. Pay invoices.

   D. Audit payment records.

19. As project manager for an international training company, you are responsible for new product development and maintenance of existing training products. Ninety percent of the development is outsourced to contract professionals. Processes are in place to consistently manage product development, and several contracts are used to control the work and ensure acceptable work is performed. After a contractor reports completion of the statement of work in their respective contract, you update contract records in the contract file. Which of the following is not a part of the contract records?

   A. Training certifications

   B. Progress reports

   C. Invoices and charges

   D. Payment records

20. Which of the following is a key input to contract closure?

   A. Record of training

   B. Project schedule

   C. Risk register

   D. Termination notice

21. Which of the following is a key output of contract closure?

   A. Verifying product acceptance based on the contract

   B. Documenting delivery of documentation for products

   C. Documenting contract termination and reasons why

   D. Vendor performance records and reports

22. You established an assumption log early in the project to record assumptions and constraints about the schedule and enhance collaboration with stakeholders. You will most likely use the assumption log to do which of the following during Close Project or Phase?

   A. Store start and end dates for project tasks in the PMIS.

   B. Create an RBS (resource breakdown structure) for staffing future projects.

C. Rebaseline scope, schedule, and cost performance.

D. Update the final lessons learned register.

23. Your project had work done by a vendor. Inspections have been performed to ensure the work conforms to quality standards. Contract documentation has been audited by the contracting office. Before the contract can be closed, it has a stipulation that 75% adoption by users be achieved in the production environment. What does this exemplify?

A. Collecting project or phase records

B. Updating lessons learned

C. Measuring stakeholder satisfaction

D. Managing knowledge sharing and transfer

24. Because you are a PMP with 19 years of manufacturing experience, you have been awarded a one-year, fixed-price contract to lead a project to design and build electric bicycles. These new bicycles will use nucleovoltaic cells. The chief scientist at the company informs you that the nucleovoltaic cell is already being sold by another country in Europe. The board of directors has decided to buy the new technology, not make it. Your project is canceled—today. What is the next thing you should do?

A. Release the project team so they can be reassigned to other projects immediately.

B. Release all resources so they can be reassigned immediately.

C. Implement the Close Project or Phase process.

D. Return the remaining budget to the accounting department for reallocation.

25. The Close Phase or Project process is used to close a contract. All the following procurement documentation is collected except:

A. Payment records

B. Information on cost performance

C. Inspection results

D. Buyer's meeting minutes

26. Your agile project team has successfully demonstrated the final deliverable of a year-long project. Your CIO is sold on the iterative/adaptive approach. The PMO is asking you to join them and support agile for all projects throughout the company. The final product is in use, and the customers love it. As part of administrative closure, what is the best thing to do?

A. Write the final report.

B. Reassign project staff.

C. Confirm data analysis techniques used in the project.

D. Control quality.

27. You are a senior project manager working on developing a new production line for ice pops. After six months of a one-year project, you are told that the company is losing money because of interest rate changes; your project is canceled, and all the team members, contractors, and full-time staff are to be let go. Until now the project was on target, on schedule, and on budget. You've seen this before—no money now, but more money next fiscal year. What is the best action to take next?

    A. Document the reason for early termination and transition the complete and incomplete deliverables to production/support/operations.

    B. Have a meeting with the executive sponsor and explain the sunk cost of your project.

    C. Use the resource management plan for guidance and release the project resources.

    D. See if another project needs a senior project manager.

28. Your project is complete. It was the first project in your company to use the agile approach. The deliverables were identified by the product owner. Some of the stakeholders are concerned about quality and have not signed off on the deliverables. The best way to collect feedback on the definition of "done" is to:

    A. Create a wiki site for five days so stakeholders can provide their comments anonymously

    B. Go back and look at all the lessons learned to evaluate strategic alignment

    C. Set up a focus group after you send out a satisfaction survey

    D. Conduct a product review meeting with the concerned stakeholders

1. C	**8.** C	**15.** C	**22.** D
2. C	**9.** B	**16.** C	**23.** C
3. C	**10.** B	**17.** D	**24.** C
4. C	**11.** C	**18.** B	**25.** D
5. A	**12.** B	**19.** A	**26.** A
6. A	**13.** B	**20.** D	**27.** A
7. B	**14.** A	**21.** C	**28.** D

1. You are at the end of a project that has been successfully delivered. One of the processes that you must manage is called the Close Project or Phase process. You are not certain what this entails. Which project document would you refer to for guidance on the process to help you close the project?

    A. The procurement management plan

    B. The project scope management plan

    C. The project management plan

    D. The quality management plan

    ☑ **C.** The Close Project or Phase process is defined within the project management plan.

    ☒ **A, B,** and **D** are incorrect because the procurement, scope, and quality management plans are specific plans for each of these areas and do not specify the Close Project or Phase process.

2. You are responsible for the Close Project or Phase process on a large project. You are asked to report the activities you are performing. These activities include defining how the project will transfer the services produced to the operational division of the organization. What term describes these activities?

    A. Contract closure

    B. The project management plan

    C. Administrative closure

    D. Deliverable acceptance

    ☑ **C.** The term for reporting activities in the Close Project or Phase process is administrative closure. This includes methodologies for how the project will transfer the services produced to the operational division of the organization.

    ☒ **A** is incorrect because contract closure is not concerned with transfer to operations. **B** is incorrect because the project management plan is the superset of these procedures. **D** is incorrect because deliverable acceptance is not part of the Close Project or Phase process.

3. You have been managing a project for some time and have been asked to identify the current stage of the project. You are reviewing a document that formally indicates that the sponsor has officially accepted the project deliverables. Which document are you reviewing?

    A. Administrative closure documents

    B. Contract closure documents

    C. Project closure documents

    D. Organizational process assets

☑ **C.** The project closure documents include sponsor/customer acceptance documentation from Validate Scope.

☒ **A, B,** and **D** are incorrect because administrative closure, contract closure, and organizational process assets are not a concern of the sponsor.

4. Your multiyear project to build the 2nd Avenue subway system is now complete. Because of your splendid work, your company has won a similar contract to build a subway extension in Toronto, Canada. As you close out the 2nd Avenue project, you should focus on:

   A. Keeping your core project team intact for the Canadian project

   B. Shutting down your project contractors

   C. Information on benefits management

   D. Holding a preliminary meeting with those involved in your project to plan the closure meeting

   ☑ **C.** Final information on project closure may include information on benefits management.

   ☒ **A** is incorrect because it is rare for a project team to stay together from one project to the next, especially a project in another country that requires work permits and visas. **B** is incorrect because you cannot shut down the contractors until you have formalized the completion of the contracts. **D** is incorrect because it is not prudent to have a meeting to discuss the next meeting. We only meet when needed, and we follow meeting type guidelines.

5. As the 2nd Avenue subway project comes to a close, as the project manager, you need to associate a time frame with the realization of benefits. Why is this important?

   A. To demonstrate that benefits can be realized by phase: short term, long term, and ongoing

   B. To provide evidence that benefits stated in the project charter have been met

   C. To provide documentation to the support group during project transition

   D. So that stakeholders can see the results of the work of your project

   ☑ **A.** It is important that project managers keep the benefits of the project clearly in mind by demonstrating realization of the benefits by phases for short-term, long-term, and ongoing benefits.

   ☒ **B** is incorrect because the project benefits management plan describes when the benefits of the project will be delivered. **C** is incorrect because the transition of the subway project from implementation to ongoing operations is part of the Close Project or Phase process. **D** is incorrect because you have shown the stakeholders project deliverables throughout the life cycle.

6. Unfortunately, your project to develop the next generation of electric bicycles was canceled because a competitor released its product before your project was scheduled to be complete. Your competitor is already selling their product. Your senior management is determining what product to pursue next. What should you do next?

A. Document the current state of contractual obligations.

B. Focus on the lessons learned from this project.

C. Show the scope of work that was completed.

D. Decide to dispose of all resources.

☑ **A.** Documenting the current state of contractual obligations as described in the project closure guidelines is the next thing to do.

☒ **B** is incorrect because you will document the lessons learned from the early termination later—in the project final report. **C** is incorrect because the work you have completed will be in documented in the Gantt chart and the activity lists. **D** is incorrect because you will need resources to help you complete the activities in the Close Project or Phase process.

7. You have completed your project in the SecureAI program. Your project's deliverables are complete and have been accepted by all stakeholders. Your next step is to:

A. Ensure lessons learned from team members are part of the project's organizational process assets

B. Hand over the product to the production support team

C. Ensure you have archived the project documentation

D. Finalize the best practices report for the PMO

☑ **B.** When the project is complete, the product, service, or result is transitioned to a production/maintenance/support group.

☒ **A** is incorrect because lessons learned are in the lessons learned register, which is part of the project final report. **C** is incorrect because the project documentation is archived after the closeout reporting meeting is held. **D** is incorrect because the best practices report is not the same as the project final report and a PMO might not be in place.

8. Your company has a new CEO and she believes in "Go Green!" You have been chosen to manage a project to replace the documentation management system as part of this paperless initiative. Requirements have been elicited, captured, and documented. Now that this phase is complete, your next step is to:

A. Call a meeting with the transition team

B. Reassign contractors to other phases in your project

C. Take a meeting with the key stakeholders

D. Request a preliminary design review

☑ **C.** Have a meeting with the key stakeholders to confirm the requirements documents have been accepted and the exit criteria for the requirements phase have been met.

☒ **A** is incorrect because there is no product, service, or result to be moved to production/maintenance/ongoing support. **B** is incorrect because you may reassign or release contractors after the requirements work is done; you will do this after the meeting to confirm deliverables. **D** is incorrect because you are not in the design phase yet; you have just completed the "what" work, that is, requirements elicitation. The "how" work begins next—the design phase.

9. On your "Go Green!" project, you have received a request for final payment on a contract. You want to make sure that there are no performance deficiencies to resolve with the contractor. This is especially important because it is the first time your organization has worked with this contractor. Your next step is to:

   A. Consult with the procurement department about adding the contractor to the prequalified sellers list

   B. Check the seller performance evaluation documentation

   C. Review the project management plan

   D. Reread the procurement management plan

   ☑ **B.** You need to check the seller performance evaluation documentation to see how well this seller is performing the project work. This documentation is an output of Control Procurements.

   ☒ **A** is incorrect because the vendors are approved or disqualified from the prequalified sellers list based on performance. **C** and **D** are incorrect because the procurement management plan is a subsidiary plan of the project management plan. The procurement management plan may be updated with seller performance data in the Control Procurements process.

10. You are concerned that all the contracted deliverables on your project may not be complete though the contractor has submitted a final payment request. If you are correct, you then need to:

    A. Terminate the contract for lack of performance

    B. Note any unaccounted variations and deviations for follow-up activities

    C. Balance your budget accordingly

    D. Notify your key stakeholders and especially the project management office

    ☑ **B.** One of the activities related to the completion of the contractual agreements is to confirm the formal acceptance of the seller's work. If you are concerned that all the deliverables from a contractor may not be complete, you need to note any unaccounted variations and deviations for follow-up activities.

☒ **A** is incorrect because common reasons for terminating a contract include unsatisfactory performance of the whole or part of the contract by the other party. We cannot be sure we have "just cause" to terminate based on our concerns. **C** is incorrect because your budget, the approved estimate for the project, has already been determined. The cost baseline could change to include contingency reserves for the incomplete deliverables. **D** is incorrect because we need more details about our "concerns" and the project management team would be notified after the project sponsor, a key stakeholder.

11. Because your budget and accounting systems are not integrated with your project management information system, it is difficult to relate expenditures, especially between different project phases. What action should you take in the best interest of your project?

   A. Assign a member of the accounting department to your project team to assist with closing all procurements.

   B. Follow your contract closure procedure as detailed in the procurement management plan.

   C. Cross-reference any differences and explain them with notes.

   D. Conduct a supplier performance review.

   ☑ **C.** You can use control accounts to cross-reference any differences compared to earned value for performance management and explain them with notes.

   ☒ **A** is incorrect because contract closure is conducted by the procurement department, not the accounting department. **B** is incorrect because contract closure procedures are part of the Close Project or Phase process; they are not in the procurement management plan. **D** is incorrect because supplier performance reviews are part of the Control Procurements process.

12. After two years, your "Go Green!" project has completed all of its multiple phases. It is time to release your project team members. What should you do first?

   A. Return staff members to their functional departments.

   B. Refer to the resource management plan.

   C. Work with the human resource department to reassign each member of your team to a new project.

   D. Notify the project management office so resources are available for other projects.

   ☑ **B.** The resource management plan provides guidance on how the project resources should be released.

   ☒ **A** is incorrect because you may not be working in a matrix environment where you are sharing resources. **C** is incorrect because the HR department is responsible for hiring team members; the IT organization is responsible for assigning resources. **D** is incorrect because the project management office facilitates the sharing of resources, not the assigning of resources for other projects.

13. You are preparing your final report on the "Go Green!" project. A key item to include in this report is:

A. Unresolved schedule issues

B. Unforeseen risks

C. Resource utilization management

D. A graph of the benefits realization by phase

☑ **B.** A summary of the unforeseen risks—and how they were addressed—can be included in the project final report.

☒ **A** is incorrect because schedule objectives as they relate to benefits achieved are in the final report. **C** is incorrect because resource utilization management is part of Plan Resource Management and is documented in the Resource Control section of the resource management plan. **D** is incorrect because benefits realization by phase may not be helpful during closure because some phases do not deliver benefits.

14. As the project manager for the "Go Green!" project, you have prepared your final project report, which includes your lessons learned. You then had a meeting with as many members of your project team that were available to review them. Your next step is to:

A. Add items as appropriate to the final report

B. Prepare your knowledge management repository

C. Promulgate meeting minutes to the members of the steering committee

D. Ask attendees if they can remain with the project as needed so closure can occur according to organizational policies

☑ **A.** Any additional items that provide more information about project performance can be added to the project final report.

☒ **B** is incorrect because knowledge gained on the project is put in the lessons learned repository. **C** is incorrect because you will officially publish the final report to the steering committee. **D** is incorrect because assigning and reallocating resources are decided during Plan Resource Management.

15. Your project is ready to be closed: all deliverables have been met, and you have met the planned benefits as described in the benefits management plan. As you are preparing the project final report, you should emphasize:

A. Benefits realized by phase

B. Transition steps to ongoing operations

C. Quality objectives—product and project

D. Scope management—actual versus baseline

☑ **C.** The project final report includes information on quality objectives—the criteria used to evaluate the product and project quality.

☒ **A** is incorrect because the project final report includes a summary of the benefits that the project was undertaken to address. **B** is incorrect because the final product, service, or result output refers to the transition steps to ongoing operations. **D** is incorrect because scope objectives are part of the final plan. Comparing actual versus baseline is part of the Control Costs process.

16. You are part of a National Health Services that has been delivering benefits to stakeholders during the last seven months. Fourteen projects are in progress, and you are managing one of them. Three will be finishing up in the next week, ten will be completing in the month following, and your project will finish six weeks from now. There have been a variety of visible results during the NHS to date. Four project managers have performed poorly, but have been able to make up for the related losses by adjusting the scope, schedule, and budgets in other projects and nonproject-related operations. Your project has met all major milestones. In your efforts to formalize acceptance of the project, you need to accomplish several activities and present the results to the stakeholder or customers. Which of the following will be least useful for this task?

    A. Analyze and document lessons learned.

    B. Capture and archive information and records.

    C. Level resources for the project.

    D. Obtain sponsor sign-off.

    ☑ **C.** Level resources for the project is not directly related to project closure and is the least useful of the choices given.

    ☒ **A, B,** and **D** are incorrect for this question because each is clearly identified as necessary activities for administrative closure.

17. You will need documentation to justify closing requirements as you shut down the various phases of your project. Which of the following is most needed to commence closure proceedings for the phase?

    A. Change requests

    B. Performance reports

    C. Variance reports

    D. Lessons learned

    ☑ **D.** The core of documentation related to closing the phase is the project archives, which will include all documentation used for the project and the lessons learned reports. This is usually a part of the project final report.

    ☒ **A** is incorrect because change requests are a part of the Perform Integrated Change Control process in the Monitoring and Controlling process group. **B** is incorrect because performance reporting may be included in agreements on the Conduct Procurements process in the Executing process group. **C** is incorrect because variance reports are produced from variance analysis—a tool and technique used in the Control Costs process.

18. As project manager for an international training company, you are responsible for new product development and maintenance of existing training products. Ninety percent of the development is outsourced to contract professionals. A system of processes is in place to consistently manage product development, and several contracts are used to control the work and ensure acceptable work is performed. After a contractor reports completion of a phase and the transfer of the completed deliverables to others, what is your next step?

A. Update the training certifications.

B. Review customer acceptance documentation.

C. Pay invoices.

D. Audit payment records.

☑ **B.** After a contractor reports completion of a phase and the transfer of the completed deliverables to others, your next step is to review customer acceptance documentation from the Validate Scope process.

☒ **A, C,** and **D** are incorrect because Close Project or Phase is the process of closing a contract executed during the project, in accordance with the contract's terms and conditions. While closing the phase, you need to update contract records in the contract file to include the contract itself, progress reports, financial records, invoices, and payment records. **A** is incorrect because training certifications may be part of source selection criteria described in the Plan Procurement Management process. **C** is incorrect because paying invoices is part of the administrative activities in Control Procurements process. **D** is incorrect because procurement audits are critical to the reliability of the procurement system. Procurement audits are a tool and technique of the Control Procurements process.

19. As project manager for an international training company, you are responsible for new product development and maintenance of existing training products. Ninety percent of the development is outsourced to contract professionals. Processes are in place to consistently manage product development, and several contracts are used to control the work and ensure acceptable work is performed. After a contractor reports completion of the statement of work in their respective contract, you update contract records in the contract file. Which of the following is not a part of the contract records?

A. Training certifications

B. Progress reports

C. Invoices and charges

D. Payment records

☑ **A.** Training certifications are not part of the contract records. Note the use of the word "not" in the question.

☒ **B, C,** and **D** are incorrect because contract closure is the process of closing a contract executed during the project, in accordance with the contract's terms and conditions. While closing the project, you need to update contract records in the contract file to include the contract itself, progress reports, financial records, invoices, and payment records.

20. Which of the following is a key input to contract closure?

A. Record of training

B. Project schedule

C. Risk register

D. Termination notice

☑ **D.** Contract closure is the process of closing a contract executed during the project in accordance with the contract's terms and conditions. While closing the project, you need to update contract records in the contract file to include the contract itself, progress reports, financial records, invoices, and payment records. Key inputs to the contract closure process include acceptance reports, contract performance records, delivery notices, and termination notices.

☒ **A** is incorrect because a record of training may or may not apply to your project and is not something required to formally close a contract. **B** is incorrect because the project schedule has been completed at this point. **C** is incorrect because a risk register is used to monitor and control a project's risks during the project and would not be a key input to closing a contract.

21. Which of the following is a key output of contract closure?

A. Verifying product acceptance based on the contract

B. Documenting delivery of documentation for products

C. Documenting contract termination and reasons why

D. Vendor performance records and reports

☑ **C.** Contract closure is the process of closing a contract executed during the project, in accordance with the contract's terms and conditions. While closing the project, you need to update the following contract records in the contract file: the contract itself, progress reports, financial records, invoices, and payment records. Key inputs to the contract closure process include acceptance reports, contract performance records, delivery notices, and termination notices.

☒ **A** is incorrect because verifying product acceptance is done before closure. **B** is incorrect because (sadly) documentation for final deliverables may not be a part of the contracted deliverables for some projects. **D** is incorrect because vendor performance records and reports are not created as a part of contract closure.

22. You established an assumption log early in the project to record assumptions and constraints about the schedule and enhance collaboration with stakeholders. You will most likely use the assumption log to do which of the following during Close Project or Phase?

A. Store start and end dates for project tasks in the PMIS.

B. Create an RBS (resource breakdown structure) for staffing future projects.

C. Rebaseline scope, schedule, and cost performance.

D. Update the final lessons learned register.

☑ **D.** As a part of closing the project, you are required to update the final lessons learned for the completed project.

☒ **A** is incorrect because the project start and end dates are recorded in the final project documents. **B** is incorrect because a resource breakdown structure for future projects is not considered during the closing phase of the current project. **C** is incorrect because projects are not rebaselined at the end of a phase or project.

23. Your project had work done by a vendor. Inspections have been performed to ensure the work conforms to quality standards. Contract documentation has been audited by the contracting office. Before the contract can be closed, it has a stipulation that 75% adoption by users be achieved in the production environment. What does this exemplify?

    A. Collecting project or phase records

    B. Updating lessons learned

    C. Measuring stakeholder satisfaction

    D. Managing knowledge sharing and transfer

    ☑ **C.** The 75% adoption rate is an example of measuring stakeholder satisfaction, which is necessary for administrative closure, especially when it is called out as a contract term.

    ☒ **A, B,** and **D** are incorrect because none of these directly measure stakeholder satisfaction.

24. Because you are a PMP with 19 years of manufacturing experience, you have been awarded a one-year, fixed-price contract to lead a project to design and build electric bicycles. These new bicycles will use nucleovoltaic cells. The chief scientist at the company informs you that the nucleovoltaic cell is already being sold by another country in Europe. The board of directors has decided to buy the new technology, not make it. Your project is canceled—today. What is the next thing you should do?

    A. Release the project team so they can be reassigned to other projects immediately.

    B. Release all resources so they can be reassigned immediately.

    C. Implement the Close Project or Phase process.

    D. Return the remaining budget to the accounting department for reallocation.

    ☑ **C.** The Close Project or Phase process is performed even if the project is terminated before objectives are met. Close Project activities must also be performed at the end of each phase to satisfy the exit criteria from the prior phase and to justify proceeding to the next phase. At project end, the Close Project process administers the transfer of the project deliverable(s) to production and/or operations. Furthermore, lessons learned are gathered throughout the project phases; however, these will be documented, analyzed, and archived within the knowledge base, part of Organizational Process Assets, during the Close Project process for use by future projects or phases.

☒ **A** is incorrect because releasing the team is a part of Close Project or Phase. **B** is incorrect because, like A, it is a part of Close Project or Phase. **D** is incorrect because it also is a part of Close Project or Phase.

25. The Close Phase or Project process is used to close a contract. All the following procurement documentation is collected except:

    A. Payment records

    B. Information on cost performance

    C. Inspection results

    D. Buyer's meeting minutes

    ☑ **D.** Buyer's meeting minutes can be used to formalize the completion of a contract. They are not usually a part of procurement documentation.

    ☒ **A** is incorrect because payment records are transactions that would be gathered during execution, and the total would be useful in closing. **B** is incorrect because cost performance is important to contract closure. **C** is incorrect because inspecting contract deliverables and results is a part of contract closure.

26. Your agile project team has successfully demonstrated the final deliverable of a year-long project. Your CIO is sold on the iterative/adaptive approach. The PMO is asking you to join them and support agile for all projects throughout the company. The final product is in use, and the customers love it. As part of administrative closure, what is the best thing to do?

    A. Write the final report.

    B. Reassign project staff.

    C. Confirm data analysis techniques used in the project.

    D. Control quality.

    ☑ **A.** Write the final report would be completed next, before the project staff are reassigned, and before the organizational process assets are updated.

    ☒ **B** is incorrect because reassigning the project staff should be one of the last activities in the Close Project or Phase process. You may need them to help with writing the final report. **C** is incorrect because the final report is not part of organizational process assets updates. The best answer is to write the final report first, with help from the project team, and then update documents and the lessons learned repository. **D** is incorrect because Control Quality, which ensures the deliverables meet stakeholder acceptance, is accomplished before the Close Project or Phase process.

27. You are a senior project manager working on developing a new production line for ice pops. After six months of a one-year project, you are told that the company is losing money because of interest rate changes; your project is canceled, and all the team members, contractors, and full-time staff are to be let go. Until now the project was on target, on schedule, and on budget. You've seen this before—no money now, but more money next fiscal year. What is the best action to take next?

A. Document the reason for early termination and transition the complete and incomplete deliverables to production/support/operations.

B. Have a meeting with the executive sponsor and explain the sunk cost of your project.

C. Use the resource management plan for guidance and release the project resources.

D. See if another project needs a senior project manager.

☑ **A.** If a project is terminated prior to completion, you are to document the reason for early termination and transition the complete and incomplete deliverables to production/support/operations.

☒ **B** is incorrect because sunk cost is money that has already been spent and cannot be recovered. Logic dictates that because sunk costs will not change—no matter what actions are taken—they should not play a role in decision making. **C** is incorrect because you will release resources after you perform the activities in the Close Project or Phase process. **D** is incorrect because yes, after you complete answers **A** and **C**, it will be time to have a look around the company for another assignment.

28. Your project is complete. It was the first project in your company to use the agile approach. The deliverables were identified by the product owner. Some of the stakeholders are concerned about quality and have not signed off on the deliverables. The best way to collect feedback on the definition of "done" is to:

A. Create a wiki site for five days so stakeholders can provide their comments anonymously

B. Go back and look at all the lessons learned to evaluate strategic alignment

C. Set up a focus group after you send out a satisfaction survey

D. Conduct a product review meeting with the concerned stakeholders

☑ **D.** Conducting a product review meeting with the concerned stakeholders is the best and fastest way to address the quality concerns.

☒ **A** is incorrect because the best way to provide honest and encouraging feedback is through face-to-face communication. **B** is incorrect because lessons learned from a previous project may not help with the current quality concerns. **C** is incorrect because sending out a survey and then organizing a focus group will take too much time. Try to solve the quality issues now.

Project Management Institute (PMI) *Code of Ethics and Professional Conduct*

While there is no domain or tasks associated with PMI's *Code of Ethics and Professional Conduct* expectations, these two areas *are* tested on the PMP certification exam. The Code addresses what is right and proper to do, and the Conduct speaks to behavior expectations of PMI members as well as anyone who holds any of the PMI certifications. The Code and Conduct also extend to certification applicants and anyone who volunteers with PMI.

There are two primary reasons the Code and Conduct areas are tested: your work as a project manager must be able to be trusted, and there are expectations of you, given your participation in the community of all other PMPs. In your work as a project manager, the *Code of Ethics and Professional Conduct* guides your behavior within a project and with your stakeholders. In participating in the community of certified PMPs, there is an expectation that your word is your bond and that you will not share insider knowledge of the actual test questions on the exam. Signing the *Code of Ethics* is mandatory, and as a PMP you agree to be held to very high standards, including in terms of professional conduct. The *Code of Ethics and Professional Conduct* instills confidence in the project management profession and helps project managers become better practitioners.

Honesty, responsibility, respect, and fairness are the four values that drive ethical conduct for the project management profession. PMI's *Code of Ethics and Professional Conduct* applies these four values to the real-life practice of project management, where the best outcome is the most ethical one. The PMP exam tests a candidate on these four values. There are two aspects to each value: aspirational standards and mandatory standards. Aspirational standards set the threshold of conduct we strive to uphold as practitioners. Mandatory standards establish firm requirements for practitioner behavior and, in some cases, limit or prohibit that behavior.

There are approximately 10 to 15 questions covering the *Code of Ethics and Professional Conduct* on the PMP exam. The 25 practice questions in this chapter are mapped to the style and frequency of question types on this topic you will see on the PMP exam.

1. Practitioners in the project management profession use the *Code of Ethics and Professional Conduct* as a reference. In this context, the statement that all project managers are committed to doing what is right and honorable refers to:

   A. Persons to whom the code applies

   B. Vision and purpose

   C. Structure of the code

   D. Values that support the code

2. What is the purpose of the *Code of Ethics and Professional Conduct* in project management?

   A. Keep unqualified project managers out of contracts.

   B. Enable prosecution of poorly performing project managers.

   C. Identify project managers who are not qualified.

   D. Instill confidence in the project management profession.

3. What was the basis used by practitioners in the project management community to develop the *Code of Ethics and Professional Conduct*?

   A. Experience of successful negotiations for budgets

   B. Contract law as practiced in participating countries

   C. International legal standards and procedures

   D. Values that formed decision making and guided actions

4. Jason knows that after he became a PMP, he needs 60 hours of professional development units (PDUs) in a three-year cycle to maintain his certification. As part of his year-end personal planning, he has a look at his profile and is shocked to discover that he needs 49 PDUs in the next four months. He has three in-class project management courses, worth 20 PDUs each, scheduled in the next six months. What is the best thing for Jason to do?

   A. Go ahead and enter the PDUs on the PMI website because he is committed to taking the courses this year.

   B. He should not attempt to enter the PDUs on the PMI website before he takes the courses. This action violates the Honesty: Mandatory Standard—it is making a false statement.

   C. According to the PMI website, once a class is paid for, it is the same as attended. Enter the PDUs on the PMI website.

   D. He should not attempt to enter the PDUs on the PMI website before he takes the courses. PMI will revoke his PMP for making misleading or false statements.

5. As a project manager, Kimberly is expected to take ownership for the decisions she makes or fails to make, the actions she takes or fails to take, and the resulting consequences. What best fits this description of the conduct of a project manager, as defined in the Project Management Institute *Code of Ethics and Professional Conduct*?

   A. Responsibility

   B. Respectability

   C. Confidentiality

   D. Consistency

6. Breck has been selected to lead a worldwide IT conversion project. Her company acquired an outsourcing group from another country. Some of her team members will be assigned as part of a matrix project environment. After the project kickoff meeting, two of her teammates are laughing and joking "about the guy in the turban." What is the best thing for Breck to do?

   A. Talk to the two teammates one on one, and maybe hold a cultural sensitivity training session for the whole team.

   B. Stop everything, call another meeting, and talk about cultural bias with the whole team.

   C. Call the human resources department and get an appointment for the two teammates and Breck.

   D. Remove the two teammates from the conversion team and request two more team members from the matrix manager.

7. It is the duty of project managers to show high regard for themselves, for others, and for the resources entrusted to them. The Project Management Institute *Code of Ethics and Professional Conduct* refers to this behavior as:

   A. Honesty

   B. Responsibility

   C. Respect

   D. Fairness

8. In project meetings, William often takes time to listen to others' points of view, seeking to understand them. In a bidder conference, he overheard a procurement officer disclose some competitor pricing information to a prospective seller. The competitor and the prospective seller are both on the prequalified sellers list. Referring to the Project Management Institute *Code of Ethics and Professional Conduct,* what is the most appropriate action for William to take next?

   A. Publish the pricing information for all bidders in the meeting minutes.

   B. Prevent the procurement officer from attending any contractor conferences in the future.

   C. Issue a procurement statement of work, including selection criteria and pricing ranges.

   D. Escalate the issue to the procurement officer's manager.

9. Olivia Rae is in a project meeting and another project manager acts in a way that is insulting to another member of the team. She knows this is a breach of the Mandatory: Respect professional standard. What is the next best thing for Olivia Rae to do?

   A. Remind the team member, inside the meeting, that it is a *Code* violation to act in an abusive manner toward others.

   B. Remind the team member, outside the meeting, that it is a *Code* violation to act in an abusive manner toward others.

   C. Act impartially and fairly by reminding all team members, outside the meeting, about prejudice.

   D. Act impartially and fairly by reminding all team members, inside the meeting, about self-interest.

10. It is "crunch time" on Isaac's special project for the CEO. Isaac and his senior business analyst (SBA) have all the PowerPoint slides ready for the big presentation on Friday. If Isaac looks good in this meeting, it could mean a promotion to program manager. He explains the "look good = promotion" scenario to the SBA, and she agrees that it is okay just to put Isaac's name on the title slide. What should Isaac do now?

    A. Don't do it. It is a failure to disclose conflicts.

    B. Sure, it's okay. It is simply an example of a coworker helping Isaac out.

    C. Don't do it. It is an example of failure to recognize and respect intellectual property.

    D. Do it. This is an example of quid pro quo.

11. Colleen is a new PMP working as a part-time project manager on a new intelligent analytics system. She is "pretty sure" this new application will allow her company to trace every phone call made throughout the world. She decides to wait a while and see if her suspicions are true. Colleen's roommate is a reporter and overheard her talking on a burner phone to her lawyer about the situation at work. What would PMI say about Colleen's behavior?

    A. Something. Colleen needs to disclose this threat to national security.

    B. Nothing. It is only Colleen's opinion that the application will jeopardize the personal information of your customers.

    C. Nothing. It is Colleen's choice to work for a company that may be violating the *Code*.

    D. Something. PMI could bring disciplinary action, use sanctions against Colleen, and revoke her PMP certification for not reporting this unethical situation.

12. While negotiating a contract with a supplier, Renee realizes that she already knows one of the other parties in a professional capacity. The professional standard of Mandatory: Fairness applies in this situation. What is the best thing for Renee to do?

    A. Ask to be reassigned to another project.

    B. Nothing. Renee can act impartially and objectively.

    C. Disclose this professional capacity as a potential conflict of interest.

    D. Recognize the conflicted loyalties and move on to the contract stage.

13. Janel is the PMP Emeritus at JLH, Inc. She lives by the ethics and values of the *Code*. In your onboarding slide deck, Janel talks about embracing the *Code* and advancing the project management profession by becoming a PMP. What is the vision and purpose of the Project Management Institute *Code of Ethics and Professional Conduct*?

A. Aspire to be a PMP; never compromise our integrity or our values.

B. Articulate ideals; provides a roadmap to advancement.

C. Collaborate values; ensures all PMI members are professional practitioners.

D. Do what is right and honorable; describes the expectations we have for ourselves and our fellow practitioners.

14. When describing the culture that Sheryl tries to encourage in the project team, she tries to create an environment in which others feel safe to tell the truth, and Sheryl uses this as an example of appropriate behavior. The Project Management Institute *Code of Ethics and Professional Conduct* refers to this behavior as Aspirational: Honesty. What can Sheryl do to encourage the reporting of unethical or illegal conduct?

A. Adopt corporate policies to protect the person who reveals *Code* violations.

B. Set up a whistleblower department.

C. Offer incentives for employees who report illegal or unethical activities.

D. Bring violations of the *Code* to the attention of project team members.

15. While managing the contracts for a project, Hudson becomes aware that a team member is engaging in dishonest behavior for personal gain. Hudson is applying the professional standard of Mandatory: Honesty in this situation. What should Hudson do?

A. Hold a team meeting.

B. Disclose this behavior.

C. File a complaint with the employee assistance program.

D. Write a report about the seller and the type of contract.

16. Harper Grace is a consulting project manager temporarily assigned to the Axis Nuclear Power project. She is a subject matter expert on water treatment in a nuclear power plant. During the execution phase, she discovers that the water from the reactor is being filtered once, not three times, as stated in the project management plan. Harper Grace checked the risk management plan, and there is nothing in the risk register about "water treatment." She fears a catastrophic effect on the local drinking water. The steering committee says it is nothing to worry about because they are using special carbon filters—one filtering is enough. What should Harper Grace do?

A. Gather the facts; report her findings to the nearest city government.

B. Polish her resume and leave the project.

C. Stay on the project; she made a firm commitment to the Axis Company.

D. Stay on the project; have a meeting with the general contractor and voice her concerns.

17. Violation of the Project Management Institute *Code of Ethics and Professional Conduct* may result in which of the following?

   A. Sanctions by the PMI

   B. Legal proceedings

   C. Salary deductions

   D. Name shame

18. Cameron has been a PMP since 2004. He is developing an in-house class for his fellow project managers called "How to Pass the PMP Exam—on Your First—and ONLY Attempt." He has downloaded the PMP *Handbook* from the Project Management Institute website—for free—because he is a PMI member. How should Cameron handle copyright compliance?

   A. Develop his course; no need to say anything about using the *Handbook*.

   B. Admit where the *Handbook* came from and include the copyright page in each handout.

   C. Print copies of the *Handbook* and distribute them to all the attendees.

   D. Do not use the *Handbook*; it is a violation of copyright law.

19. The *Code of Ethics and Professional Conduct* from PMI describes the professional standards to which members and certificants must adhere. These professional standards fall into all the following categories except:

   A. Earnestly seek to understand the truth.

   B. Be truthful in our conduct.

   C. Strive to create an environment in which others feel safe to tell the truth.

   D. Take credit as the project manager for achievements of the team members.

20. Connor is a PgMP, and his former college roommate, Mitzie, is a PMP. Mitzie posted on Facebook that she is an expert C++ programmer. And in the same post she says she worked on the NSA Cyber Project. Connor knows that one of these statements is not true. What should Connor do about Mitzie?

   A. When Mitzie gets her next job, Connor must tell PMP. Until then, do nothing; there is no ethics problem.

   B. Deal with Mitzie and tell her that he knows that she is guilty of false advertising. Ask her to delete the post, or Connor will report her to PMI.

   C. Do a screen print of the post and send it to PMI.

   D. This is not a problem for him. It is the buyer's problem. Do nothing.

21. Kelly ordered 12 laptops for her customers from an old-time supplier who has a lower cost than amazon.com. In October, Kelly gets a surprise visit from the owner of the laptop company. The owner hands Kelly an envelope with the words "World Series tickets" printed on the outside of the envelope. What is the best thing for Kelly to do?

    A. Accept the tickets. She knew nothing about tickets when she purchased the laptops.

    B. Give the envelope back immediately; it is an unacceptable bribe.

    C. Report the owner to the Better Business Bureau.

    D. Keep the tickets and share them with her boss and other corporate officers.

22. Ryan is a certified PMP and a PMI-ACP running a project using Scrum and lean Agile. He has developed a "how to" manual using Chapter 4 from the PMBOK Guide and the glossary from the *Agile Practice Guide*. When you read over the manual, you don't see any registered trademark symbols from either source. What is the best thing for you do at this point?

    A. Have a meeting with the legal department and bring the manual.

    B. Take a picture of three pages of the manual and send it to PMI.

    C. This is not a problem. The manual is only being used internally. Intellectual property rights are an external issue.

    D. Meet with Ryan, face to face, and show him the PMI *Code of Ethics and Professional Conduct*. Ryan must get permission to use PMI materials.

23. Harley, your boss, has been a project manager for nearly 30 years and is nearing retirement. At happy hour on Friday, you saw Harley drink six beers in one hour. Then he stubbed out his cigar, fumbled in his pocket for his car keys, and stumbled out the door, ignoring your petition to call him a cab, and then drove 14 miles home. On Monday, what do you tell Harley about his status with PMI?

    A. Nothing. Harley is your boss and what he does outside of work is his own business and no concern of PMI.

    B. PMI is only concerned with professional conduct at work, and Harley must be an effective project manager if he has been at the same company for nearly 30 years.

    C. Harley violated one of the PMI responsibilities of membership, which is to "make decisions and take actions based on the best interests of society, public safety, and the environment."

    D. Harley is violating his social responsibilities to the company and to PMI.

24. Ethan is a new PMP. After a long, tiring budget meeting, he whines about the professional conduct requirements of PMI. What do you tell Ethan about why it is important to be an ethical PMI member?

   A. It maintains the integrity of PMI as an organization.

   B. It is good for morale, job security, and profits.

   C. It ensures all PMPs make ethical decisions and behave in a professional manner.

   D. It instills confidence in the project management profession and helps an individual become a better practitioner.

25. Leslie is the president of the PMI chapter in a capital city of a South America country. She is a senior project manager for a U.S.-based oil company. The company is bidding on offshore oil rights. Leslie knows that it is a "generally accepted business practice" to pay a "service fee" to the members of the preferred buyers selection committee. What is Leslie to do?

   A. Pay the "service fee." PMI agrees that Leslie should obey local customs.

   B. Pay the "service fee." Because it is a "generally accepted business practice," Leslie has no problem.

   C. Do not pay the "service fee." It is a bribe in the United States, and Leslie works for a U.S.-based oil company.

   D. Do not pay the "service fee." Find another way to pay a "service fee" based on the preferred buyer list that does not violate U.S. law.

1. B
2. D
3. D
4. B
5. A
6. A
7. C

8. D
9. B
10. C
11. B
12. C
13. D
14. A

15. B
16. A
17. A
18. B
19. D
20. B
21. B

22. D
23. C
24. D
25. C

1. Practitioners in the project management profession use the *Code of Ethics and Professional Conduct* as a reference. In this context, the statement that all project managers are committed to doing what is right and honorable refers to:

   A. Persons to whom the code applies

   B. Vision and purpose

   C. Structure of the code

   D. Values that support the code

   ☑ **B.** Practitioners in the project management profession are committed to doing what is right and honorable as defined in the *Code of Ethics and Professional Conduct* vision statement.

   ☒ **A, C,** and **D** are incorrect because they are details of applicability, structure, and values.

2. What is the purpose of the *Code of Ethics and Professional Conduct* in project management?

   A. Keep unqualified project managers out of contracts.

   B. Enable prosecution of poorly performing project managers.

   C. Identify project managers who are not qualified.

   D. Instill confidence in the project management profession.

   ☑ **D.** One of the purposes of the *Code of Ethics and Professional Conduct* is to instill confidence in the project management profession.

   ☒ **A, B,** and **C** are incorrect because keeping unqualified project managers out of contracts, enabling prosecution of poorly performing project managers, and identifying project managers who are not qualified are not the purposes of this *Code*.

3. What was the basis used by practitioners in the project management community to develop the *Code of Ethics and Professional Conduct*?

   A. Experience of successful negotiations for budgets

   B. Contract law as practiced in participating countries

   C. International legal standards and procedures

   D. Values that formed decision making and guided actions

   ☑ **D.** The basis used to develop the *Code of Ethics and Professional Conduct* were values that formed decision making and guided actions.

   ☒ **A, B,** and **C** are incorrect because there are no contract law, international legal standards, or personal value statements in the *Code*.

4. Jason knows that after he became a PMP, he needs 60 hours of professional development units (PDUs) in a three-year cycle to maintain his certification. As part of his year-end personal planning, he has a look at his profile and is shocked to discover that he needs 49 PDUs in the next four months. He has three in-class project management courses, worth 20 PDUs each, scheduled in the next six months. What is the best thing for Jason to do?

   A. Go ahead and enter the PDUs on the PMI website because he is committed to taking the courses this year.

   B. He should not attempt to enter the PDUs on the PMI website before he takes the courses. This action violates the Honesty: Mandatory Standard—it is making a false statement.

   C. According to the PMI website, once a class is paid for, it is the same as attended. Enter the PDUs on the PMI website.

   D. He should not attempt to enter the PDUs on the PMI website before he takes the courses. PMI will revoke his PMP for making misleading or false statements.

   ☑ **B.** Jason must follow the *Code*. In the next four months, he may be able to earn more PDUs in another Education or Giving Back category.

   ☒ **A** is incorrect because any misrepresentation may lead to disciplinary action. **C** is incorrect because when reporting PDUs, Jason attests that the information he provides is correct. **D** is incorrect because, although Jason may consider it, he is making misleading or false statements. PMI may or may not revoke his PMP credential.

5. As a project manager, Kimberly is expected to take ownership for the decisions she makes or fails to make, the actions she takes or fails to take, and the resulting consequences. What best fits this description of the conduct of a project manager, as defined in the Project Management Institute *Code of Ethics and Professional Conduct*?

   A. Responsibility

   B. Respectability

   C. Confidentiality

   D. Consistency

   ☑ **A.** Taking ownership for the decisions we make or fail to make, the actions we take or fail to take, and the resulting consequences is defined as the responsibility of project managers.

   ☒ **B** is incorrect because respectability is not defined. **C** and **D** are incorrect because confidentiality and consistency are not described and are not values as defined in the *Code*.

6. Breck has been selected to lead a worldwide IT conversion project. Her company acquired an outsourcing group from another country. Some of her team members will be assigned as part of a matrix project environment. After the project kickoff meeting, two of her teammates are laughing and joking "about the guy in the turban." What is the best thing for Breck to do?

A. Talk to the two teammates one on one, and maybe hold a cultural sensitivity training session for the whole team.

B. Stop everything, call another meeting, and talk about cultural bias with the whole team.

C. Call the human resources department and get an appointment for the two teammates and Breck.

D. Remove the two teammates from the conversion team and request two more team members from the matrix manager.

☑ A. It is our duty to deal with others who engage in disrespectful behaviors. It is the PM's responsibility to correct the disrespectful behavior and take preventive action. Knowing the norms and customs of others is part of the Respect: Aspirational Standard of the *Code of Ethics and Professional Conduct.*

☒ B is incorrect because talking to the whole team takes time away from their project work and is an example of "reward the guilty and punish the innocent." C is incorrect because conflict should be addressed early, in private, and using a collaborative (win-win) approach with the team members. If the negative action(s) continue, then formal procedures may be used. D is incorrect because replacing the two teammates on the conversion team will not foster an environment where diversity is valued. In fact, this decision could result in lower productivity and negative working relationships.

7. It is the duty of project managers to show high regard for themselves, for others, and for the resources entrusted to them. The Project Management Institute *Code of Ethics and Professional Conduct* refers to this behavior as:

A. Honesty

B. Responsibility

C. Respect

D. Fairness

☑ C. As project managers, showing high regard for ourselves, for others, and for the resources entrusted demonstrates respect.

☒ A, B, and D are incorrect because honesty, responsibility, and fairness are the other three values described in the Project Management Institute *Code of Ethics and Professional Conduct.*

8. In project meetings, William often takes time to listen to others' points of view, seeking to understand them. In a bidder conference, he overheard a procurement officer disclose some competitor pricing information to a prospective seller. The competitor and the prospective seller are both on the prequalified sellers list. Referring to the Project Management Institute *Code of Ethics and Professional Conduct,* what is the most appropriate action for William to take next?

   A. Publish the pricing information for all bidders in the meeting minutes.

   B. Prevent the procurement officer from attending any contractor conferences in the future.

   C. Issue a procurement statement of work, including selection criteria and pricing ranges.

   D. Escalate the issue to the procurement officer's manager.

   ☑ **D.** We report unethical or illegal conduct to appropriate management.

   ☒ **A** is incorrect because not all bidders are authorized to have the pricing information. **B** is incorrect because preventing the procurement officer from attending any contractor conferences in the future might be needed; this action does not address the abuse of intellectual property. **C** is incorrect because procurement statement of work, selection criteria, and pricing ranges could be used in proposal evaluation—long after the bidder conference is held.

9. Olivia Rae is in a project meeting and another project manager acts in a way that is insulting to another member of the team. She knows this is a breach of the Mandatory: Respect professional standard. What is the next best thing for Olivia Rae to do?

   A. Remind the team member, inside the meeting, that it is a *Code* violation to act in an abusive manner toward others.

   B. Remind the team member, outside the meeting, that it is a *Code* violation to act in an abusive manner toward others.

   C. Act impartially and fairly by reminding all team members, outside the meeting, about prejudice.

   D. Act impartially and fairly by reminding all team members, inside the meeting, about self-interest.

   ☑ **B.** Acting in a way that is abusive to another member of the team is a breach of the Mandatory Respect Standard. And this type of conflict is best handled in private.

   ☒ **A** is incorrect because this conflict is personal and, if managed properly, the resolution can build trust and strengthen relationships. **C** is incorrect because this action is breach of the Mandatory Respect Standard, not Fairness: Conduct Free From Prejudice. **D** is incorrect because this is a breach of the Mandatory Respect Standard, not Fairness: Conduct Free From Self-Interest.

10. It is "crunch time" on Isaac's special project for the CEO. Isaac and his senior business analyst (SBA) have all the PowerPoint slides ready for the big presentation on Friday. If Isaac looks good in this meeting, it could mean a promotion to program manager. He explains the "look good = promotion" scenario to the SBA, and she agrees that it is okay just to put Isaac's name on the title slide. What should Isaac do now?

A. Don't do it. It is a failure to disclose conflicts.

B. Sure, it's okay. It is simply an example of a coworker helping Isaac out.

C. Don't do it. It is an example of failure to recognize and respect intellectual property.

D. Do it. This is an example of quid pro quo.

☑ **C.** Recognizing and respecting intellectual property is a Responsibility: Mandatory Standard in the Project Management Institute *Code of Ethics and Professional Conduct*.

☒ **A** is incorrect because this situation is not about a conflict of interest. **B** is incorrect because although the SBA may have given Isaac permission to not put her name on the title slide, still he is taking credit for someone else's work. **D** is incorrect because Isaac doesn't know whether the research was done properly.

11. Colleen is a new PMP working as a part-time project manager on a new intelligent analytics system. She is "pretty sure" this new application will allow her company to trace every phone call made throughout the world. She decides to wait a while and see if her suspicions are true. Colleen's roommate is a reporter and overheard her talking on a burner phone to her lawyer about the situation at work. What would PMI say about Colleen's behavior?

A. Something. Colleen needs to disclose this threat to national security.

B. Nothing. It is only Colleen's opinion that the application will jeopardize the personal information of your customers.

C. Nothing. It is Colleen's choice to work for a company that may be violating the Code.

D. Something. PMI could bring disciplinary action, use sanctions against Colleen, and revoke her PMP certification for not reporting this unethical situation.

☑ **B.** Only filing ethics complaints when they are substantiated by facts is an example of Mandatory: Responsibility.

☒ **A** is incorrect because in Aspirational: Respect, we do not gossip. **C** is incorrect because in Aspirational Honesty, we make decisions on correct and appropriate information. **D** is incorrect because Colleen hasn't done anything wrong or dishonorable.

12. While negotiating a contract with a supplier, Renee realizes that she already knows one of the other parties in a professional capacity. The professional standard of Mandatory: Fairness applies in this situation. What is the best thing for Renee to do?

A. Ask to be reassigned to another project.

B. Nothing. Renee can act impartially and objectively.

C. Disclose this professional capacity as a potential conflict of interest.

D. Recognize the conflicted loyalties and move on to the contract stage.

☑ **C.** Disclosure of potential conflict of interest is an example of Mandatory: Fairness.

☒ **A** is incorrect because it does not recognize that Renee has placed herself in a conflict-of-interest situation. **B** is incorrect because Renee must take corrective action even though she may believe she can act impartially and objectively. **D** is incorrect because recognizing the conflicted loyalties is one thing and taking corrective action (disclosure) is appropriate.

13. Janel is the PMP Emeritus at JLH, Inc. She lives by the ethics and values of the *Code*. In your onboarding slide deck, Janel talks about embracing the *Code* and advancing the project management profession by becoming a PMP. What is the vision and purpose of the Project Management Institute *Code of Ethics and Professional Conduct*?

    A. Aspire to be a PMP; never compromise our integrity or our values.

    B. Articulate ideals; provides a roadmap to advancement.

    C. Collaborate values; ensures all PMI members are professional practitioners.

    D. Do what is right and honorable; describes the expectations we have for ourselves and our fellow practitioners.

    ☑ **D.** To do what is right and honorable is the vision and describes the expectations we have for ourselves and our fellow practitioners, which is the purpose of the *Code*.

    ☒ **A** is incorrect because even though aspiring to be a PMP is a great idea, it is not in the *Code*. **B** is incorrect because articulate ideals, both aspirational and mandatory, is in the *Code*; providing a roadmap to advancement is not mentioned in the *Code*. The PMP certificate may lead to advancement. **C** is incorrect because the *Code* helps you become a better practitioner; it does not ensure professionalism.

14. When describing the culture that Sheryl tries to encourage in the project team, she tries to create an environment in which others feel safe to tell the truth, and Sheryl uses this as an example of appropriate behavior. The Project Management Institute *Code of Ethics and Professional Conduct* refers to this behavior as Aspirational: Honesty. What can Sheryl do to encourage the reporting of unethical or illegal conduct?

    A. Adopt corporate policies to protect the person who reveals *Code* violations.

    B. Set up a whistleblower department.

    C. Offer incentives for employees who report illegal or unethical activities.

    D. Bring violations of the *Code* to the attention of project team members.

    ☑ **A.** Adopting corporate policies to protect the person who reveals *Code* violations creates an environment in which others feel safe to tell the truth. It is an example of Aspirational: Honesty

☒ **B** is incorrect because setting up a whistleblower department will not make reporting easier. It lacks anonymity. **C** is incorrect because offering incentives for employees who report illegal or unethical activities may result in lack of trust by rewarding the act of reporting more than the truth of the report. **D** is incorrect because bringing violations of the *Code* to the attention of project team members may result in negative consequences.

15. While managing the contracts for a project, Hudson becomes aware that a team member is engaging in dishonest behavior for personal gain. Hudson is applying the professional standard of Mandatory: Honesty in this situation. What should Hudson do?

    A. Hold a team meeting.

    B. Disclose this behavior.

    C. File a complaint with the employee assistance program.

    D. Write a report about the seller and the type of contract.

    ☑ **B.** We are not dishonest and do not allow personal gain based on dishonesty. This is an example of Mandatory: Honesty.

    ☒ **A** is incorrect because team meetings are for decision making, issue resolution, lessons learned, and status updates. **C** is incorrect because the employee assistance program does not handle unethical/illegal behavior. **D** is incorrect because writing a report is not needed—yet. We disclose the dishonest behavior immediately.

16. Harper Grace is a consulting project manager temporarily assigned to the Axis Nuclear Power project. She is a subject matter expert on water treatment in a nuclear power plant. During the execution phase, she discovers that the water from the reactor is being filtered once, not three times, as stated in the project management plan. Harper Grace checked the risk management plan, and there is nothing in the risk register about "water treatment." She fears a catastrophic effect on the local drinking water. The steering committee says it is nothing to worry about because they are using special carbon filters—one filtering is enough. What should Harper Grace do?

    A. Gather the facts; report her findings to the nearest city government.

    B. Polish her resume and leave the project.

    C. Stay on the project; she made a firm commitment to the Axis Company.

    D. Stay on the project; have a meeting with the general contractor and voice her concerns.

    ☑ **A.** Gathering the facts and reporting her findings to the nearest city government is part of her Responsibility: Aspirational standard to make decisions and take actions based on public safety.

    ☒ **B** is incorrect because leaving the project may be an option for Harper Grace and her career, but it does not address the possible harm to the city residents from the improper filtering of the nuclear water. **C** is incorrect because she has a duty to report the problem after she knows about it. **D** is incorrect because reporting a problem is first; she can attempt to fix it later.

17. Violation of the Project Management Institute *Code of Ethics and Professional Conduct* may result in which of the following?

A. Sanctions by the PMI

B. Legal proceedings

C. Salary deductions

D. Name shame

☑ **A.** Violation of the Project Management Institute *Code of Ethics and Professional Conduct* may result in sanctions by the PMI.

☒ **B** is incorrect because there are no legal implications directly implied by the *Code*. **C** is incorrect because salary deductions are for the employer to consider. **D** is incorrect because name and shame may be done by the press.

18. Cameron has been a PMP since 2004. He is developing an in-house class for his fellow project managers called "How to Pass the PMP Exam—on Your First—and ONLY Attempt." He has downloaded the PMP *Handbook* from the Project Management Institute website—for free—because he is a PMI member. How should Cameron handle copyright compliance?

A. Develop his course; no need to say anything about using the *Handbook*.

B. Admit where the *Handbook* came from and include the copyright page in each handout.

C. Print copies of the *Handbook* and distribute them to all the attendees.

D. Do not use the *Handbook*; it is a violation of copyright law.

☑ **B.** Copyright law states that "each copy includes a notice of copyright" of the *Handbook* must be noted. It would be a clever idea to check with PMI and explain your use of the *Handbook* in your not-for-profit/educational course.

☒ **A** is incorrect because Cameron cannot abuse the intellectual property of others. **C** is incorrect because distributing a copy to all attendees does not address copyright compliance. **D** is incorrect because it is okay to use the *Handbook* if you follow the copyright law, such as acknowledging authorship and ownership.

19. The *Code of Ethics and Professional Conduct* from PMI describes the professional standards to which members and certificants must adhere. These professional standards fall into all the following categories except:

A. Earnestly seek to understand the truth.

B. Be truthful in our conduct.

C. Strive to create an environment in which others feel safe to tell the truth.

D. Take credit as the project manager for achievements of the team members.

☑ **D.** We avoid taking credit for others' work or achievements.

☒ **A, B,** and **C** are incorrect because they are subcategories of the Honesty: Aspirational Standards category.

20. Connor is a PgMP, and his former college roommate, Mitzie, is a PMP. Mitzie posted on Facebook that she is an expert C++ programmer. And in the same post she says she worked on the NSA Cyber Project. Connor knows that one of these statements is not true. What should Connor do about Mitzie?

   A. When Mitzie gets her next job, Connor must tell PMP. Until then, do nothing; there is no ethics problem.

   B. Deal with Mitzie and tell her that he knows that she is guilty of false advertising. Ask her to delete the post, or Connor will report her to PMI.

   C. Do a screen print of the post and send it to PMI.

   D. This is not a problem for him. It is the buyer's problem. Do nothing.

   ☑ **B.** We accept only those assignments that are consistent with our background, experience, skills, and qualifications.

   ☒ **A** and **D** are incorrect because, as a PMI member or certificant, Connor has a responsibility to report possible violations of the *Code of Ethics and Professional Conduct*. **C** is incorrect because Connor needs to first discuss the situation with Mitzie, following the "reasonable and clear factual basis" rule.

21. Kelly ordered 12 laptops for her customers from an old-time supplier who has a lower cost than amazon.com. In October, Kelly gets a surprise visit from the owner of the laptop company. The owner hands Kelly an envelope with the words "World Series tickets" printed on the outside of the envelope. What is the best thing for Kelly to do?

   A. Accept the tickets. She knew nothing about tickets when she purchased the laptops.

   B. Give the envelope back immediately; it is an unacceptable bribe.

   C. Report the owner to the Better Business Bureau.

   D. Keep the tickets and share them with her boss and other corporate officers.

   ☑ **B.** It is illegal to accept the envelope with "World Series tickets." It is a kickback.

   ☒ **A** and **D** are incorrect because although it might be tempting, we obey the law and the envelope should be avoided. **C** is incorrect because unless the laptop company has done something illegal, we would not do this.

22. Ryan is a certified PMP and a PMI-ACP running a project using Scrum and lean Agile. He has developed a "how to" manual using Chapter 4 from the PMBOK Guide and the glossary from the *Agile Practice Guide*. When you read over the manual, you don't see any registered trademark symbols from either source. What is the best thing for you do at this point?

A. Have a meeting with the legal department and bring the manual.

B. Take a picture of three pages of the manual and send it to PMI.

C. This is not a problem. The manual is only being used internally. Intellectual property rights are an external issue.

D. Meet with Ryan, face to face, and show him the PMI *Code of Ethics and Professional Conduct*. Ryan must get permission to use PMI materials.

☑ **D.** Talking to Ryan is the best thing to do.

☒ **A** and **B** are incorrect. If Ryan refuses to act on lifting sections from the documents, these actions might be required. **C** is incorrect because intellectual property rights apply to internal and external use.

23. Harley, your boss, has been a project manager for nearly 30 years and is nearing retirement. At happy hour on Friday, you saw Harley drink six beers in one hour. Then he stubbed out his cigar, fumbled in his pocket for his car keys, and stumbled out the door, ignoring your petition to call him a cab, and then drove 14 miles home. On Monday, what do you tell Harley about his status with PMI?

A. Nothing. Harley is your boss and what he does outside of work is his own business and no concern of PMI.

B. PMI is only concerned with professional conduct at work, and Harley must be an effective project manager if he has been at the same company for nearly 30 years.

C. Harley violated one of the PMI responsibilities of membership, which is to "make decisions and take actions based on the best interests of society, public safety, and the environment."

D. Harley is violating his social responsibilities to the company and to PMI.

☑ **C.** You saw Harley breaking the law (public safety) and you are bound by the *Code* to talk to him about it.

☒ **A** and **B** are incorrect because even though they might sound good, they are not true. **D** is incorrect because you do not have a social responsibility to your company or to PMI.

24. Ethan is a new PMP. After a long, tiring budget meeting, he whines about the professional conduct requirements of PMI. What do you tell Ethan about why it is important to be an ethical PMI member?

A. It maintains the integrity of PMI as an organization.

B. It is good for morale, job security, and profits.

C. It ensures all PMPs make ethical decisions and behave in a professional manner.

D. It instills confidence in the project management profession and helps an individual become a better practitioner.

   ☑ **D.** This is in the Vision and Purpose section of the *Code of Ethics and Professional Conduct*.

   ☒ **A, B,** and **C** are incorrect because they are consequences of ethical behavior.

25. Leslie is the president of the PMI chapter in a capital city of a South America country. She is a senior project manager for a U.S.-based oil company. The company is bidding on offshore oil rights. Leslie knows that it is a "generally accepted business practice" to pay a "service fee" to the members of the preferred buyers selection committee. What is Leslie to do?

   A. Pay the "service fee." PMI agrees that Leslie should obey local customs.

   B. Pay the "service fee." Because it is a "generally accepted business practice," Leslie has no problem.

   C. Do not pay the "service fee." It is a bribe in the United States, and Leslie works for a U.S.-based oil company.

   D. Do not pay the "service fee." Find another way to pay a "service fee" based on the preferred buyer list that does not violate U.S. law.

   ☑ **C.** Leslie works for a U.S.-based oil company and she is subject to U.S. laws.

   ☒ **A** is incorrect because, although PMI approves of obeying local customs, it does not approve of breaking the law. Leslie works for a U.S.-based oil company and she is subject to U.S. laws. **B** and **D** are incorrect because they are attempting to use other ways to pay the "service fee"—which is really a bribe.

Pre-Assessment Test

Instructions

Before completing the practice questions in the chapters of this book, you should first complete this pre-assessment test to gauge your knowledge of the project management terms and concepts that you need to know and understand to pass the PMP® exam.

The 30 questions in this pre-assessment test are mapped to the content, style, tone, difficulty, and frequency of question types you will see on the PMP exam.

The weighting of Chapters 1, 2, and 3 of the *PMBOK Guide, Sixth Edition*, the PMI *Code of Ethics and Professional Responsibility*, and the PMP *Examination Content Outline* used in the real PMP exam are also mirrored in this activity, as shown in the following table:

Chapters	Number of Pre-Assessment Items
1.0 PMP Foundations	3
2.0 The Initiating Domain	2
3.0 The Planning Domain	6
4.0 The Executing Domain	8
5.0 The Monitoring and Controlling Domain	7
6.0 The Closing Domain	1
7.0 Project Management Institute (PMI) Code of Ethics and Professional Conduct	3
Total:	**30**

To mimic the real exam environment, you should allocate 40 minutes of uninterrupted time to answer these questions. Make sure you are in a quiet space with no distractions. Then set a timer for 40 minutes and begin this activity. Allowing more than 40 minutes will yield inaccurate results.

Do not use any reference materials or assistance while taking the pre-assessment test. Complete all 30 questions before checking your results.

When you are done, you can use the Quick Answer Key along with the in-depth Answers sections to evaluate your responses. Keep track of the number of questions you answer correctly and compare this number with the table found in the Analyzing Your Results section at the end of this activity. This table will give you valuable feedback based on the number of correct answers you gave. You should also compare the answers you missed with the objective map at the end of this activity to identify areas that you need to focus on as you study.

Are you ready? Set your timer for 40 minutes and begin!

1. You must present your project budget to the project sponsor for approval. You are anticipating some of the questions that she may ask about how the project benefits the organization. The following table shows expected cash flow for five years, given project completion in Year 1. What is the payback period for this project?

End of Year	Cash In	Cash Out
1	–	450,000
2	250,000	200,000
3	450,000	50,000
4	350,000	50,000
5	300,000	50,000

   A. Two years

   B. Three years

   C. Four years

   D. Five years

2. You have been assigned as project manager for a project to develop a new line of microwave cooking devices. You understand that projects drive change in organizations. The project seems to be a clever idea. What is the next thing you should do?

   A. Determine the link to the strategic objectives of the organization and the business value of the project.

   B. Progressively elaborate the project management plan.

   C. Start developing the project charter.

   D. Set up a portfolio review board to engage with the right stakeholders.

3. You have been asked by the project management team to determine the best development life cycle for the new microwave cooking devices project. Customer value and quality will be incorporated in real time during development. Your most appropriate response to this request is to:

   A. Indicate that this is not a normal project manager decision; you are willing to discuss the request with the project sponsor.

   B. Appoint a committee to investigate the idea and then interview key stakeholders about high-level business requirements.

   C. Choose an adaptive life cycle: agile, iterative, or incremental. The key stakeholders will be continuously involved, and the requirements will be elaborated frequently during delivery.

   D. Draw a continuum of project life cycles and consider the risk and cost of the initial planning effort.

4. You have been asked to create an end-to-end manufacturing process for your company's next-generation semiconductor fabrication line. This new fabrication line is time critical, and industry competition is fierce. Many of the older employees who have traditionally worked on the fabrication lines have helped the company be successful using ad hoc processes and heuristic knowledge. As the project manager, you want to use comprehensive project management best practices wherever possible to maximize the chances of success. Which of the following would you do first?

   A. Calculate the project timeline and initial budget.

   B. Recruit the key project skills as early as possible.

   C. Develop the project charter and scope of work.

   D. Write a comprehensive change control process.

5. You are a newly hired project manager working on your first project at a law firm with the goal of upgrading information security. The two managing partners at the law firm are used to getting their way and are pressuring you to meet only their needs and not to involve the remaining 30 lawyers in the project. How will the Identify Stakeholders process assist you with the task?

   A. Planning how you will control stakeholders and their impact throughout the project

   B. Establishing an approach to increase the support and minimize opposition of stakeholders

   C. Creating a systematic approach to identifying stakeholders

   D. Setting the tone for document creation to be used on the project

6. A residual risk is assessed to have a probability of 0.1 and an impact value of $50,000. What is the EMV of the residual risk?

   A. $1,000

   B. $5,000

   C. $50,000

   D. EMV does not apply to residual risk.

7. You are a construction project manager working on a new office building in the outskirts of your city. You are developing your project management plan that assumes a dedicated project team. The plan for the project forecasts a two-year schedule. As part of the plan, you need to consider:

   A. Potential increases in resource costs

   B. The payback period for every year of the project

   C. Design changes based on external dependencies

   D. The need for annual cost/benefit analyses

8. Given the planning data for your project, SEMAJ, you have identified the need to use several contractors for three parts of the multiyear project. As you determine specific procurement strategies after analyzing the involved WBS elements, your next step is to:

A. Analyze the project scope statement

B. Analyze the product description

C. Prepare a procurement management plan

D. Consider make-or-buy analysis

9. You have a team of 12 people who are working on various parts of a project whose purpose is to facilitate the buying and selling of big-box stores that have closed. You have a WBS, and now you are developing your scope baseline. Which of the following should you include in your project schedule?

A. Schedule decomposition

B. Stakeholder issue tracking

C. Activities related to stakeholder engagement

D. A requirements traceability matrix

10. You just graduated from a prestigious university and you have been appointed to your first job as a project manager. Your project charter has been approved, and you now have a dedicated team who is working with you in planning the project. So far, you have prepared your scope and quality management plans and now are beginning to work on other plans that will be included in your project management plan. In the project management plan, you need to describe how performance reports will be prepared and distributed. Your program manager pointed out that she wanted regular updates, but she did not want to see many metrics collected that did not add value. You and your team have decided that the best approach is to choose metrics that:

A. Show how your project contributes to the organization's bottom line

B. Show the progress according to the triple constraints

C. Use earned value management to assess project performance and progress

D. Show project management and team delivery rates

11. The project has produced a requirements traceability matrix that links requirements to their origin and traces them throughout the project life cycle. Which statement describes the purpose of the requirements traceability matrix?

A. It describes in detail the project's deliverables and the work required to create those deliverables and includes product and project scope description.

B. It ensures that requirements approved in the requirements documentation are delivered at the end of the project and helps manage changes to the product scope.

C. It is a narrative description of products or services to be delivered by the project and is received from the customer for external projects.

D. It provides the necessary information from a business standpoint to determine whether the project is worth the required investment.

12. You are leading and performing the work defined in the project management plan. Which of the following actions would be least helpful to you?

   A. Allocate available resources.

   B. Manage organizational interfaces.

   C. Analyze work performance data.

   D. Leverage prior organizational knowledge.

13. A key benefit of the Manage Team process is that it:

   A. Requires subject matter experts to create sustainable solutions

   B. Selects team members who can deal with high rates of change

   C. Implements a zero-sum reward and recognition system for the team

   D. Influences team behavior to optimize project performance

14. Which of the following trends and emerging practices in procurement management could have a negative effect on the success of your project?

   A. Advances in tools

   B. Permanent engagements

   C. More advanced risk management

   D. Changing contracting processes

15. Seller proposals is an input to:

   A. Plan Procurement Management

   B. Request Procurements

   C. Procurement Strategy

   D. Conduct Procurements

16. Finally, after three months of negotiating with the resource allocation manager, a new business analyst, Sharon, has been added to your current project team. Given the introduction of a new team member, which team development stage might your team fall into?

   A. Forming

   B. Storming

   C. Norming

   D. Performing

17. The Manage Project Knowledge process consists of:

   A. Managing tacit and explicit knowledge

   B. Knowledge sharing and codifying implicit knowledge

   C. Making sure tools and techniques are shared by the stakeholders

   D. Ensuring that all stakeholder knowledge needs are met

18. Design for X (DfX) is a(n):

    A. Set of technical guidelines for the optimization of a specific aspect of the product design

    B. Situational guideline for using agile approaches

    C. Specific design tool that addresses specific aspects of a mature product

    D. Agile tool used by everybody throughout the project

19. You are working in an adaptive environment. You want to streamline team member access to information and have transparent decision making. The most effective project reporting technique in this situation would be to:

    A. Set up an intranet site

    B. Email and fax project status reports

    C. Form an online community

    D. Use information radiators

20. You have been assigned as the project manager on a project focused on developing a new process for your organization called configuration management. Which of the following identifies the functions this process performs?

    A. Identifying, submitting, approving, tracking, and validating changes

    B. Submitting, approving, tracking, measuring, and validating changes

    C. Identifying, requesting, assessing, validating, and communicating changes

    D. Reviewing, approving, tracking, validating, and proving changes

21. You have been working on defining the procedures by which the project scope and product scope can be changed. In which process is your team engaged?

    A. Validate Scope

    B. Plan Configuration Management

    C. Initial Scope Definition

    D. Control Scope

22. A consultant has been reviewing your Monitor Risks process outputs. She lists many actions that are required to bring the project into compliance with the project management plan. What are these actions called?

    A. Recommended preventive actions

    B. Risk register updates

    C. Recommended corrective actions

    D. Project management plan updates

23. The project you are managing has a problem that requires the contract with a seller to be modified. The alteration to the contract is in accordance with the change control terms of the contract and project. The best time to make this change to the contract is:

    A. Never; the contract cannot be modified at any time

    B. At any time, regardless of the response from the seller

    C. At any time prior to the contract being awarded to the seller

    D. At any time prior to contract closure by mutual consent

24. What is the objective of the use of a procurement audit on a project when conducted in the Close Project or Phase process?

    A. Identify when legal action should be started.

    B. Terminate the nonperforming suppliers' contracts.

    C. Identify who signed the nonperforming contracts.

    D. Identify success and failure for use in future contracts.

25. You assign one of your junior staff to track the actual start and finish of activities and milestones to ensure they are being performed against the planned timeline. They report regularly any deviations and keep the plan updated as changes occur. Which of the following processes is most consistent with these activities?

    A. Control Scope

    B. Control Schedule

    C. Monitor Communications

    D. Monitor Risks

26. It is imperative that you keep your budget in control. Project governance has been established to keep budgets within 10% of what was planned and report weekly when costs are more or less than this threshold. Which of the following facets of cost control is least useful in controlling your budget?

    A. Contracting outsource services vs. using capable in-house staff

    B. Holding down costs so the project remains on budget

    C. Bringing the project back on budget when an overrun occurs

    D. Identifying opportunities to return project funding to the enterprise

27. As the project manager for the "Go Green!" project, you have prepared your final project report, which includes your lessons learned. You then had a meeting with as many members of your project team that were available to review them. Your next step is to:

    A. Add items as appropriate to the final report

    B. Prepare your knowledge management repository

    C. Promulgate meeting minutes to the members of the steering committee

    D. Ask attendees if they can remain with the project as needed so closure can occur according to organizational policies

28. Joe knows that after he became a PMP, he needs 60 hours of professional development units (PDUs) in a three-year cycle to maintain his certification. As part of his year-end personal planning, he has a look at his profile and is shocked to discover that he needs 49 PDUs in the next four months. He has three in-class project management courses, worth 20 PDUs each, scheduled in the next six months. What is the best thing for Joe to do?

   A. Go ahead and enter the PDUs on the PMI website if he is committed to taking the courses this year.

   B. Do not attempt to enter the PDUs on the PMI website before he takes the courses. This action violates the Honesty: Mandatory Standard—it is making a false statement.

   C. According to the PMI website, once a class is paid for, it is the same as attended. Enter the PDUs on the PMI website.

   D. Do not attempt to enter the PDUs on the PMI website before he takes the courses. PMI will revoke his PMP for making misleading or false statements.

29. It is "crunch time" on your special project for the CEO. You and your senior business analyst (SBA) have all the PowerPoint slides ready for the big presentation on Friday. If you look good in this meeting, it could mean a promotion to program manager. You explain the "look good = promotion" scenario to the SBA, and she agrees that it is okay just to put your name on the title slide. What should you do?

   A. Don't do it. It is a failure to disclose conflicts.

   B. Sure, it's okay. It is simply an example of a coworker helping you out.

   C. Don't do it. It is an example of failure to recognize and respect intellectual property.

   D. Do it. This is an example of quid pro quo.

30. You are a PgMP, and your former college roommate, Mitzie, is a PMP. Mitzie posted on Facebook that she is an expert C++ programmer. And in the same post she says she worked on the NSA Cyber Project. You know that one of these statements is not true. What should you do about Mitzie?

   A. When Mitzie gets her next job, you must tell PMP. Until then, do nothing; there is no ethics problem.

   B. Deal with Mitzie and tell her that you know that she is guilty of false advertising. Ask her to delete the post, or you will report her to PMI.

   C. Do a screen print of the post and send it to PMI.

   D. This is not a problem for you. It is the buyer's problem. Do nothing.

1. B	**11.** B	**21.** D
2. A	**12.** D	**22.** A
3. C	**13.** D	**23.** D
4. C	**14.** B	**24.** D
5. B	**15.** D	**25.** B
6. B	**16.** B	**26.** A
7. A	**17.** A	**27.** A
8. D	**18.** A	**28.** B
9. C	**19.** D	**29.** C
10. A	**20.** C	**30.** B

1. You must present your project budget to the project sponsor for approval. You are anticipating some of the questions that she may ask about how the project benefits the organization. The following table shows expected cash flow for five years, given project completion in Year 1. What is the payback period for this project?

End of Year	Cash In	Cash Out
1	–	450,000
2	250,000	200,000
3	450,000	50,000
4	350,000	50,000
5	300,000	50,000

   A. Two years

   B. Three years

   C. Four years

   D. Five years

   ☑ **B.** One common method a project manager uses to do an economic analysis of project benefits is the payback method. This method identifies where on the project schedule income exceeds the outgoing plus the initial investment. Brigham and Houston indicate that "The payback period, defined as the expected number of years required to recover the original investment, was the first formal method used to evaluate capital budgeting projects." For this project, it will take three years for the Cash In (0 + 250,000 + 450,000) to equal the Cash Out (450,000 + 200,000 + 50,000).

   ☒ **A, C,** and **D** are incorrect because the answers do not match the formula.

2. You have been assigned as project manager for a project to develop a new line of microwave cooking devices. You understand that projects drive change in organizations. The project seems to be a clever idea. What is the next thing you should do?

   A. Determine the link to the strategic objectives of the organization and the business value of the project.

   B. Progressively elaborate the project management plan.

   C. Start developing the project charter.

   D. Set up a portfolio review board to engage with the right stakeholders.

   ☑ **A.** After the project initiation context has been mapped to one of the four fundamental categories, you need to determine the link to the strategic objectives of the organization and the business value of the project.

☒ **B** is incorrect because progressively elaborating the project management plan happens during the Planning process group. **C** is incorrect because the project charter is developed in the Initiating process group. **D** is incorrect because you do not know if you will manage this project as a project, program, or portfolio. It is not time to set up a portfolio review board to engage with the right stakeholders.

3. You have been asked by the project management team to determine the best development life cycle for the new microwave cooking devices project. Customer value and quality will be incorporated in real time during development. Your most appropriate response to this request is to:

   A. Indicate that this is not a normal project manager decision; you are willing to discuss the request with the project sponsor.

   B. Appoint a committee to investigate the idea and then interview key stakeholders about high-level business requirements.

   C. Choose an adaptive life cycle: agile, iterative, or incremental. The key stakeholders will be continuously involved, and the requirements will be elaborated frequently during delivery.

   D. Draw a continuum of project life cycles and consider the risk and cost of the initial planning effort.

   ☑ **C.** The key stakeholders will be continuously involved, and the requirements will be elaborated frequently during delivery. Customer value and quality will be incorporated in real time during development. An adaptive life cycle—agile, iterative, or incremental—maps to these elements.

   ☒ **A** is incorrect because it is normal for the project manager and the project management team to determine the best life cycle for each project. **B** is incorrect because appointing a committee to investigate the idea and then interviewing key stakeholders about high-level business requirements does not fit with the project manager's roles in the sphere of influence. **D** is incorrect because drawing a continuum of project life cycles and considering the risk and cost of the initial planning effort depend on the life cycle being employed.

4. You have been asked to create an end-to-end manufacturing process for your company's next-generation semiconductor fabrication line. This new fabrication line is time critical, and industry competition is fierce. Many of the older employees who have traditionally worked on the fabrication lines have helped the company be successful using ad hoc processes and heuristic knowledge. As the project manager, you want to use comprehensive project management best practices wherever possible to maximize the chances of success. Which of the following would you do first?

   A. Calculate the project timeline and initial budget.

   B. Recruit the key project skills as early as possible.

C. Develop the project charter and scope of work.

D. Write a comprehensive change control process.

> ☑ **C.** A project charter with a well-defined scope of work is necessary to calculating timelines, calculating budgets, recruiting skills, and creating a change management process. The development of the project charter is part of the project initiation process.

> ☒ **A, B,** and **D** are incorrect because they are part of scope control and detailed planning, which follow project charter creation. **A** is incorrect because a project timeline and budget cannot be created without knowing what is in scope for the project. **B** is incorrect and should be undertaken as early as possible, but skills cannot be determined until the scope of the effort is determined. **D** is incorrect because the timing for a change control process is after an understanding of the scope of the effort is complete.

5. You are a newly hired project manager working on your first project at a law firm with the goal of upgrading information security. The two managing partners at the law firm are used to getting their way and are pressuring you to meet only their needs and not to involve the remaining 30 lawyers in the project. How will the Identify Stakeholders process assist you with the task?

A. Planning how you will control stakeholders and their impact throughout the project

B. Establishing an approach to increase the support and minimize opposition of stakeholders

C. Creating a systematic approach to identifying stakeholders

D. Setting the tone for document creation to be used on the project

> ☑ **B.** Stakeholder analysis is performed during the Identify Stakeholders process to define strategies to promote stakeholder engagement. It includes key stakeholders and their impact/influence, level of participation, and stakeholder groups.

> ☒ **A** is incorrect because the goal is not to control stakeholders. **C** is incorrect because the stakeholders should have already been identified; however, new ones may be added. **D** is incorrect because the stakeholder management strategy information is too sensitive to share.

6. A residual risk is assessed to have a probability of 0.1 and an impact value of $50,000. What is the EMV of the residual risk?

A. $1,000

B. $5,000

C. $50,000

D. EMV does not apply to residual risk.

> ☑ **B.** $5,000. The three steps to calculate EMV are as follows: 1. Assign a probability of occurrence for the risk. 2. Assign a monetary value for the impact of the risk when it occurs. 3. Multiply Step 1 and Step 2. The value you get after performing Step 3 is

the expected monetary value (EMV). This value is positive for opportunities (positive risks) and negative for threats (negative risks). Project risk management requires you to address both types of project risks.

☒ **A**, **C**, and **D** are incorrect because the answers do not come from following the three steps for calculating EMV.

7. You are a construction project manager working on a new office building in the outskirts of your city. You are developing your project management plan that assumes a dedicated project team. The plan for the project forecasts a two-year schedule. As part of the plan, you need to consider:

A. Potential increases in resource costs

B. The payback period for every year of the project

C. Design changes based on external dependencies

D. The need for annual cost/benefit analyses

☑ **A.** Direct costs include the salaries for dedicated team members on your project and contractors that provide support exclusively to your project. In multiyear projects it is likely that resource costs will increase each year, and a prudent project manager will budget for these increases.

☒ **B.** The payback period formula is used to determine the length of time it will take to recoup the initial amount invested on a project or investment. It is calculated at the beginning of the project. **C** is incorrect because "design changes based on external dependencies" may affect the project, but the PM controls these changes. **D** is incorrect because cost/benefit analysis is part of the business case and completed in the initiation stage of the project.

8. Given the planning data for your project, SEMAJ, you have identified the need to use several contractors for three parts of the multiyear project. As you determine specific procurement strategies after analyzing the involved WBS elements, your next step is to:

A. Analyze the project scope statement

B. Analyze the product description

C. Prepare a procurement management plan

D. Consider make-or-buy analysis

☑ **D.** Make-or-buy analysis (which can lead to a make-or-buy decision) is a process that PMs follow to know whether it's better for them to do the work in-house or pay for a third-party company to help the project team.

☒ **A** is incorrect because you have already analyzed the project scope statement to determine specific procurement strategies. **B** is incorrect because the product scope description is completed as part of scope definition. **C** is incorrect because the procurement management plan will include your procurement decisions after you complete the make-or-buy analysis.

9. You have a team of 12 people who are working on various parts of a project whose purpose is to facilitate the buying and selling of big-box stores that have closed. You have a WBS, and now you are developing your scope baseline. Which of the following should you include in your project schedule?

A. Schedule decomposition

B. Stakeholder issue tracking

C. Activities related to stakeholder engagement

D. A requirements traceability matrix

☑ C. The project schedule should include activities related to stakeholder engagement, risk mitigation, and project reviews.

☒ A is incorrect because the activities/tasks are already decomposed in a project schedule to work packages and then aggregated to build a project schedule. B is incorrect because stakeholder issues are listed in the stakeholder issue log. D is incorrect because a requirements traceability matrix is not included in a project schedule.

10. You just graduated from a prestigious university and you have been appointed to your first job as a project manager. Your project charter has been approved, and you now have a dedicated team who is working with you in planning the project. So far, you have prepared your scope and quality management plans and now are beginning to work on other plans that will be included in your project management plan. In the project management plan, you need to describe how performance reports will be prepared and distributed. Your program manager pointed out that she wanted regular updates, but she did not want to see many metrics collected that did not add value. You and your team have decided that the best approach is to choose metrics that:

A. Show how your project contributes to the organization's bottom line

B. Show the progress according to the triple constraints

C. Use earned value management to assess project performance and progress

D. Show project management and team delivery rates

☑ A. Key performance indicators (KPIs) should measure how the project contributes to tangible and intangible, as well as internal and external, benefits, such as profitability, goodwill, loyalty, etc.

☒ B is incorrect because reaching a reasonable trade-off among the three project constraints does not necessarily mean that the project is delivering business value. C is incorrect because EVM is used at the project level and does not show the direct and indirect measurements used to show the benefits (business value) realized. D is incorrect because there is no indication

11. The project has produced a requirements traceability matrix that links requirements to their origin and traces them throughout the project life cycle. Which statement describes the purpose of the requirements traceability matrix?

A. It describes in detail the project's deliverables and the work required to create those deliverables and includes product and project scope description.

B. It ensures that requirements approved in the requirements documentation are delivered at the end of the project and helps manage changes to the product scope.

C. It is a narrative description of products or services to be delivered by the project and is received from the customer for external projects.

D. It provides the necessary information from a business standpoint to determine whether the project is worth the required investment.

☑ **B.** The requirements traceability matrix ensures that requirements approved in the requirements documentation are delivered at the end of the project. The requirements traceability matrix also provides a structure for managing changes to product scope.

☒ **A** is incorrect because it describes the project scope statement. **C** is incorrect because this is the project statement of work used in developing the project charter. **D** is incorrect because it describes the project business case.

12. You are leading and performing the work defined in the project management plan. Which of the following actions would be least helpful to you?

A. Allocate available resources.

B. Manage organizational interfaces.

C. Analyze work performance data.

D. Leverage prior organizational knowledge.

☑ **D.** The question is asking about the Direct and Manage Project Work process. Leveraging prior organizational knowledge is expertise that could be considered in the expert judgment technique.

☒ **A**, **B**, and **C** are incorrect in this case because they are all project activities to complete project deliverables and accomplish established objectives.

13. A key benefit of the Manage Team process is that it:

A. Requires subject matter experts to create sustainable solutions

B. Selects team members who can deal with high rates of change

C. Implements a zero-sum reward and recognition system for the team

D. Influences team behavior to optimize project performance

☑ **D.** The Manage Team process influences team behavior, manages conflict, and resolves issues.

☒ **A** is incorrect because subject matter experts are used for expert knowledge based on an application area. **B** is incorrect because selecting change-tolerant team members would be useful in an agile environment. **C** is incorrect because project managers should avoid zero-sum awards where only one project team member can win the award, such as project team member of the month. These rewards can damage trust among the project team.

14. Which of the following trends and emerging practices in procurement management could have a negative effect on the success of your project?

    A. Advances in tools

    B. Permanent engagements

    C. More advanced risk management

    D. Changing contracting processes

    ☑ B. Trial engagements are used to evaluate potential partners.

    ☒ A, C, and D are incorrect because all three are recognized as major trends in procurement that positively affect the success rate of projects.

15. Seller proposals is an input to:

    A. Plan Procurement Management

    B. Request Procurements

    C. Procurement Strategy

    D. Conduct Procurements

    ☑ D. Seller proposals are an input to the Conduct Procurements process.

    ☒ A is incorrect because Plan Procurement Management is a process in the Planning process group. B is incorrect because request procurements is not an activity of Plan Procurement Management. C is incorrect because procurement strategy is the planned approach to cost-effectively purchasing a company's required goods and supplies.

16. Finally, after three months of negotiating with the resource allocation manager, a new business analyst, Sharon, has been added to your current project team. Given the introduction of a new team member, which team development stage might your team fall into?

    A. Forming

    B. Storming

    C. Norming

    D. Performing

    ☑ B. Project team members who have worked together in the past might skip a stage; instead of starting with forming, the team could move up the ladder to storming.

    ☒ A, C, and D are incorrect because it is common for the Tuckman team stages to occur in order: forming, storming, norming, performing, and adjourning (reforming).

17. The Manage Project Knowledge process consists of:

    A. Managing tacit and explicit knowledge

    B. Knowledge sharing and codifying implicit knowledge

C. Making sure tools and techniques are shared by the stakeholders

D. Ensuring that all stakeholder knowledge needs are met

☑ **A.** Explicit knowledge can be readily codified, and tacit knowledge is personal and difficult to express. The Manage Project Knowledge process is concerned with managing both explicit and tacit knowledge.

☒ **B** is incorrect because codifying implicit knowledge is part of work done by a business analyst to create explicit knowledge. Codified explicit knowledge can be used in lessons learned. **C** is incorrect because tools are something tangible used in producing a product or result, and techniques are defined procedures used by a human resource to perform an activity to produce a product or result or deliver a service. **D** is incorrect because knowledge management is about making sure all the skills and expertise of the stakeholders are used throughout the project.

18. Design for X (DfX) is a(n):

A. Set of technical guidelines for the optimization of a specific aspect of the product design

B. Situational guideline for using agile approaches

C. Specific design tool that addresses specific aspects of a mature product

D. Agile tool used by everybody throughout the project

☑ **A.** This is the definition of design for X (DfX).

☒ **B** is incorrect because DfX is not a situational guideline, but rather a tool/technique of the Manage Quality process. **C** is incorrect because DfX is used in new product development. **D** is incorrect because DfX is not an agile tool.

19. You are working in an adaptive environment. You want to streamline team member access to information and have transparent decision making. The most effective project reporting technique in this situation would be to:

A. Set up an intranet site

B. Email and fax project status reports

C. Form an online community

D. Use information radiators

☑ **D.** Information radiators are visible, physical displays that provide up-to-the-minute knowledge sharing without having to disturb the team.

☒ **A** is incorrect because setting up a SharePoint site, wiki, or intranet site requires additional resources. **B** is incorrect because electronic communications will be either push or pull methods, and stakeholders will participate based on cost and time constraints. **C** is incorrect because forming an online community gives the opportunity to engage with stakeholders who are members of that community, and stakeholders may not have familiarity with the tools.

20. You have been assigned as the project manager on a project focused on developing a new process for your organization called configuration management. Which of the following identifies the functions this process performs?

A. Identifying, submitting, approving, tracking, and validating changes

B. Submitting, approving, tracking, measuring, and validating changes

C. Identifying, requesting, assessing, validating, and communicating changes

D. Reviewing, approving, tracking, validating, and proving changes

☑ **C.** Configuration management is the process of identifying, requesting, assessing, validating, and communicating changes to the project management plan.

☒ **A**, **B**, and **D** are incorrect. Configuration management does not include measuring and does not include proving.

21. You have been working on defining the procedures by which the project scope and product scope can be changed. In which process is your team engaged?

A. Validate Scope

B. Plan Configuration Management

C. Initial Scope Definition

D. Control Scope

☑ **D.** Defining the procedures by which the project scope and product scope can be changed is known as Control Scope.

☒ **A**, **B**, and **C** are incorrect. Validate Scope is done at the end of a project or phase to confirm the deliverables are as contracted. Configuration management is the process of considering changes before they are put into change control. Initial scope definition is not about Control Scope.

22. A consultant has been reviewing your Monitor Risks process outputs. She lists many actions that are required to bring the project into compliance with the project management plan. What are these actions called?

A. Recommended preventive actions

B. Risk register updates

C. Recommended corrective actions

D. Project management plan updates

☑ **A.** Actions that are required to bring the project into compliance with the project management plan are known as recommended preventive actions.

☒ **B**, **C**, and **D** are incorrect. Recommended corrective actions include contingency plans and work-around plans. Risk register updates and project management plan updates are also outputs of the Monitor Risks process, but do not fit the question posed.

23. The project you are managing has a problem that requires the contract with a seller to be modified. The alteration to the contract is in accordance with the change control terms of the contract and project. The best time to make this change to the contract is:

   A. Never; the contract cannot be modified at any time

   B. At any time, regardless of the response from the seller

   C. At any time prior to the contract being awarded to the seller

   D. At any time prior to contract closure by mutual consent

   ☑ **D.** The contract with a seller can be modified at any time, in accordance with the change control terms of the contract and project.

   ☒ **A**, **B**, and **C** are incorrect. Contracts usually are varied or modified during a project for practical reasons. The contract is not in place until it has been awarded.

24. What is the objective of the use of a procurement audit on a project when conducted in the Close Project or Phase process?

   A. Identify when legal action should be started.

   B. Terminate the nonperforming suppliers' contracts.

   C. Identify who signed the nonperforming contracts.

   D. Identify success and failure for use in future contracts.

   ☑ **D.** The objective of the use of the procurement audit process is to identify success and failure for use in future contracts on this or other projects. This is performed as part of the project closure process.

   ☒ **A**, **B**, and **C** are incorrect. Identifying when legal action should be started, terminating the nonperforming suppliers' contracts, and identifying who signed the nonperforming contracts are part of contract administration.

25. You assign one of your junior staff to track the actual start and finish of activities and milestones to ensure they are being performed against the planned timeline. They report regularly any deviations and keep the plan updated as changes occur. Which of the following processes is most consistent with these activities?

   A. Control Scope

   B. Control Schedule

   C. Monitor Communications

   D. Monitor Risks

   ☑ **B.** Control Schedule is the process of ensuring that the project will produce its required deliverables and solutions on time. The activities in this process include tracking the actual start and finish of activities and milestones against the planned timeline and updating the plan so that the comparison to the plan is always current.

   ☒ **A**, **C**, and **D** are incorrect because Control Scope, Monitor Communications, and Monitor Risks include other activities to support their respective processes.

26. It is imperative that you keep your budget in control. Project governance has been established to keep budgets within 10% of what was planned and report weekly when costs are more or less than this threshold. Which of the following facets of cost control is least useful in controlling your budget?

A. Contracting outsource services vs. using capable in-house staff

B. Holding down costs so the project remains on budget

C. Bringing the project back on budget when an overrun occurs

D. Identifying opportunities to return project funding to the enterprise

☑ **A.** This is least helpful, given the importance of staff in any effort to add value to an organization; however, project managers should keep the focus on long-term impact, not short-term costs.

☒ **B, C,** and **D** are incorrect; these are the most helpful because there are three facets to controlling costs: holding down costs so the project remains on budget, bringing the project back on budget when an overrun occurs, and identifying opportunities to return project funding to the organization.

27. As the project manager for the "Go Green!" project, you have prepared your final project report, which includes your lessons learned. You then had a meeting with as many members of your project team that were available to review them. Your next step is to:

A. Add items as appropriate to the final report

B. Prepare your knowledge management repository

C. Promulgate meeting minutes to the members of the steering committee

D. Ask attendees if they can remain with the project as needed so closure can occur according to organizational policies

☑ **A.** Any additional items that provide more information about project performance can be added to the project final report

☒ **B** is incorrect because knowledge gained on the project is put in the lessons learned repository. **C** is incorrect because you will officially publish the final report to the steering committee. **D** is incorrect because assigning and reallocating resources are decided during Resource Management.

28. After Joe became a PMP, he knows he needs 60 hours of professional development units (PDUs) in a three-year cycle to maintain his certification. As part of his year-end personal planning, he has a look at his profile and is shocked to discover that he needs 49 PDUs in the next four months. He has three in-class project management courses, worth 20 PDUs each, scheduled in the next six months. What is the best thing for Joe to do?

A. Go ahead and enter the PDUs on the PMI website if he is committed to taking the courses this year.

B. Do not attempt to enter the PDUs on the PMI website before he takes the courses. This action violates the Honesty: Mandatory Standard—it is making a false statement.

C. According to the PMI website, once a class is paid for, it is the same as attended. Enter the PDUs on the PMI website.

D. Do not attempt to enter the PDUs on the PMI website before he takes the courses. PMI will revoke his PMP for making misleading or false statements.

☑ **B.** Joe must follow the *Code*. In the next four months, he may be able to earn more PDUs in another Education or Giving Back category.

☒ **A** is incorrect because any misrepresentation may lead to disciplinary action. **C** is incorrect because when reporting PDUs, Joe attests that the information he provides is correct. **D** is incorrect because, although he may consider it, Joe is making misleading or false statements. PMI may or may not revoke his PMP credential.

29. It is "crunch time" on your special project for the CEO. You and your senior business analyst (SBA) have all the PowerPoint slides ready for the big presentation on Friday. If you look good in this meeting, it could mean a promotion to program manager. You explain the "look good = promotion" scenario to the SBA, and she agrees that it is okay just to put your name on the title slide. What should you do?

A. Don't do it. It is a failure to disclose conflicts.

B. Sure, it's okay. It is simply an example of a coworker helping you out.

C. Don't do it. It is an example of failure to recognize and respect intellectual property.

D. Do it. This is an example of quid pro quo.

☑ **C.** Recognizing and respecting intellectual property is a Responsibility: Mandatory Standard in the Project Management Institute *Code of Ethics and Professional Conduct*.

☒ **A** is incorrect because this situation is not about a conflict of interest. **B** is incorrect because although the SBA may have given you permission to not put her name on the title slide, still you are taking credit for someone else's work. **D** is incorrect because you don't know whether the research was done properly.

30. You are a PgMP, and your former college roommate, Mitzie, is a PMP. Mitzie posted on Facebook that she is an expert C++ programmer. And in the same post she says she worked on the NSA Cyber Project. You know that one of these statements is not true. What should you do about Mitzie?

A. When Mitzie gets her next job, you must tell PMP. Until then, do nothing; there is no ethics problem.

B. Deal with Mitzie and tell her that you know that she is guilty of false advertising. Ask her to delete the post, or you will report her to PMI.

C. Do a screen print of the post and send it to PMI.

D. This is not a problem for you. It is the buyer's problem. Do nothing.

☑ **B.** We accept only those assignments that are consistent with our background, experience, skills, and qualifications.

☒ **A** and **D** are incorrect because, as a PMI member or certificant, you have a responsibility to report possible violations of the *Code of Ethics and Professional Conduct*. **C** is incorrect because you need to first discuss the situation with Mitzie, following the "reasonable and clear factual basis" rule.

Analyzing Your Results

Congratulations on completing the PMP Exam pre-assessment! Now that you're done, let's analyze your results with two objectives in mind:

- What resources you should use to prepare for your PMP exam
- Which objectives you may need to spend some extra time studying

First, use the following table to help gauge your overall readiness for the PMP exam. Total your score from the pre-assessment questions for an overall score out of 30.

Number of Answers Correct	Recommended Course of Study
1–11	If this had been the actual PMP exam, you would not have passed. Considerable study is necessary before taking the real exam. It is recommended that you thoroughly review the *PMBOK Guide, Sixth Edition* and *Project Management: The Managerial Process* by Erik W. Larson before proceeding with use of this book.
12–17	If this had been the actual PMP exam, you would not have passed. Additional study is necessary before taking the PMP exam. It is recommended that you thoroughly review the *PMBOK Guide, Sixth Edition* and *Project Management: The Managerial Process* by Erik W. Larson before proceeding with use of this book.
18–23	If this had been the actual PMP exam, you probably would not have passed. Additional study and targeted review is recommended. At this level it will be helpful to know which exam objectives are points of weakness to tailor your studies based on your needs. Use the following Objective Map to determine which objectives are targets for further study and allocate extra time to review the questions related to these objectives and the in-depth answer explanations that accompany them.
24–30	Congratulations! If this was the actual PMP exam, you probably would have passed. It is still recommended that you work through all the questions included in this book to refresh your knowledge and prepare for the types of questions that may appear on the actual exam.

Once you have determined your readiness for the exam, you can use the following table to determine which objectives need further study:

Domain	Weight	Objective	Chapter	Question Number in Pretest
Included in the Initiating domain	Although no domain tasks are associated with the first three chapters of PMI's *PMBOK Guide, Sixth Edition*, these three areas are tested on the PMP certification exam.	PMP Foundations The first three chapters of PMI's *PMBOK Guide, Sixth Edition*, present the core foundation information tested on the PMI exam. From positioning project management and introducing the project documents, to discussing the environmental factors of a given enterprise, to the role of the project manager within the enterprise, the PMBOK guides project managers in core aspects that help them become oriented to a project.	1	1, 2, 3
Initiating	13%	The Initiating process group is the start of the project journey and consists of defining and authorizing the project and identifying the stakeholders.	2	4, 5
Planning	24%	The Planning process group is all about thinking through the aspects of the project at hand before moving into the execution phase. Project managers perform the planning domain with the goal of reducing project risk.	3	6, 7, 8, 9, 10, 11
Executing	31%	The Executing process group is the place where all the project work takes place. It involves carrying out all the work that was planned in the Planning process group to satisfy the project requirements. Most of the budget is used, and most of the project team's time is spent here. As the project manager, you and the project team create the unique product, service, or result planned in the Planning process group and brought to life in the Executing process group.	4	12, 13, 14, 15, 16, 17, 18, 19

Domain	Weight	Objective	Chapter	Question Number in Pretest
Monitoring and Controlling	25%	The Monitoring and Controlling process group consists of those processes required to measure and correct the progress and performance of the project; identify any areas in which changes to the plan are required; and trigger change requests.	5	20, 21, 22, 23, 24, 25, 26
Closing	7%	The Closing domain includes all the activities necessary to close the project. Closing may be signified by system acceptance and transfer to the support organization, or by official system retirement or replacement. Closing marks the end of the project, including transferring operations and/or data to a follow-on system (as applicable) and retirement of any legacy system. Closing includes archiving project data and documenting final lessons learned.	6	27
Included in the Executing Domain	While there is neither a domain nor tasks associated with PMI's *Code of Ethics and Professional Conduct* expectations, these two areas are tested on the PMP certification exam.	Code of Ethics and Professional Conduct. The Project Management Institute has defined a Code of Ethics and Professional Conduct that all members of PMI are expected to adhere to when managing projects. This Code is intended to address moral, ethical, and cultural competencies.	7	28, 29, 30

About the Online Content

This book comes complete with Total Tester Online customizable practice exam software with 600 practice exam questions.

System Requirements

The current and previous major versions of the following desktop browsers are recommended and supported: Chrome, Microsoft Edge, Firefox, and Safari. These browsers update frequently and sometimes an update may cause compatibility issues with the Total Tester Online or other content hosted on the Training Hub. If you run into a problem using one of these browsers, please try using another until the problem is resolved.

Single User License Terms and Conditions

Online access to the digital content included with this book is governed by the McGraw-Hill Education License Agreement outlined next. By using this digital content you agree to the terms of that license.

Access To register and activate your Total Seminars Training Hub account, simply follow these easy steps.

1. Go to hub.totalsem.com/mheclaim.
2. To Register and create a new Training Hub account, enter your email address, name, and password. No further information (such as credit card number) is required to create an account.
3. If you already have a Total Seminars Training Hub account, select "Log in" and enter your email and password.
4. Enter your Product Key: gf3f-jgcp-b4dp.
5. Click to accept the user license terms.
6. Click "Register and Claim" to create your account. You will be taken to the Training Hub and have access to the content for this book.

Duration of License Access to your online content through the Total Seminars Training Hub will expire one year from the date the publisher declares the book out of print.

Your purchase of this McGraw-Hill Education product, including its access code, through a retail store is subject to the refund policy of that store.

The Content is a copyrighted work of McGraw-Hill Education and McGraw-Hill Education reserves all rights in and to the Content. The Work is © 2018 by McGraw-Hill Education, LLC.

Restrictions on Transfer The user is receiving only a limited right to use the Content for user's own internal and personal use, dependent on purchase and continued ownership of this book. The user may not reproduce, forward, modify, create derivative works based upon, transmit, distribute, disseminate, sell, publish, or sublicense the Content or in any way commingle the Content with other third-party content, without McGraw-Hill Education's consent.

Limited Warranty The McGraw-Hill Education Content is provided on an "as is" basis. Neither McGraw-Hill Education nor its licensors make any guarantees or warranties of any kind, either express or implied, including, but not limited to, implied warranties of merchantability or fitness for a particular purpose or use as to any McGraw-Hill Education Content or the information therein or any warranties as to the accuracy, completeness, correctness, or results to be obtained from, accessing or using the McGraw-Hill Education content, or any material referenced in such content or any information entered into licensee's product by users or other persons and/or any material available on or that can be accessed through the licensee's product (including via any hyperlink or otherwise) or as to non-infringement of third-party rights. Any warranties of any kind, whether express or implied, are disclaimed. Any material or data obtained through use of the McGraw-Hill Education content is at your own discretion and risk and user understands that it will be solely responsible for any resulting damage to its computer system or loss of data.

Neither McGraw-Hill Education nor its licensors shall be liable to any subscriber or to any user or anyone else for any inaccuracy, delay, interruption in service, error or omission, regardless of cause, or for any damage resulting therefrom.

In no event will McGraw-Hill Education or its licensors be liable for any indirect, special or consequential damages, including but not limited to, lost time, lost money, lost profits or good will, whether in contract, tort, strict liability or otherwise, and whether or not such damages are foreseen or unforeseen with respect to any use of the McGraw-Hill Education content.

Total Tester Online

Total Tester Online provides you with a simulation of the PMP exam. Exams can be taken in Practice Mode or Exam Mode. Practice Mode provides an assistance window with references to the book, explanations of the correct and incorrect answers, and the option to check your answer as you take the test. Exam Mode provides a simulation of the actual exam. The number of questions, the types of questions, and the time allowed are intended to be an accurate representation of the exam environment. The option to customize your quiz allows you to create custom exams from selected domains or chapters, and you can further customize the number of questions and time allowed.

To take a test, follow the instructions provided in the previous section to register and activate your Total Seminars Training Hub account. When you register you will be taken to the Total Seminars Training Hub. From the Training Hub Home page, select **PMP Practice Exams** from the "Study" dropdown at the top of the page, or from the list of "Products You Own" on the Home page. You can then select the option to customize your quiz and begin testing yourself in Practice Mode or Exam Mode. All exams provide an overall grade and a grade broken down by domain.

Technical Support

For questions regarding the Total Tester software or operation of the Training Hub, visit **www .totalsem.com** or email **support@totalsem.com**.

For questions regarding book content, email **hep_customer-service@mheducation.com**. For customers outside the United States, email **international_cs@mheducation.com**.